SHERLOCK'S SQUADRON

THE INCREDIBLE TRUE STORY OF THE UNSUNG RAF HEROES OF WORLD WAR TWO

STEVE HOLMES
WITH KEN SCOTT

JOHN BLAKE

ISBN: 978-1-78219-421-7

British Library Cataloguing-in-Publication Data:

A catalogue record for this book is available from the British Library.

Design by www.envydesign.co.uk

Printed in Great Britain by CPI Group (UK) Ltd

1 3 5 7 9 10 8 6 4 2

Papers used by John Blake Publishing are natural, recyclable products made from wood grown in sustainable forests. The manufacturing processes conform to the environmental regulations of the country of origin.

Every attempt has been made to contact the relevant copyright-holders, but some were unobtainable. We would be grateful if the appropriate people could contact us.

Although you are no longer with us I am sure these words will somehow filter their way back to you. Wherever you are, this book is for you.

John, William and Sandra

'My strength has now been reduced to the equivalent of 36 squadrons...we should be able to carry on the war single-handed for some time if not indefinitely.'

Sir Hugh Dowding, RAF Fighter Command
May 1940

'Air superiority is the ultimate expression of military power.'

Winston Churchill

'Air superiority is a condition for all operations, at sea, on land, and in the air.'

Air Marshal Arthur Tedder

'Anyone who fights, even with the most modern weapons, against an enemy who dominates the air, is like a primitive warrior who stands against modern forces with the same limitations and the same chance of success.'

Field Marshal Erwin Rommel

'We shall not flag or fail. We shall go on to the end. We shall fight in France, we shall fight on the seas and oceans, we shall fight with growing confidence and growing strength in the air. We shall defend our island, whatever the cost may be. We shall fight on the beaches, we shall fight on the landing grounds, we shall fight in the fields and in the streets, we shall fight in the hills; we shall never surrender.'

Winston Churchill June 4, 1940

'No enemy plane will fly over the Reich Territory.'

Hermann Goering

'Never in the field of human conflict was so much owed by so many to so few.'

Winston Churchill on the Battle of Britain,
August 20, 1940

CONTENTS

ACKNOWLEDGEMENTS

There are many people I'd like to thank who helped me bring this book to life. I was lucky enough to stumble on a chance meeting with the author Ken Scott and we shared a few beers as I told him about my many years of research and the website I'd pulled together. It was Scotty who first suggested there may be a book in my father's story. He had previously 'ghosted' two World War Two novels, one of which I'd read and had been suitably impressed. I liked his style, the way he brought the characters to life and somehow almost got inside their heads. By the end of the second beer I'd already made my mind up, I wanted to give it a shot.

Ken Scott worked with me for little over four months, I'd like to think we gave it more than a shot and I enjoyed every minute we spent together, especially the Tuesday afternoon 'research' lunches with his wife Hayley and his children Callum and Emily. He has taught me much about writing and the book industry and I am more than pleased at what we have produced. From the bottom of my heart Scotty, thanks for being patient and pulling it altogether... one of my lifetime's achievements.

I would like to say a special thank you to my daughter Kayleigh Louise Holmes for her work and encouragement throughout my time working on this book.

There are many more people to thank and mention, far too many to call. I would however like to say a special thanks to everyone who gave me encouragement and my proof readers and critics too.

My research brought me into contact with the sons and daughters of the men who flew with my dad. It was a humbling experience and at times very emotional. They were more than happy to help with the finer details and character descriptions of their fathers. Judy Vanrenen, Steph Handley, Cathy (Jones) Cameron, Ros (Tammas) Flaxman and Russell and Bev Tickner. I owe you all so much and I'm just more than a little apprehensive that this book reads well to you all, particularly you Judy. Your father may not have appeared to have been the most popular member of the crew but I'm 100% certain he was the most respected and his crew wouldn't have swapped him for his weight in gold. His skill in bringing that plane down on that final doomed mission undoubtedly saved everyone's lives and well they knew it, well I know it. I will be forever in debt to 'Van the Man' for bringing my father back to Blighty in one piece and allowing me to build such a special relationship with him. I cherished every moment I spent with him... he was my best mate.

And finally to all my researchers, I hope you don't mind me labelling you with that title. To John Reid, Bruce Gommersall, Bruno Lecaplain, Mike Stimson, Dave Coates, Warren Tickner, Johans Verhagen and Arie-Jan Hees, Sally and Richard Halon... enjoy, my friends!

FOREWORD

It has taken me fifteen years to complete this book in memory of my late father Flight Engineer John Holmes and his comrades who flew with him and those on the ground who supported them. My father was fascinated by aircraft from a young age and I suppose as a chip off the old block I followed suit. It was when I discovered his exact role in World War Two that I concentrated on and fell in love with the aircraft he flew twenty four sorties in. The Stirling. My father never talked too much about the war and 196 Squadron or the brave men he came into contact with. I wish he had because I've spent literally thousands of hours on research, read over a hundred books and called upon the personal memories from the daughters and sons and nieces and nephews of those great men who are sadly no longer with us. However, a portion of this book has what we call *poetic licence*. Let me explain.

I wanted this book to be an accurate account of what happens when young men go to war. I wanted to capture not just the statistics and records of the sorties but the emotion, the camaraderie, the sense of fear and of pride and at times disillusionment. And I wanted so much more than that, I wanted this book to be a complete read, a story with a beginning, a middle and an end. We all know the beginning and we all know the end but how many of us are truly aware of what the middle was like? I wanted the sons, daughters, grandsons and granddaughters of these men to pick up my book and read it like a novel but I wanted it to be real and I wanted it to be a fitting tribute to the men who fought against an evil regime hell bent on world domination so that we could continue to live as free men and women. I'll give an example.

My father never mentioned a rear gunner called Curly Mason and I know he didn't fly with him. But through my extensive research I know Curly Mason was almost certain to have come in contact with my father during their training. Therefore, in Chapter Four of this book I have introduced Curly Mason as a friend of my father. I have brought in other characters too, such as Lofty Matthews. Again my father never mentioned Lofty but I'm pretty sure he bumped into him somewhere along the way and I feel a special bond with him that I can't explain, but at times I feel I knew Lofty Matthews on a personal level and I wanted to bring him and his tragic tale into this book.

These men are heroes; I had to bring them alive again as a fitting tribute to their courage and fortitude. I make no apologies for doing so. I remember reading somewhere, that to live on in the hearts and minds of the reader is truly not to die. This was my sole purpose in writing this book. We owe them everything, we must never forget them.

In the pages of this book they all live on.

Steve Holmes

CHAPTER ONE

The modern world is still living with the memories and indeed the consequences of World War Two, the most titanic conflict in history. On September 1st 1939, Germany invaded Poland without warning, sparking the start of the war. The clues and undercurrents, however, had been bubbling since the early 1930s.

John Holmes listened with interest to news reports from the BBC World Service prior to 1939. He was the youngest of five children, son of William and Georgina, and he sat in the comfortable, clean and tidy lounge in the Skerton area of Lancaster as the family huddled around the radio.

It was difficult to describe John's feelings; his excitement, for want of a better word. Something told him that a major war was inevitable and not only that, despite the fact that he was still a schoolboy, he instinctively knew that he would play a major part in it. He knew where his destiny lay. His destiny lay in the sky. He was simply fascinated by the images of the RAF fighters and bombers – especially the bombers, clumsy looking, hulking, gigantic pieces of machinery. He wondered what law of nature made them defy gravity and propelled the huge beasts up into the sky.

Life prior to 1939 was pleasant enough for the Holmes family. John's father William was a joiner who worked at the prestigious Waring and Gillow furniture manufacturer. It was a respected occupation and paid well. Whilst not rich, the Holmes family would probably be described as bordering on the middle class element of pre-war England.

Little did William know at the time, but ultimately as the war in Europe escalated the factory would be handed over to war production making ammunition chests and interior fittings for aircraft. Therefore William Holmes never went to war as he had a reserved occupation. Naturally he advised his son to follow in his footsteps or at least get a trade, preferably one that would keep him out of the war they all suspected could break out soon. John heeded his father's advice as always and tried to do as he suggested. It was expected and John respected his father's wishes, a sign of the times perhaps.

John would think about life and work and war as he swam in the River Lune, which was less than five minutes' walk from his house. This was John's escape, the greatest pleasure in his life. He was at one with nature as he struck out against the fast flowing river. It was a challenge battling against the water – and of course against the cold. In the height of summer the River Lune was cold enough, but in winter it was positively Arctic. It mattered not. November, December, January and February John would still discard his clothes above the ramparts where the tidal river from its inlet at Morecambe Bay became a fresh water river.

It was a four-mile walk from the weir adjacent to his house to the beautiful spot at the Crook O' Lune but it was four miles that John never tired of and when he got there it was always worth it. It gave him time to think, time to imagine; a place where he could lose himself in a daydream. The four miles never felt that long and every so often he would look up and gaze into the clouds. That's what his Mum would say to her neighbours every now and again. 'Our John... always has his head in the clouds.' And in a strange sort of way she was right, though John wasn't about to tell her the exact reason why his head was in the clouds quite so often.

John became a very good swimmer and developed a strong physique for someone so young. The Crook O' Lune had to be his favourite spot in the whole world. He'd leave his clothes behind a bush where no one would find them and, dressed only in his underpants, dive into the dark waters a few feet below the bank. He'd swim several strokes underwater. Slow strokes, until he was sure that his body had adjusted to the cold and he hadn't died from a heart attack (as his mum sometimes warned him he would). Then he'd resurface and open his eyes and take in the beautiful scenery that seemed to explode in front of him.

Someone had told him that the Crook O' Lune was painted by the famous artist JMW Turner, the so called painter of light. And of course John went along to his local library and looked up the English Romantic landscape painter, because if the Crook O' Lune was good enough for Turner then it was good enough for him. John first spotted the painting in an obscure book that a kindly librarian had ordered in for him especially. Turner's painting of Crook O' Lune, looking towards Hornby Castle, took John's breath away. He sat on the same banks as Turner had many years ago and he wondered – no, he knew –

that Turner had the same feeling of being at one with nature in this beautiful place.

In 1937 John left school and took up an apprenticeship as a fitter at a local Lancashire mill. He maintained and repaired the huge machines at the mill and at first took great interest in the mechanics of every single one, priding himself on his ability to diagnose specific breakdown problems. He still found time to swim in the Crook O' Lune despite the long hours his new employer insisted he work and, to be truthful, once he'd learned and mastered what he needed to know his heart was never in it. This was not what he wanted to be, it was not where he wanted to be.

Nevertheless John took on board his new-found responsibility and confessed he felt good about contributing to the Holmes family budget. Their standard of living seemed to improve slightly, his mother able to treat the family every now and again. It was 1938 and after the evening meal John would huddle around the Emporic four valve radio that took pride of place in the lounge, listening to world developments that appeared to be gathering at an unstoppable pace. He listened along with his father and his brothers; James and Ernie, while his mother and sisters, Alice and Mary, busied themselves with the chores around the house.

It was mid-September 1938 when John came home to his favourite meal of the week; ham, egg and chips. It wasn't the fanciest meal on the Holmes menu but his mother's chips were to die for and ham and eggs were surely invented to compliment Georgina Holmes's culinary masterpiece. It had been a tough day at work for everyone; was John imagining it or were the employers demanding a little bit more recently? The family tried to avoid the one topic on everyone's mind but John kept glancing at the kitchen clock, willing the hands round to nine o'clock when the BBC would broadcast a detailed account of international world affairs. He noticed his father with one eye on the clock too. He tried to shake the word 'war' from his mind and his mother scolded her boys each time they mentioned it, but even she realised that world events were being influenced by a certain man called Adolf Hitler. John's brother James spoke.

'Chamberlain's over there now Dad, talking with Adolf Hitler. He'll sort him out, Dad, won't he?'

John was all too aware that at 23 years of age James would be the first of the brothers to be called up if war broke out. James enjoyed family life in Skerton and his job as a store-man in the town's biggest department store. He had a little bit of money in his pocket and a pretty girlfriend, enjoyed a few beers at the weekend and dancing at the local Roxy. He didn't want to go and fight this fellow Hitler.

'I certainly hope so, son,' his father said. 'I certainly hope so.'

On 15th September 1938, as William Holmes and his sons sat listening to the world news, there was a collective sigh of relief as Neville Chamberlain announced that Adolf Hitler 'appears to be a man who could be relied upon when he had given his word'. It was what everybody wanted to hear. Hitler was an honest chap after all. Georgina Holmes breezed into the lounge polishing a large dinner plate with a tea-towel.

'You hear that, Mum?' said Ernie. 'Hitler's given his word to Mr Chamberlain.'

Georgina Holmes gave a half-smile. The look didn't convince young John. He was only 15 and far too young to be called up into the armed forces, but he was already plotting the future. Hitler couldn't be trusted; John didn't know why but he knew. He had seen the pictures of him in the newspapers and hated everything about him right down to his silly little half-moustache. And he had seen him on the Pathé news reels at the picture house in the middle of the Saturday afternoon matinée, banging his fist on the rostrum he spoke from while he ranted and raved in a language John couldn't understand while thousands of soldiers yelled 'Heil Hitler,' with their right arms pointing to the sky.

Every time John heard the man speak a shiver ran the length of his spine. It wasn't a shiver of fear; it was adrenalin because John Holmes knew that his life in the mill wouldn't last long and destiny would take over and pitch him into conflict with this evil man. He knew that Hitler wasn't to be trusted. He wanted to invade Czechoslovakia, the radio announcer had said, that's why Chamberlain had made the trip to Germany along with other heads of state. The theory was that if Hitler was made fully aware that other countries opposed his invasion plan then he would have to back down. John knew Hitler wouldn't back down, he would invade Czechoslovakia – and after Czechoslovakia, where next?

The radio announcer said goodbye and asked his listeners to join him at the same time the following evening. John was tired and said his goodnights to the family. He spent twenty minutes reading before drifting off to sleep. The book fell to the floor with a thud. John had read the book from cover to cover several times but his interest never waned. It was a book on aviation, *The A-Z of the Aeroplane*. He had picked it up several weeks before at the local church jumble sale. John dreamt that night. He dreamt of soldiers and of conflict and he dreamt about Adolf Hitler. He was looking down on the German Chancellor from a great height as he shouted and gesticulated to the masses. John looked down on him through the clouds. He could not shake off the unmistakable drone of aircraft engines echoing in the background of his dream.

Later that month Chamberlain was back in Germany. In London, on home soil, Winston Churchill warned of the futility of appeasing Adolf Hitler.

'The belief that security can be obtained by throwing a small state to the wolves is a fatal delusion,' he said, referring to Hitler's wish to invade Czechoslovakia.

The conference had been chaired by Adolf Hitler with Italy's Benito Mussolini, Britain's Neville Chamberlain, and France's Edouard Daladier discussing German demands on Czechoslovakian territory. At the end of the two days the Munich Agreement was signed. It allowed Germany to annex the Sudetenland portion of Czechoslovakia. Prime Minister Neville Chamberlain said 'I believe it is peace for our time.'

The Holmes brothers and their father sat in their familiar chairs as the announcement was made. Ernie breathed a sigh of relief while James busied himself polishing his shoes for the next working day. William Holmes was quiet, almost stoic. John drained the last of his tea and walked through to the kitchen. He washed the cup and placed it onto the drainer.

'I'm off to bed,' he announced, before kissing his mother gently on the cheek. And as he climbed the stairs wearily he mumbled to himself. 'Czechoslovakia... where next?'

Events in Nazi Germany were gathering pace. The public school tones of the radio announcer almost faltered as he detailed an event known as *Kristallnacht*, night of broken glass. The Nazi authorities had orchestrated a nationwide protest against the Jews in Germany and Austria. It followed the murder of German diplomat Ernst vom Rath, killed allegedly by Herschel Grynszpan, a French Jew in the German Embassy in Paris. Jewish homes and synagogues were looted and burned. Hardly a Jewish shop or business survived the bricks and petrol bombs of the fired up mob. By the end of the night

91 Jews were killed and by the end of the week 20,000 had been taken away to concentration camps.

Christmas came and went. Georgina Holmes had made a real effort that year and John wondered if his mother suspected it might be their last together as a family, at least for a while. James, Alice, Mary and Ernie all had good jobs but their mother was well aware that every one of them was liable for call up should war break out.

On the stroke of midnight on December 31st, 1938 turned into 1939. It was a time for good cheer, a little alcohol and best wishes for the year to come. The Holmes family sat together in the well-kept lounge of their semi-detached home in front of a roaring log fire. It was a bitterly cold evening and a fine covering of snow lay on the cobbled streets outside. Ernie's girlfriend Dorothy was there and a young man called Jimmy, who had his eye on Alice. James had brought a couple of friends back from the pub and the assembled group sang 'Auld Lang Syne'. William sat in his big comfortable armchair by the fire. He was nursing a whisky and looked on with approval at his sons and daughters happy smiling faces. He'd given his youngest son a bottle of best bitter and although not quite the most wonderful tasting drink in the world, John had been only too happy to join his older brothers and sisters and enjoy his first drop of alcohol.

'Just the one now, John,' his father had warned him and John had nodded before taking a long drink. The alcohol kicked in immediately, making him feel light-headed, a little giggly even, but he was happy to be a part of the adult crowd. The lounge seemed particularly dark that night, probably something to do with all the bodies blocking out the light from the fire and the standard lamp that stood in the corner of the room. If it had been a little lighter someone may have noticed the tears that ran silently down his mother's cheeks.

It was early spring 1939 when John began to notice the very visible signs that the country was preparing for war. The workforce at the mill had been reduced significantly and young men from the age of twenty one were disappearing at a rapid rate of knots joining the Army, the Navy or the RAF. Some joined up voluntarily, some were conscripted, they had no choice yet no one seemed to object.

Hitler was still in the news and some hacks from the press were suggesting he was hell bent on world domination. They mentioned something about a white supremacist Aryan race; blond-haired blue-eyed individuals, powerful, tall, strong and athletic. John almost laughed as he thought about the man whose vision this was… a five foot eight, unhealthy-looking Austrian with black hair and dark eyes. Hardly the perfect role model.

The radio was still the favoured place to congregate after each evening meal and now the men of the Holmes family were joined by the ladies of the house. One evening John's father announced that his factory had had a visit from the men from the War Office. They were to stop making furniture for the foreseeable future.

'Then what will you be making?' John asked.

'Oh there's plenty to make, son, plenty of stuff needed for the war. Waring & Gillow have furnished ships and boats before, lots of famous ones like the *Lusitania*, *Heliopolis* and the *Queen Mary*.'

'So you'll be fitting out ships for the war?'

William nodded. 'Pretty much so. The upholstery department will lend a hand too, making kit-bags, tents and camouflage nets. It's nothing new, the same thing happened during the

Great War, we even made wooden propellers for De Havilland DH9 aircraft.'

John knew all about the De Havilland DH9, there was even a picture of it in his aircraft book. To think Dad's factory had made those propellers. Ernie and James, Alice and Mary all detailed the changes that had occurred in their own workplace, their factories and offices. James and Ernie talked about how they wouldn't hesitate to join up if it came to all-out war with Germany. John wished he was just that little bit older. Almost on cue the familiar music of the BBC World Service permeated the room and the Holmes family fell silent.

The station played a recent speech by Adolf Hitler. It was in German, of course, and the translator let the tape play for a few seconds before interpreting.

'Czechoslovakia has ceased to exist' he said, 'The glorious German troops now occupy the rest of Czechoslovakia.'

The invading German Storm-Troopers had annexed Bohemia and Moravia too. This was all in violation of the Munich Agreement of the previous year. The dulcet tones of the broadcaster announced that needless to say the British and French governments had protested strongly. Several days later Neville Chamberlain told the Cabinet that continuing negotiations with Adolf Hitler was impossible.

William Holmes spoke. For the first time John's father acknowledged that war was inevitable. His statement took everyone by surprise, not least John.

'We'll be at war within three months,' he predicted. 'Mark my words… everyone will be at war on a scale we've never seen before.'

His words would become strangely prophetic.

'Who'll be at war?' John asked.

William Holmes leaned across and ruffled John's hair.

'Everyone, son… everyone in the whole damned world.'

And so they sat night after night. They listened to Hitler demanding the return of the Polish Corridor and Danzig and they listened to the BBC as they announced that German troops had occupied the city of Memel, which was situated on the border of East Prussia and Lithuania. Poland warned Germany that any attempt to seize Danzig would mean all-out war. They listened with admiration as Chamberlain told the House of Commons that France and Britain had declared they would stand by Poland and support Polish independence.

It was early June and John continued to swim in the Crook O' Lune. On this day in particular he was recalling the words of Winston Churchill as he wrote in a magazine called *The Collier*. John had studied the words in the magazine during a trip to the barber shop in Lancaster town centre. Churchill had said that unless there was a change of regime in Nazi Germany, war was inevitable. The Germans were spoiling for a fight, he wrote. He went on to say that the war would undoubtedly start before the end of the year. John powered on up the river stroke after stroke drawing inspiration and energy from the words he had heard Mr Churchill speak of late. There was nothing finer than when the BBC announcer introduced a speech by Winston Churchill. Whilst he had nothing personal against Mr Chamberlain it seemed that Churchill knew how to stir up a little emotion, ruffle a few feathers and he talked sense. He made the hairs on the back of John's neck stand on end.

John swam longer and faster than he could ever recall swimming before. As he climbed from the water he was out of breath and after a minute or two the cool river water mingled with his perspiration. He walked down to where he had hidden his clothes, dried himself off and changed, then made his way up to the mill preparing for another long and monotonous day. As he walked through the gates he sighed and wondered how long it would be before he could say goodbye to the place. He looked up to the sky as always and said a silent prayer.

On August 22nd 1939 Hitler authorized the killing 'without pity or mercy, all men, women and children of Polish descent or language.' By the end of the month the Royal Navy was put on full alert and Army and Navy mobilisation commenced. The conscription age was lowered to age 20.

Hitler received the Polish Ambassador to Berlin, mainly to appease Mussolini, who was trying to establish a peace formula. The talks lasted no longer than a few minutes. Hitler had already made up his mind to invade Poland. He declared to his generals a few hours later that at 4:45am on 1st September 1939, the German Armed Forces would invade Poland.

On 2nd September Neville Chamberlain issued an ultimatum to Nazi Germany that Hitler must withdraw his troops from Poland with immediate effect. Chamberlain would broadcast live to the nation the following day.

John could hardly wait to get home on September 3rd 1939. His work that day had been shoddy, like many others he was unable to concentrate or focus on the task in hand. After all, it's not every day that your country is on the brink of war. His supervisor understood and sent him home early. For once he wasn't hungry; for once his mother understood and didn't scold him for leaving good food on his plate.

They sat and waited for the appointed hour. William, Georgina, James, Alice, Ernie, Mary and John sat in a stony yet deafening silence. The radio crackled into life and the commentator announced that they were going across to the House of Commons. It seemed like a poor connection, a little distorted but after several seconds Neville Chamberlain spoke.

'This morning the British Ambassador in Berlin handed the German Government a final note stating that unless we heard from them by eleven o'clock that they were prepared at once to withdraw their troops from Poland, a state of war would exist between us.'

Chamberlain paused for dramatic effect or was John just imagining it.

'I have to tell you that no such undertaking has been received and that consequently this country is at war with Germany.'

CHAPTER TWO

By the evening of September 3rd, Britain and France were at war with Germany and within a week, Australia, New Zealand, Canada and South Africa had also joined the conflict. The world had been plunged into its second world war in 25 years. No one, not John, not his father, mother or his brothers or sisters would have believed that the war would last six long and bloody years. No one would have predicted it would be so fierce and fought over many thousands of square miles or would claim so many innocent lives. It would be fought from the hedgerows of Normandy to the streets of Stalingrad, the icy slopes of Norway and Finland to the sweltering heat of North Africa and the insect infested jungles of Burma and the tropics of Java. It would affect every single family in Great Britain.

Towards the end of September, John made his way home from work and lingered on his boss's words that it would be over by Christmas. He hoped that was the case, he hoped everyone would return home safely and they would enjoy the festivities like he'd remembered from the year before. But something welling in the pit of his stomach told him that wouldn't be the case.

He recalled the history lessons at school as his teacher, Mr Mackenzie, gave him the facts on World War One. 'The War To End All Wars,' 'The Great War.' The teacher said as he pontificated at the front of the classroom. What a stupid name, thought John; which idiot named it 'The Great War?' It didn't appear very 'great' after listening to his lessons.

It was the Germans again who had antagonised half of Europe by invading Belgium, Luxembourg and France. The war was fought mainly in the trenches of Northern France, young men and boys massacred like toy soldiers. Cannon fodder, Mr Mackenzie had said, and by the war end, Great Britain had lost five million military personnel. John couldn't even contemplate those sorts of figures. One of his classmates said there wasn't a million minutes in a year; he wondered if that were true?

His boss was wrong; the war hadn't ended by Christmas. John still listened to the radio reports about the battles and the push for territory, the successes and the losses sustained by the Allies. He hated to admit it but he was almost disappointed that the war hadn't seemed to have reached Lancaster. Why hadn't the war arrived here?

Lancaster was so distant, it had never seen any real action. It was like there wasn't a war going on at all, as if it was happening somewhere else in some far-off distant land. No strategic bombing, no soldiers patrolling the streets or air wardens shining small torches through gaps in windows ordering people to block out lights. Nothing. No munitions factories here. Just warehouses, textile mills, cobbled streets and the Crook O' Lune.

But the war was happening in Lancaster, and it was happening in Skerton too as one by one, young men and women in their early twenties gradually disappeared from the grey cobbled streets to do their duty for King and Country fighting a war in a foreign land. John recalled Mrs Roberts from a few doors down standing in the kitchen of her home as she proudly boasted to John's mother that her son Frank was one of the first to be called up. And she had been proud, mighty proud as the day for Frank's departure arrived. John watched from his bedroom window as close relatives and extended family arrived at number 43 to wave Frank off until eventually a small crowd gathered around the step to the front door. And they sang songs and waved flags and bunting adorned the doorway and hung from lampposts nearby. And how Mrs Roberts smiled and beamed with pride as Frank set off along the street.

And then it was John's brothers' turn as they received their papers. The papers told them to report to various drill halls in the North West. James, the eldest, received his call-up first. It was spring 1940. The letter advised him to report to a church hall in Lancaster on a specified date, unless he was in one of the reserve occupations listed, in which case he had to notify the war office within 48 hours. Georgina Holmes looked at the list. Dock-workers, miners, farmers, merchant seamen, firemen, railwaymen and utility workers in the water, gas, or electric industry. James had always wanted to be a fireman but she had discouraged him; she thought it was a dangerous occupation. She was so proud when he left school and took up his position as a store-man. Within a few short years he headed the department.

No one in the house knew of the torment she was going through as her eyes hovered over the word *fireman*. No one knew of the anguish she would suffer during the six years of conflict that would claim 60 million lives and devastate most of Europe and large parts of Asia and Africa.

James reported for duty and basic training at Squire's Gate Camp in Blackpool. He had chosen the East Lancashire Regiment. After eight weeks' basic training he would find himself fighting the Germans in a muddy field in northern France. Latterly he would be posted to Malaya and Burma. He was 25 years of age when he kissed goodbye to his family. His sister, Alice, held his girlfriend Marjorie tight as James walked to the end of the street. Marjorie cried as if the world had come to an end. She was inconsolable.

Ernie was next. His papers arrived two weeks later. Ernie's girlfriend Dorothy Mossop was having tea with the family when William placed the envelope on the kitchen table.

'This came this morning,' he announced. 'I thought I'd wait until we'd finished our tea.'

Ernie had forked the last piece of potato into his mouth, which was just as well because his appetite vanished immediately. There was a prolonged silence. It was only an envelope, yet everyone who crowded around the small kitchen table knew of its significance, not least his girlfriend Dorothy who burst into tears as she dropped a knife onto her plate causing everyone to jump. Ernie laughed it off.

'Don't be stupid lass, we knew this day would come and you know how much I want to go and give Hitler the kicking he deserves.'

John smiled. He wanted to go and give Hitler a good kicking too. John wanted to join his two older brothers, wherever, whenever. Why couldn't he go? He could work, he could get served in the local pubs and hotels in Lancaster and he was even old enough to get married and yet he couldn't go and serve his country, protect it from a man and a country hell bent on destruction.

'It'll be over soon, don't you fret Dot, and I'll be back before you know it.'

John admired his older brother's courage and dignity, even if he was just putting on a brave face. John was always close to Ernie despite the five-year gap. It had been Ernie who took him into the Greaves Hotel in town and bought him his first pint of bitter a few weeks back and it had been Ernie who first encouraged him to ask the attractive-looking barmaid, Joyce, out on a date even if she was quite a few years older than him. John would miss Ernie, that was for sure. He'd miss his guidance and his protection, his humour too. He had accepted a small packet from Ernie the third time he had taken Joyce out.

'I got these from the barber, John. I think you'll need them soon.'

John unwrapped the stiff brown paper. He was about to open the packet in full view of the regulars in the pub. Ernie reached across and clamped his hand on the packet.

'Not here, our kid… later,' he grinned.

John sensed from Ernie's smile that they were something to be opened in private though at the time didn't know exactly what it was he held in the palm of his hand. He slid the packet in his pocket and promised himself he would take a peek the next time he needed to go to the toilet.

Ernie joined the Loyal North Lancashire Regiment. He read up on the regiment at the local library and was very proud to be joining such a famous and well respected outfit. During the weeks before he left for their headquarters at Fulwood Barracks, Preston, he reminded anyone who would listen that during World War One three members of the Regiment had been awarded the Victoria Cross. He said that the regiment recruited from the towns of Central Lancashire, including Preston, Chorley, Bolton and Wigan. What more could he ask for than to go to war with a bunch of his blood brothers, salt of the earth Lancashire lads?

'Don't worry,' he called out to his parents as he walked out of the front door en route to the railway station. 'We'll look out for each other. You'll see me quicker than you think.'

Georgina Holmes tried her best not to cry. It was the last thing her son would want to see. She fought the tears; she fought harder than she'd ever fought anything before and just about managed to carry it off. Ernie was 22. He promised to write to his mother as often as he could. But as Ernie turned the corner of Ashton Drive, he turned and gave a final wave. As he disappeared from view her legs gave way, not unlike a heavyweight boxer caught on the ropes with nowhere to hide. It took her husband all his strength to keep her from collapsing in a heap on their front doorstep.

John noticed the subtle differences in the house, particularly in his mother's attitude towards him. She would hardly let him out of her sight and fussed around him like an old mother hen. John knew how difficult it was for her, having lost two sons, and even his sisters appeared to treat him a little differently. There was no name calling or teasing which was always par for the course and each week, on pay day, Mary and Alice would bring him a little treat, a bar of chocolate or a magazine. He thanked them of course but then always reminded them there wasn't any need to bring him gifts, he wasn't a baby anymore and he had his own wages now. He was wrong, thought Georgina Holmes. He was the baby, always had been and always would be.

Mary and Alice were lucky; although they weren't in reserved occupation they had escaped being called up into the Women's

Auxiliary Air Force, the Nursing Corps or indeed to factories further afield making munitions. Mary worked at K shoes at Lancaster and had done since she left school at 15. She had risen to the rank of supervisor and had 25 people working under her. In 1939 K shoes had been contracted to produce aircraft covers, tents, service boots, kit bags, gaiters and even RAF flying boots. Production was stepped up and an extra hour put onto the working day. The government deemed that Mary would be best placed to remain in her current employment and help with the war effort that way. John adored Mary, who reminded him very much of his mother. In fact it was as if he had two mothers at number 59 Ashton Drive.

Alice, on the other hand, was totally different to Mary, like chalk and cheese but just as special to John.

Alice took great pride in her appearance, always dressed immaculately whenever she left the house and although the smallest of the brothers and sisters at just under five foot, she carried herself high. John's mother would sometimes have a little laugh at her expense, announcing 'here's her majesty a'coming' if she spotted her in the street from the bay window of the lounge. The jackets and skirts from her wardrobe were carefully tailored, more contoured to the shape of her figure, and consequently looked more feminine than the other box-cut fashions some of her friends and colleagues wore. One particular favourite of Alice's was a suit that many women wore during the war years. The suits were made from a tartan cloth and would later be nicknamed 'siren suits' when hordes of tartan-clad girls would be seen running for the air raid shelters when the sirens sounded. Alice demanded everything neat and tidy and took her tea in a delicate china cup. She positively frowned with displeasure when John and his dad took theirs from white tin mugs. John's dad said it made no sense.

'Give me a mug,' he'd command. 'Can't get any more than a gob full out of those bloody thimbles.'

Alice, aged 23, was office manager in the accounts department of the local council. She helped set the budgets, kept essential services financed and made sure the wages were paid to the workers. Again the government thought it prudent that she stayed put in Lancaster. Georgina Holmes was luckier than most; three out of five at home isn't bad, she thought. But as the three remaining siblings settled down to listen to the evening news from the BBC she wondered just how long it would be before she was left with two. John sat down on the rug and crossed his legs. He leant up against his mother's knees as she put down her knitting and rubbed a weary hand through his hair.

John had to get used to being the only boy in the household. His chores were increased to make up for the fact that his two older brothers were away to war and suddenly there was only him and his dad to cut wood, bring in the coal, clean the fire and tend to the allotment. All in all John didn't mind; he moaned occasionally but it was just a front to cover the fact that he missed his brothers so much.

John continued to swim in the Crook O' Lune and was selected for the legendary Lancaster water polo team, arguably the top club in England. They would win every game John played but sadly travelling to events and competitions was restricted because of the war. Nevertheless it was another small release for John who desperately wanted to join his brothers fighting for his country.

John had also struck up a friendship with a local boy, Norman Shaw. Norman was quite a small lad, as were most of his family, or so Norman said. Norman lived with his parents, brothers and sisters in a very imposing three storey, four bedroomed end terrace house. It was in Belle Vue Terrace, in the Greaves area of Lancaster. The house was elevated up from the main A6 road on a terrace known locally as the Monkey Rack. It was definitely the posh end of town. Norman and John got on like a house on fire and met most evenings for a couple of pints in the Greaves Hotel after the nine o'clock BBC news briefing. The war was the one subject on everyone's lips and Norman and John were no different. The two young men knew that the war wasn't going as well as expected.

'They're evacuating the Allied troops at Dunkirk, John.'

John took a mouthful of beer, replaced his glass on the table. 'So I heard. Probably nothing, you can't win every battle in the war, Norm'.'

'Perhaps not. Any idea where Ernie and James are?'

John shook his head. 'No, heard nothing since they left their billets.'

Both brothers had written a couple of times during their basic training but the family had heard nothing since they were put on troop trains at Liverpool Lime Street Station some weeks back. Their destination was top secret.

The British Government hadn't disclosed the full facts about the evacuation at Dunkirk, for obvious reasons. Great Britain and the Allies had been on the verge of defeat. 300,000 Allied troops were stranded on the beaches at Dunkirk. They had not eaten in days, they were low on ammunition and their dead and wounded colleagues lay all around. The might of a fully equipped and confident German Army had pinned them on the beaches and encircled them. The German Luftwaffe was ready to take off and obliterate the beaches and the bodies on them as soon as their Fuhrer gave the order. Hitler spoke to his victorious troops.

'Dunkirk has fallen… with it has ended the greatest battle of world history. Soldiers! My confidence in you knows no bounds. You have not disappointed me.'

In the House of Commons Winston Churchill put on a brave face.

'We must be very careful not to assign to this deliverance the attributes of a victory. Wars are not won by evacuations.'

He also praised the RAF. The Royal Air Force played a pivotal role protecting the retreating troops from the Luftwaffe. It was said that the sandy beaches softened the explosions from the German bombs, minimising casualties, but there is no doubt that the pilots and crews of the RAF bought the time necessary to get British, French and Belgian troops back to the southern shores of Hampshire, Kent and Sussex in order that they could live to fight another day. Between 26th May and 4th June during the evacuation, the RAF flew a total of 4,822 sorties over Dunkirk. They claimed 262 Luftwaffe aircraft.

In the wake of the evacuation of Dunkirk in the summer of 1940, Hitler's generals proposed that the German army should invade Britain. The operation was codenamed Sea Lion but the Generals quite rightly conceded that it could only be achieved with full superiority in the air over the British Isles.

Hitler sent out the order to prepare the Luftwaffe for action with the prime objective to destroy the British Royal Air Force. The Luftwaffe was unquestionably much greater than their British counterpart with much more experience too. The German pilots were well blooded in the bombing raids on Spain towards the end of the Civil War and the Blitzkrieg in France had also served them well. As the German generals addressed the key people of the Luftwaffe in Berlin towards the beginning of June 1940 they reassured them that victory would be theirs very soon. They reminded them that the German aircraft superiority outnumbered that of the RAF by nearly four to one. A slight exaggeration perhaps, but not a million miles from the truth. Goering went a step further; he estimated that it would take just four days to defeat the RAF Fighter Command in southern England. He would follow it up with a four-week offensive during which the bombers and long-range fighters would destroy all military installations throughout the country. In addition they would attempt to wreck the British aircraft industry. The campaign would start with attacks on airfields near the coast, gradually moving inland to attack the ring of airfields defending London.

The British people were gearing up for a German invasion. On 18th June 1940, Winston Churchill spoke in the House of Commons.

'The Battle of France is over,' he said. 'I expect the Battle of Britain is about to begin. The whole fury and might of the enemy must very soon be turned on us. Hitler knows he will have to break us in this island or lose the war. If we can stand up to him, all Europe may be free and the life of the world may move forward into broad sunlit uplands. But if we fail, then the whole world, including the United States, including all that we have known and cared for, will sink into the abyss of a new Dark Age made more sinister and perhaps more protracted, by the lights of perverted science. Let us therefore brace ourselves to our duties, and so bear ourselves that, if the British Empire and its Commonwealth last for a thousand years, men will still say *this was their finest hour.*'

Over the summer of 1940, in the skies in the south of England, dogfights could regularly be seen between RAF and German fighters and the fighter airfields of the south were relentlessly bombed by the Luftwaffe. The losses on both sides were great. At one point, unknown to Goering, the RAF were on their knees, but after Bomber Command attacks on Berlin, Goering decided to turn the might of the Luftwaffe on London giving the RAF respite and much needed time to rearm. In late September the Battle of Britain had ended and Operation Sea Lion had been postponed indefinitely. Against overwhelming odds the RAF fighter command had overcome the might of the Luftwaffe. It led to another important address to the nation by Winston Churchill, the British Prime Minister. He ended with the immortal line:

'Never in the field of human conflict was so much owed by so many to so few.'

John Holmes rushed home every night, had a quick bite to eat and literally ran to the Roxy Cinema, which was replaying footage of the Battle of Britain. It was a 'Movietone' production that he sat watching as he munched through a chocolate bar, unable to take his eyes from the screen. The footage showed a group of Canadian pilots being scrambled as news of a German attack came in. The narrator proudly exclaimed that Fighter Command had already performed wonders and John watched as the Spitfires and Hurricanes roared down the runways and up into the air to engage the German aircraft. The footage switched to the air as it focused on a group of German bombers protected by Messerschmitt fighters. John knew that the Movietone production was heavily weighted towards the British successes but then again pictures didn't lie and the film reel clearly showed dozens of clips of burning German aircraft hitting the ground with airfield fireman extinguishing the fires of German planes as the tail pieces, adorned with huge swastikas, took centre stage.

'169 German aircraft lost in one day,' the voice announced. The narrator said that the figures were compiled by the pilots who shot down the aircraft and an independent witness. John had to laugh; an independent witness, where would they find one of them? And still he waxed lyrical about the stricken German planes in his monotone public school voice.

'Equivalent to twelve or fourteen squadrons, how long can the Nazis stand such losses? The Bosch got what was coming to them.'

The crews rested and played football between raids, a portable telephone on standby to warn them of the next attack. John wondered when they slept. *A graveyard of Nazi hopes*, the letters on the screen announced from a new film reel, this time a different production. The camera filmed a 20-acre scrap yard somewhere in southern England where the wreckage of hundreds of German planes were being dismantled for valuable scrap metal. In an incredible piece of footage the movie makers explained and detailed the tactics of a spitfire taking out a Heinkel bomber. The narrator explained the vulnerability of the Heinkel who had three gunners, one in the front, one in the rear and one underneath. The Heinkel design was poor he claimed, giving a clear arc of attack on the pilot should a spitfire come in from above at the correct angle. The guns of the bomber were effectively useless if the pilot of the Spitfire got his coordinates correct. And then the footage showed exactly the angle the pilot would fly in from. Pure genius thought John, pure genius. It was no accident that the casualties were running at around five to one in favour of the Allied aircraft. It then showed a real clip of a Spitfire doing exactly what the narrator had previously explained. The Spitfire powered in on the Heinkel and the bullets concentrated on the enemy cockpit. A little smoke poured from the cockpit, the pilot clearly dead and then the bomber burst into flames much to the delight of the assembled cinemagoers that started applauding loudly.

John returned to the cinema night after night during July, August, September and October 1940. His father claimed he was becoming obsessed, spending his entire wage packet on cinema tickets. John didn't care and he was almost disappointed when the battle of Britain ended towards the end of October when the Luftwaffe turned their attention to British cities once again.

The two friends sat in silence for a few moments. Norman's brother, Cliff, had also joined the East Lancashire Regiment along with James and had slept in the same billet during basic training. It only came out in a letter that Cliff sent home. In it he mentioned a 'James Holmes' from Skerton. Norman had brought the letter along to the pub to show John and the two friends had put two and two together. It was an amazing coincidence that the two soldiers had got on so well together, as had their two brothers back home in Civvy Street. It gave them a little reassurance knowing that they would look out for each other.

'I wish I could be there with them, Norman; I feel so useless sat in a fucking factory ten hours a day,' said John.

'Me too, mate, but our time will come. Another few months and we'll both get our chance. Will you be joining the East Lancaster's?'

John shook his head. 'Not me, Norman.'

'What mob are you joining then?'

'The RAF.'

Norman Shaw nearly choked on his beer. 'The fucking Brylcreem Boys! I knew you were watching too much bloody footage at the pictures. The Battle of Britain is over mate, we won. You're too late.'

Norman put his glass down onto the table, gazed across at his friend. 'You can't be serious?'

'You bet I am. I've never been so serious about anything in my life.'

John and his dad grew ever closer, as they never missed a single night by the radio. It had become a sort of tradition. They sat together in November 1940 as the BBC announced the destruction of the city of Coventry, the Coventry Blitz as it would be known. 515 German bombers had flown over the city in an operation codenamed *Mondscheinsonate* (Moonlight Sonata). It was an innovative raid which would influence all future strategic bombing raids. The Luftwaffe used pathfinder aircraft with electronic aids to mark the munitions factory targets before the main bombers went into action. The first wave of follow-up bombers dropped high explosive bombs, knocking out utilities, the gas, water and electricity networks. They deliberately cratered the roads, making it difficult for the fire engines to reach fires, and determined that the city of Coventry would burn like a firestorm. The bombers dropped a combination of high explosive and incendiary bombs. They damaged roofs, making it easier for the incendiary bombs to fall into buildings and ignite them. They may have struck lucky that night as they scored a direct hit on the fire brigade headquarters. The city burned for three days, the firemen unable to cope. The raid on Coventry claimed over 1,000 lives, the vast majority civilian women working a shift in the factories. An incredible 60,000 buildings were destroyed or damaged. It wasn't surprising; the Germans had dropped 500 tons of high explosives and 36,000 incendiary bombs within a few hours. Mission accomplished for the pilots and aircrews of the Nazi air force.

John couldn't contemplate the sheer scale of destruction. For once his father couldn't bring himself to discuss the evening radio reports. He got up from the table shaking his head and as he walked out of the door John heard him mumble.

'Coventry…Coventry… God help the poor bastards in Coventry.'

It was the first time John had heard his father curse in anger.

Two days later John and Norman were back together in the Greaves Hotel. Norman asked why John hadn't appeared the night before and he explained that he'd had a hastily-arranged date with Joyce.

'What was so hasty you couldn't meet up with your pal?'

John smiled. 'Her parents were out for the evening.'

Norman's brow furrowed; he had a puzzled look etched across his face. He looked over to the bar where Joyce pulled a pint for one of the regulars. Then the penny dropped.

'You didn't?'

John grinned, signalled over to Joyce, put two fingers up and pointed to Norman and himself.

'Two pints, John?' she called over.

John nodded and stood up. 'I'll just pay for them mate.'

Norman grabbed his jacket as he stepped from behind the table.

'You didn't answer me, John.'

'Answer what?'

'You didn't, did you?'

John bent over and whispered in his ear.

'You bet I did mate. At least half a dozen times, she rode me like a jockey in the Derby, the Grand National and the St Ledger all rolled into one.'

For a few seconds Norman lost the power of speech as his jaw fell open but no words came.

John took a few paces towards the bar. 'That reminds me, I'll be needing a haircut soon to pick up some more military hardware.'

'Well I never,' mumbled Norman as he picked up his glass. 'The dirty... rotten...*lucky* bastard.'

The meetings continued for some weeks, as did John's dates with Joyce, and by this time he had another two girls on the go and he never tired of giving Norman a blow-by-blow account of each passionate encounter.

'You're some fellow, John Holmes,' he joked. 'You want to be careful – that cock of yours will drop off.'

The two friends sat at their regular table in the bar. The door opened to the street and a shape appeared in the doorway. It was a pleasant interlude. The girl took a step forward and gazed around the bar, obviously looking for someone. The only girls that came into the pubs and clubs of Lancaster at that particular time generally stood behind the bar and pulled pints. John's jaw dropped. Suddenly Joyce had lost her appeal.

'Look Norman, look.' John pointed over to the girl.

Norman put his beer glass on the table and peered over, curious as to what John was so interested in.

The girl in the doorway couldn't have been more than five feet tall, very petite, but extremely good looking and smartly dressed in a close fitting jacket, a tight pencil skirt and black high heels. John caught his breath as she seemed to recognise him and smiled. And to his absolute joy she closed the door and started walking towards their table.

'Look Norm, she's coming this way, she's absolutely gorgeous.'

Norman turned to face him.

'That she is, John...that she is. But I'll thank you to keep your dirty fucking paws off her. That's my sister Dorothy.'

CHAPTER THREE

'I'm warning you John, you keep your bloody eyes in your head and your hands in your pocket. She's my sister and she is strictly off limits. End of story.'

'Spoken like a father, Norm,' John said as he slapped Norman on the back. Norman shied away, making John well aware his body language had purpose and meaning.

'Fuck off John and stop patronising me.'

John edged forward in his seat and rested his elbows on the table, his face barely inches from his good friend's. He took a quick mischievous look around the bar and then stared back at Norman as he cautiously glared over the top of his pint pot.

'Don't you worry Norman, I'm an honourable man.'

'I'm glad to hear it.'

'After all, mates are mates.'

'Good.'

'And you are like a brother to me.'

Norman leant forward with heavy shoulders as he reluctantly

showed his approval but a facial twitch also displayed a tiny hint of suspicion.

'And?'

'I cross my heart in God's honour.' John made the sign of the cross on his chest.

'You don't believe in God.'

John hesitated.

'You're right…I'd forgotten about that.' He grinned again. 'Doesn't matter, I'll swear on my Mam's life, anything.'

'Swear what?'

'I swear, my best mate Norman, that I'll keep my hands off your sister Dot.' John rose from the table, placed his cap on his head as he looked at his watch.

'Got to get going old mate. It's a long walk home.'

Norman was nodding; he smiled for the first time that evening.

'The thing is, Norman…' he stood up, leant over the table and slapped his friend gently on the cheek. 'Can she keep her hands off me?'

John Holmes had timed it perfectly. Norman jumped up from the table, spilling what was left in his glass onto the table.

'You cheeky little bastard, I'll fucking brain you.'

He sprinted across the room to the doorway but John was already running away into the night gloom laughing mockingly as he went. Norman reached the doorway and peered out into the darkness. John had disappeared.

John's initial sprint had turned into a jog. There was no way Norman Shaw would ever have caught up with him even if he could have seen him. It was at least half a mile before his chuckles had died away. Norman Shaw was the easiest man in the world to wind up. John Holmes looked up into the night sky. A fine drizzle began to fall, the tiny droplets stood out against the dull glow of the street lights. He pulled up the collar

of his coat to protect him from the cold, damp night air. As he
did he gazed up into the sky. He wondered where his brothers
were, if they were okay or if they too were cold and wet in a
trench somewhere in France. As he turned the corner into
Ashton Drive a GPO telegram bike stood outside the door of
number 43.

'It's bad news, I'm telling you,' said his father.

'It could be anything, Bill…' his mother replied.

William Holmes sat with an untouched cup of lukewarm tea.

'Not at this time of night. They don't send a telegram
announcing a birth or an engagement at this time of night.'

Georgina Holmes stood motionless, her thumb and
forefinger stroking at a troubled chin.

'Do you think I should call on her?' she eventually said.

'I'll come with you, get your coat, it's turned into a horrible
night.'

He took his big overcoat from the hook on the back of the
kitchen door, pulled his cap from the pocket and John was left
sitting in the kitchen on his own.

John was still sitting in the same spot two hours later. Alice
and Mary had joined him and they sat in stony silence until
they heard the front door slam. Alice stood up.

'That's Mam back now, I'll go and…'

'Sit down,' John interrupted. 'I'll put the kettle on.'

The two statuesque faces of William and Georgina Holmes
as they walked through the door told the three siblings
everything they needed to know. Georgina Holmes's eyes were
red and moist. She had been crying for some time. As she
looked into the vacant stares of her children she broke down
again and collapsed on a seat next to the kitchen table. William
Holmes went to comfort her. He turned to his children.

'Your Mam remembers Frank being born, playing out in the street in short pants.'

He didn't need to tell his son and daughters what they already knew but he did.

'He's been killed in France.'

The war had truly arrived in Skerton.

But life went on. Life had to go on. The shops and the factories continued to operate, the picture houses and pubs opened as normal, even the local dance halls continued to flourish, young men and women eager for release, keen to show the Germans that they would never break their resolve.

Norman and John had gone to the local dance at the Roxy on Market Street the following Saturday night. Norman's sister Dorothy also sat on a table over the far side of the room with at least a dozen of her friends. The atmosphere in the hall was a little sombre at first; it seemed everyone knew Frank Roberts or at least knew someone that knew him. The band leader gave out the bad news and called for one minute's silence. But afterwards he called for an air of normality, said it was what Frank would have wanted, and almost ordered the crowd to enjoy themselves as he conducted the band to open with 'A String of Pearls', one of Glenn Miller's most popular tunes. By the third or fourth tune the dance floor was beginning to fill, and by tune six – with the gentle persuasion of a few beers, not to mention the ladies' favourite, port and lemon – it was in full swing.

Dorothy Shaw nudged her best friend Mavis Walsh.

'Hey Mave, that's John Holmes over there sitting with my brother.'

'Oh yeah, so it is. He's gorgeous isn't he?'

'Think I stand a chance?'

'No way, he's hooked up with Joyce from the Greaves Hotel.

34

They reckon she's teaching him the tricks of the trade.' Mavis laughed. 'He's a couple more on the go too, I'm told.'

Mavis looked her friend up and down and a mocking smile flicked across her face.

'And Dot, I think he's a bit young for you anyway. Best leave him alone, nothing but trouble, that one.'

Dorothy Holmes found a burst of courage as she laughed and rose to her feet. She'd gazed across the darkened room, peered in between the dancing figures. The dance floor was one big jumping, pounding, bouncing Jitterbug as a thousand sparkles from a revolving silver ball suspended from the ceiling lit up a hundred happy, smiling faces. They looked as if they didn't have a care in the world. Frank Roberts was a memory now and the war a million miles away. Dorothy Shaw could barely pick out the shape of her brother and his friend but she was on a mission and nothing was going to stop her.

Another friend chipped in.

'Where are you going, Dot? The bar's over there.' She pointed in the opposite direction to where Dorothy was looking.

Dorothy Shaw didn't answer; already halfway across the crowded dance floor she dodged flailing limbs and twisting bodies as the five piece band from Lancaster mimicked the sounds of Benny Goodman's Big Band. As she reached the table Dorothy realised how unprepared she was. What was she going to say, what would she do? There was a pregnant pause as she looked at her young brother and then at his friend. She looked almost hypnotically into his piercing blue eyes as they held her gaze there for a moment and she felt an uncontrollable but pleasant shiver run the length of her spine.

Norman's voice brought her back to the present.

'What you after, our lass?'

'Nothing Norman, just wondering what you were doing here. I didn't know you could dance.'

'I can't, neither can John here but we heard the beer was good and anyway we like the music.'

It was the perfect opening, a gift from the Gods. Good old Norman, she thought, and the words came to her as naturally as asking for a loaf of bread at the local shop.

'I could teach you if you like John.'

Norman's head fell into his two hands and he shook it from side to side. He'd never seen his sister look this way before. It was his worst nightmare and there was nothing he could do to stop it.

As Dorothy took John by the hand and prepared to walk onto the dance floor she stopped and turned to face her brother.

'By the way Norman, there's a girl on my table called Laurena. I think you should ask her to dance.'

'And why's that?'

Dorothy leaned forward and whispered into his ear.

'Because she fancies you, you twit.'

John Holmes and Dorothy Shaw danced all evening. They danced to the Jitterbug, did the Foxtrot and smooched to the Waltz. When they weren't dancing they stood at the bar drinking and talking, mostly talking. By the end of the night they were inseparable and despite the best efforts of Norman and Dorothy's friends they would not return to their respective tables. When the evening ended John asked if he could walk his new girl home. Norman had long gone, as had Dorothy's friends. She agreed. By the time they turned right onto Penny Street and set off in the direction of Greaves Road their hands were entwined and by the time they reached the junction of Ashton Road John knew, just knew, that he had met the girl he was going to marry. They turned left into Greaves Park. They walked through slowly, glad of the silence and the loneliness of the park. As they neared the exit on the far side a lodge house loomed up through the darkness blocking out the lights from the nearby streets. Dorothy turned to face him.

'I think it's best you leave me here. Belle Vue Terrace is just around the corner.'

John nodded.

'No problem, Dorothy, no problem at all.'

He was trying to act the gentleman, be polite. He was trying his hardest not to put his foot in it, not to do anything that would spoil this beautiful, beautiful evening. Dorothy gave him a little peck on the cheek and bid him goodnight. It was a long walk home but it mattered not. John Holmes would walk home floating on air.

John was pleased he'd had so many conversations with Norman. Norman had given him the entire history of every member of his family – including Dorothy. He knew what she did and where she worked and even what time she clocked on and off. Good old Norman.

The textile mill where Dorothy worked was on South Road. It backed onto the Lancaster to Preston Canal. John had completed his routine maintenance in double quick time that day and the supervisor saw no reason not to let him out of work 30 minutes early. He arrived outside the gates of Storey Brothers' Mill with five minutes to spare. The entrance was impressive, a big old white stone fronted facade, the name Storey Brothers carved deep into the stone and painted red. Behind the stunning entrance it was a mill just like any other, a huge, imposing dirty grey bricked building that seemed to block out the whole landscape. He looked up to the elegant edifice, noticed turrets standing proudly at each end. He had been told it had been home for a Battalion in the Crimean War but now it housed only a workforce who didn't want to be there. It shouldn't have been depressing, but it was.

Spot on six o'clock the security guard unlocked the huge padlock that secured a thick chain around the gates, unwrapped the chain and swung the gates open. A few minutes later the workers drifted out into the huge compound eager to make their way home. Dorothy spotted him before he spotted her. She stopped at the gates.

'Well well, John Holmes, what are you doing here?'

'I've come to ask my girl if she would like to go out on a date.'

'Your girl. Is that what I am?' She broke into a forced laugh. 'You dance with me a few times and I'm your girl?'

'Fourteen dances actually.'

'You were counting?'

John nodded and grinned. 'And anyway I was wondering if my girl would like to come and join me for a picnic this weekend?'

'A picnic, are you mad? It's November, its freezing! Where, when, what time?'

John held up a hand, 'Whoa… steady on, no more questions. Just tell me you'll go and I'll pick you up at home around one on Sunday.'

Dorothy stood with her hands on her hips. 'Very well then if you insist.'

'I do.'

'One more question though.'

'Yes.'

'Where are we going?'

John fell back against the mill wall and looked into the sky.

'That's an easy one, Dorothy Shaw. I'm taking you to the most beautiful place in the world.'

The World, and Europe in particular, were far away from being described as a beautiful place in the spring of 1941. It was clear from the radio reports that the war was far from over. John and his father listened with dismay as the BBC announced that Swansea and Glasgow on the River Clyde had been sought out for special treatment by the German Luftwaffe and the worst bombing of the year had taken place in London, the Luftwaffe bombs even managing to hit Buckingham Palace. German and British troops had also confronted each other for the first time in North Africa, at El Agheila in western Libya. John's father shook his head.

'What is it, Dad?' asked John.

His father's chin rested on the palm of his hand as he let out a sigh.

'I don't know, John, I just don't know. When this bloody war started I was convinced it would be over in a matter of months. We're fighting all over the bloody world now, even in Africa.'

Despite the doom and gloom of the BBC man, as always he finished on a bright note, the irony not lost on John. He always ended with some good news as he informed the listeners that the United States President Franklin Delano Roosevelt had signed a lease act allowing Britain, China and other Allied nations to purchase military equipment and to defer payment until after the war.

'That's good news isn't it Dad, the Americans on our side, giving us weapons?'

'Yes son… good news indeed.'

And yet John noticed something in his father's eyes, a look that said he wanted more than that. The BBC would not tell their listeners that the spring of 1941 was not a good time for the Allies. Their troops were being run ragged. Portsmouth had also suffered heavy casualties after another night of heavy bombing by the Luftwaffe and huge convoy losses had been suffered in the mid-Atlantic. Rommel had also reoccupied El Agheila, Libya in his first major offensive against British troops. The British retreated and were driven back into Egypt. Hitler could have been forgiven for thinking he had the upper hand against the Allies; his confidence was at an all-time high and he ordered his military leaders to plan for the invasion of Yugoslavia and sets his sights further afield on the Soviet Union. At the same time he gave the order for the expansion of Auschwitz prison camp, to be run by Commandant Rudolph Hess.

So William Holmes wanted more; he wanted the bloody Americans to come in and help the Allies. The Germans were sinking their merchant ships by the score but still they sat on the sidelines. What was wrong with them?

The BBC announcer wrapped up his report. There was a two or three second delay and a beautiful American big band sound filled the room. William grinned sarcastically.

'Glenn Miller,' he said pointing at the radio. 'Glenn bloody Miller. Why doesn't he put his trombone away and pick up a bloody gun?'

John turned down the sound on the radio, turned to face his father. 'Do you think the Yanks will come in to the war, Dad?' he asked.

William's head was back in his hands as he raked his fingers through his hair. He looked up at his son, pulled him towards him and ruffled at his hair just like he had when he was a small boy. John leaned into him and his father's arms wrapped around him tightly.

'I hope so son…I hope so.'

John tried to look at the situation logically. Surely the Americans wouldn't sit on the fence for ever. Another ship sunk perhaps? Maybe something bigger?

It was March 27th 1941 and John bid his father goodnight and climbed the stairs to bed. On the other side of the world, the Japanese spy Takeo Yoshikawa arrived in Honolulu, Hawaii and began to study the United States fleet at Pearl Harbor.

John had never expected to meet Dorothy's parents on this their first real date but Dorothy had insisted he come in and meet the family. It was only when she took his hand and pulled him into the house that his resolve broke. Her soft tiny hand felt so good in his. He never wanted to let it go.

Dorothy's father stood with his elbow resting on the mantelpiece of the black cast iron range, bedecked in a steel grey three-piece suit complete with waistcoat and a gold Albert chain hanging from the pocket. He wore a crisp, starched, brilliant white shirt and a bottle green tie and he smoked a pipe. It was the quintessential look of that particular time. He eyed John up and down purposely, as if to say *watch your step my lad, be very careful with my daughter.* If he'd wanted to frighten John Holmes then it worked a treat. John was petrified. The white smoke from the pipe drifted into the air before disappearing, as if by magic, into the recesses of the room. And then he spoke.

'What does your father do, young man?'

'Furniture maker for Waring and Gillow, Mr Shaw,' he said nervously.

John Shaw took another pull on his pipe, peered at John through the smoke as he blew it out through the side of his mouth.

'Hmmm… very good, fine job.'

There then ensued another uncomfortable silence. He could hear what he thought was Dorothy's mother busying herself in the kitchen but the rest of the house was deathly silent. He squeezed on Dorothy's hand; she squeezed back and he was glad of the reassurance. It was all rather bizarre meeting Dorothy's father when they hadn't even been out on a real date, and yet he knew – they both did – that it was something that needed to be done. It was as if they were both displaying how serious they were about the future. They knew they had a future; they wanted to be with each other forever, to marry and to have children. They hadn't told each other at that point but they would, very soon. In fact they would declare their undying love for each other that very day in the most beautiful place on earth. John Shaw spoke.

'And where are you taking my daughter today, young man?'

'The Crook O' Lune, Mr Shaw.'

John Shaw smiled and nodded with approval. 'I know it well lad. I know it well.'

James Holmes was home on leave. There was a purpose; he was getting married to his long term sweetheart Marjorie Nelson. His brother Ernie had also been granted leave for the event. It was an unusual occurrence. Three brothers home together during the war. It was the perfect opportunity for John to introduce Dorothy to the family. The reception was held in the local church hall; it was a magnificent feast and for once no one mentioned the war. John had approached Ernie several times; he wanted to find out first-hand what it was really like over there. But Ernie had flatly refused to talk about it. It was a long day but an enjoyable one because he was never far away from Dorothy's side. They sat together holding hands in the church, they dined together, danced together and shared an awful lot of drinks together. Afterwards he walked Dorothy home and he told her all about his desire to join the RAF, to be one of the Brylcreem Boys. Air crew, not ground crew; he wanted to be one of the best. Dorothy said she believed he was the type of man who could be anything he wanted to be. Prophetic words. Confident words. Trusting words. And as he kissed her goodnight he swore he'd make those words come true.

On 22nd June 1941, Hitler's Third Reich Army invaded Russia in an operation called Barbarossa. To many military experts it was a fatal mistake in that Hitler opened up two war fronts. He sent over 4.5 million troops of the axis powers, nearly 600,000 motor vehicles and 750,000 horses. On 19th September the Nazis took Kiev. Nearly the entire south western front of the Red Army was encircled and the Germans took nearly 600,000 Russian POWs. They treated them dreadfully. Some of them were immediately executed in the field by the German forces, while many simply died of starvation in German prisoner of war camps and during the ruthless death marches from the front lines. The camps were often simply open areas, fenced off with barbed wire and the crowded prisoners dug holes with their bare hands in a vain attempt to protect themselves from the elements. Many died from exposure as the weather turned colder.

The Kiev disaster was an unprecedented defeat for the Red Army and Hitler's confidence then knew no bounds. He decided to set his sights further afield and ordered his troops to advance onwards towards Moscow. His senior generals urged caution advising on the severity of the Russian Winter. Hitler ignored them.

Towards the end of November the German forces fighting for control of Moscow were worn out and frozen, with only a third of their motor vehicles still operable. Their infantry divisions were at one-third to one-half strength and serious logistics issues prevented the delivery of winter equipment to the front. Warm clothing and decent boots were in short supply. Even Hitler seemed to concede that the idea of a long struggle seemed futile. The daily casualties were extremely high, many German troops simply froze to death during the cold nights where temperatures regularly touched -35°C. German losses were estimated between 300,000 and 450,000 men. Operation Barbarossa was the largest military operation in human history in terms of both manpower and casualties.

On 7th December 1941, the Japanese Imperial Navy attacked the USA pacific fleet at Pearl Harbor, Hawaii. The Japanese raid on Pearl Harbor has been described as one of the less noble moments in the history of World War Two, but one that could have led to victory for the Axis powers had it not been for the resolve and determination of the Allies afterwards. An American General likened it to a boxing match where one of the prize-fighters sat on his stool blinded, deafened and completely unaware that his opponent had started the fight. The Japanese were roundly condemned around the world for not declaring war on the US before the attack. However, what no one could deny was that it was a well-orchestrated, well-executed plan which all but removed the United States Navy's force as a possible threat to the Japanese Empire's southward expansion.

The Japanese Navy secretly sent one of its biggest aircraft carriers across the Pacific with a greater aerial striking power than had ever been seen on the World's oceans before. Its planes hit just before 8am on 7th December 1941. The Americans were taken completely by surprise and within a short time, five of its eight battleships were seriously damaged, all of which would eventually settle into the dark murky silt deep at the bottom of Pearl Harbor. Three destroyers were wrecked, a minelayer and a target ship destroyed and two cruisers were also badly damaged. Many other smaller ships suffered major structural damage.

Such was the ferocity of the Japanese attack it also accounted for most of the Hawaii-based combat planes and as the Japanese turned tail for home satisfied with their day's work over 2,400 Americans were dead. Soon after, Japanese planes eliminated much of the American air force in the Philippines.

The 'sneak' attacks shocked and enraged the previously divided American people and fuelled a determination to fight, and in Congress the following day, President Roosevelt asked for a declaration of war against Japan. He referred to the attacks as a 'date that will live in infamy'. Vice Admiral Halsey brought his Enterprise task force into Pearl Harbor and when he witnessed the sheer destruction first hand said, 'Before we're through with 'em, the Japanese language will be spoken only in hell.'

At last, the United States of America had joined the war.

In the spring of 1942 the Government introduced the rationing of electricity, coal and gas. It did not go down well in the houses of Great Britain. John's father was practical as he read the Sunday papers announcing the date of introduction.

'It's a sensible precaution,' he announced to his son and wife. 'The more power we save the more we can use to produce armaments.'

He scanned the rest of the news and read the salient points out loud.

'Those RAF lads are doing their bit, John. I see Hamburg has had a taste of Bomber Command medicine.'

The RAF had also sent out raids against Lübeck, almost destroying the medieval city centre. Adolf Hitler was outraged and ordered 'Baedeker raids' on historic British sites in revenge for the Lübeck bombing. Around the same time, with sinister undertones he ordered the Jewish population in Berlin to wear the yellow Star of David at all times.

A few months later, the first reports began to filter through to the west that gas was being used to kill the Jews sent to the east.

Autumn 1942 was an eventful month for Dorothy Shaw and John Holmes. John had sat the test for the RAF in Liverpool. It had seemed to take forever to get there on the bus and while most of his friends including Norman had joined the local infantry regiments where an examination wasn't necessary, John had at least wanted to give it a go. He recalled the conversation with Norman the previous evening in the Greaves Hotel. Norman had said it wasn't worth it.

'Our sort don't join the RAF John, the RAF is for toffs, public school boys and those with money,' he'd said.

The bus approached the outskirts of the city and John began to get a few pangs of doubt. Perhaps Norman was right he thought to himself, a waste of a day, a waste of a bus fare and a day's pay lost too. Then he recalled Dorothy's words. *I can do it*, he told himself; *I will do it*, he mouthed as the bus pulled into the depot in Lime Street. It was a ten-minute walk to the recruiting office in Victoria Street and as he walked in the desk sergeant, a portly balding man in his mid-fifties, looked over the top of his bi-focal glasses.

'Name.' he bellowed.

'Holmes, Sir.'

John found himself coming to attention, poking out his chest though he hadn't a clue where it had come from.

'I'm here to take a test, Sir.'

The sergeant scrolled down the sheet of paper in front of him and rested his pen halfway down the sheet.

'John Holmes. Born 1923, 59 Ashton Drive, Skerton in Lancaster. Is that you, boy?'

'Yes Sir.' John smiled.

The sergeant pointed to a row of chairs.

'Then take a seat and wait your turn, and stop fucking smiling boy. I didn't ask you to smile.'

John could have done no more. The exam had been as expected, not easy but then again he didn't think it had been too difficult. And he'd been glad of his knowledge of engineering and the mechanics that made the machines in the mill work as quite a few questions referring to that sort of thing had cropped up on the paper. Next was his interview. He sat another twenty minutes before the desk sergeant called his name.

'Holmes. Room four.'

Wing Commander RG Wilson, the brass plaque read on the door. He seemed a friendly enough chap at first, totally different from the desk sergeant he'd first met. He warned John about how difficult it was to get into the RAF and how he mustn't be disappointed if he wasn't accepted.

John explained that both his brothers were fighting in the war and he was desperate to join them.

'But why the RAF, Holmes? Why not join one of your brothers' regiments? You'll be with your pals, chaps from your own neighbourhood.'

'I'm not interested Sir, I want to join the RAF, I want to be the best. I feel that's where I belong, don't ask me why or how, it's just how I feel.'

John's eyes oozed sincerity and determination, the look was not lost on Wing Commander Wilson.

John continued. 'I've been fascinated by aircraft, especially bombers, since I was a small boy, I've always felt destined to fly and I…'

'Whoa, just a minute here old chap,' the Wing Commander interrupted. 'You're getting a little ahead of yourself now. Who said anything about flying?'

John opened his mouth but the words wouldn't form.

'There are seven crew members flying in one of those Stirling Bombers including the pilot. Those boys are the elite, sonny. You can forget that straight away. If you're serious, and I mean really serious then you'll set your sights on being one of the ground crew.'

John gulped. He felt his eyes moisten just a little and hoped the Wing Commander hadn't noticed.

'But I don't want to be ground crew, Sir. I…'

The Wing Commander interrupted again

'It takes at least sixty ground crew to keep those chaps in the air Holmes, are you insulting my ground crew?'

'No Sir, but…'

'You are; you've just told me you don't want to join our ground crew.'

John felt physically sick. He'd blown it. How had the conversation tailed off so badly? He needed to somehow rescue the situation, he was thinking on his feet.

'Yes Sir, I'd be truly honoured to be a member of the ground crew.'

The Wing Commander jotted a few notes on the writing pad in front of him. There was a deafening silence before he eventually spoke.

'I'm glad to hear it. Coming in here insulting my boys. Ha!' He mocked a fake laugh. 'Delusions of grandeur no doubt.'

The Wing Commander closed his pad.

'Okay, here's what happens next. We mark your test and post

you a letter within the next few days. If you've passed then we'll send you to Blackpool on a two-week selection course. It won't be any fun, I warn you, not a Stirling Bomber or a Spitfire to be seen. Just hours and hours of square bashing and dozens more competency tests, a lot of study in the classroom and a final examination.'

John was nodding his understanding.

'Some won't make it, we'll send them home and they'll go into their local regiments. The rest –' he looked John Holmes in the face. '– the *elite* – will join the RAF.'

'Yes Sir.'

The Wing Commander opened his note pad once again and began referring to his notes. Without looking up he told John Holmes to go.

As John reached the door he turned around and paused. He took a sharp intake of breath.

'Sir…'

'Yes, Holmes?'

'I apologise, Sir, I really do.'

He looked up. 'Glad to hear it boy, now be off with you.'

'It's just…'

'Yes, Holmes?'

'It's just that I want to be in air crew so badly.'

'Holmes,' the Wing Commander announced in a voice that was a few decibels louder than his usual tone. 'Have you ever flown in an aircraft before, even as a passenger?'

'No, Sir.'

'I thought as much. Now fuck off out of my office and close the door quietly as you do.'

For five days John Holmes was the first out of bed every morning waiting for the postman to bring a letter postmarked

Liverpool. Jimmy French, the local postman, walked towards the door on a cold blustery morning. He waved a letter at the bay window as John Holmes peered out. John could just about make out his words.

'Letter from Liverpool, John. RAF stamp on the back. It's the one you've been waiting for I think.'

Jimmy French waited while John opened the letter. His face broke out into a broad grin.

'Yes. Yes!' he repeated over and over again.

'What, what is it?' Jimmy asked.

'I'm off to Blackpool next week, on an RAF selection course.'

Jimmy's face fell.

'Is that it? Is that what all the fucking fuss is about, a bloody selection course? Jesus Christ John, I thought the letter was telling you you'd been made up to Flight Commander!'

There's an expression in life that says, 'it's a perfect day, watch some bastard spoil it'. If John's encounter with the postman hadn't exactly spoiled what to him was a perfect day then his meeting with Dorothy certainly did. He was full of enthusiasm as he showed her the letter and although she did her best to share his exuberance John knew something wasn't quite right. They were soul mates, lovers and best friends. It was as if he could almost read her mind.

'Do you want to tell me what's wrong, Dot?'

The tears welled up in Dorothy's eyes and she pulled a handkerchief from her sleeve.

'Is it not obvious, John?'

'Tell me what it is darling, we'll get through it together.'

'I'm sure we will John, I'm sure we will.' She sniffed, dabbed at the corner of her eyes with the handkerchief.

'They're sending me off to Coventry.'

Hearing the name of the West Midlands city hit John like a blow from a sledgehammer.

'I'll be working in a munitions factory in the city centre... living in digs.'

No, no, no, this couldn't be happening. His father's words came back to haunt him. *Coventry...Coventry... God help the poor bastards living in Coventry.*

CHAPTER FOUR

The bus to Blackpool for the Aircrew Candidates Selection Board (ACSB) had taken just over three hours, stopping in various towns en route picking up other young RAF hopefuls along the way. It was a long three hours and John's head was in the clouds – or rather it was in Coventry. *Why Coventry?* he'd asked himself a hundred times. Dorothy would be lodging in the Bishopsgate Green part of the city and although she would be home every other weekend it didn't make it any easier.

He'd had his first letter from her and she missed him, couldn't wait to get back to Lancaster. When would they see each other again? It was anyone's guess. Although Dorothy's leave was precisely documented, his wasn't. Whether he passed or failed the RAF's stringent entrance procedures he didn't have a clue where he'd end up. His life was in the lap of the Gods.

John did what he'd always done. He blocked out the turbulent forces that controlled his life, things he could do nothing about, and knuckled down. One thing he could control was his own destiny in the RAF…perhaps. He would give it his best shot. If it wasn't to be, if he wasn't cut out for RAF life, then he could live with that as long as he'd given it his all.

The first two weeks were a breeze, and John loved every minute. In the army it would be called square bashing but the RAF boys didn't bash around squares. No. Up and down Blackpool promenade they marched mile after mile, their clothes pristine, ties ironed to perfection, buttons polished until they were almost smooth and black boots bulled up so that you could see your face in them. John was in his element, beaming with pride, even though he wasn't yet kitted out in the uniform of Her Majesty's Royal Air Force. The civilians on the promenade always had a kind word or two as if they knew how much it meant to the young men marching past. John suppressed an almost permanent smile. A smile of pride. It wouldn't do to be seen smiling; the drill sergeant would think you were some sort of village idiot. He wouldn't have understood. It was okay for him, he had his uniform on his back, the uniform John craved so badly.

The third and fourth weeks were a lot tougher. John struggled in the classroom and struggled to complete the tasks set for the candidates each evening. On the third day of the third week, two of his mates failed one of the examinations and were sent home. He breathed a sigh of relief; at least he wasn't one of them. There were eight left in the section. It was back to school, homework to be handed in the very next morning, so that when his fellow candidates nipped out for a few pints at the end of the working day John confined himself to barracks in a vain attempt to perfect the job in hand. Perhaps Norman had been right. He hadn't the education some of his colleagues had and yes there were one or two toffs in his section, more than a few who spoke with marbles in their mouths, calling him 'old bean' instead of 'mate' or 'pal'. *Old bean*, he thought to himself, *why call someone an old bean?*

It was decision day and John wondered if he could have pushed it just a little harder. It was too late, no use thinking about what might have been. Squadron Leader Phelps stood in front of the assembled men. He said that they'd all worked very hard and that they were a credit to the towns and cities from which they had come. And then his voice dropped a little. It became a little softer and John Holmes detected a note of sympathy.

'Unfortunately there are winners and losers in all walks of life.'

He read out six names.

'Gilbert, Jackson, Valentine, Graham, Wilson-Morgan, Devonshire.'

He asked them to walk out to the front of the class. The nervous young men did as they were told and stood at ease while the Squadron Leader examined his clipboard.

'Gentlemen…' he paused for dramatic effect and then he grinned.

'Well done, you've made it.'

There was a collective cheer as they slapped each other on the back, and one or two caps flew into the air. John hung his head; this wasn't happening, he'd worked so hard. He looked at Curly Mason, a MP's son from the Wirral. Curly shrugged his shoulders as if to say 'so what, we gave it our best'. The Squadron Leader dismissed the assembled happy, smiling men. Something told John the beer would flow in gallons that evening. They'd made it, he hadn't. End of story.

John rose from his seat as the last body exited the room. He directed his plea to the Squadron Leader.

'Sir, if I could just have a few more days I promise I'll make the grade, I'll work harder and smarter. I'll –'

The Squadron Leader raised his hand.

'Holmes, please stop.'

'But, Sir! I –'

'Stop talking and listen, that's an order.'

'I'll do better!'

'Shut up, I'm ordering you Flight Engineer, shut up.'

It took a moment to register…was that a smile on the Squadron Leader's face? *He called me Flight Engineer*, thought John. What was he talking about?

'Flight Engineer Holmes. You'll report for duty at 0700 hours at Redcar in seven days' time.'

He turned to Curly Mason.

'You, Gunner Mason, are heading to a pretty little spot on the south coast.'

John Holmes could only point at the door.

'But Sir, the others…you said they'd made it. I don't understand.'

Now the Squadron Leader was smiling, there was no mistake.

'Ground crew, gentlemen. They are the lucky ones. Your colleagues are staying on the ground. You poor bastards are going up into the sky to give Jerry a taste of his own medicine.'

Thank God Dorothy had made it home on leave two days before John was ready to head off to Redcar. It had been almost like torture being without her, worse, knowing that she was in Coventry. Although the bombing in the West Midlands city had never been as bad as that terrible night in 1940, the bombs still rained down on a regular basis. John spent the weekday evenings with Norman in the Greaves Hotel counting down the days until the weekend and those two precious days with Dorothy before he commenced his official training in Redcar.

He met Dorothy at the bus station in Lancaster; she'd taken

the early morning bus from Coventry which arrived a little before ten. Dorothy was a little tearful when she got off the bus. It wasn't the sort of reaction John expected, okay it was only two days but nevertheless his heart was full of the joys off spring, beaming like a Cheshire cat as he spotted her coming down the steps. He was also looking forward to starting his training in Redcar. It was all he'd ever wanted to do for as long as he could remember. Two action packed days with the woman he loved and then the start of his own personal dream. It couldn't get much better.

They embraced and kissed as Dorothy threw herself into his arms, the tears falling ever harder as she sobbed on his shoulder. He held her there for a few moments before he took her hand and led her away in the direction of home.

'What is it Dorothy, what's wrong?'

She looked at him incredulously.

'You don't know, John?' He shrugged his shoulders.

'Let me begin,' she said as if about to deliver a lecture.

'Firstly there's a war on, my brother's God knows where getting shot at and bombed by the Germans, I'm stuck in a city that Hitler sees fit to bomb every other night, I hate my job and the tip of a place where I lay my head every night and you're not there with me. I'm home for two days, *two whole days,*' she announced with a hint of sarcasm, 'and first thing on Monday morning you're off to a place I've never heard of and I've no idea when I'll see you again. Once you've completed your training I'm assuming they'll send you over to Germany in an aeroplane and the Nazis will take pot shots at you just for the hell of it. And you have the nerve to ask me what's wrong.'

Dorothy had finished her tirade and her head was back on John's shoulder. He held her tight while she cried herself out until eventually the tremors subsided. She took a handkerchief and cleaned herself up, took John's hand and they began to walk again.

'I'm sorry, John, it's just beginning to get to me a little.'

John remained silent and more than a little puzzled. Dorothy had never been like this on the previous occasions she came home and she knew how much he wanted to join the RAF. Something had happened in Coventry, he was sure. Was the bombing beginning to get to her? Other thoughts filled his head, thoughts that he couldn't shake off, his worst nightmares imaginable. Dorothy's tears had filled him with despair; something was wrong, terribly wrong and it was as if the feelings Dorothy harboured deep inside had somehow manifested themselves in John. He had been looking forward to this weekend so much and suddenly it had lost its appeal. The rest of the weekend was much the same. They went to the pictures and to visit both families but every time they found themselves alone the floodgates opened. Dorothy found the courage to tell him what was wrong as she went to wave him off on the bus to Redcar on a wet and windy Monday morning at six thirty.

'I'm pregnant, John.'

The news hit him like a thunderbolt and suddenly nothing else mattered. He wanted to turn back, wanted to stay with Dorothy and work things out but she wouldn't hear of it.

'Get on that bus John Holmes, it's all you've ever wanted to do since I've known you.'

'But Dorothy, I need to –'

'Get on that bus,' she said, physically forcing him onto the steps. The bus driver shouted to him to move along. Still he protested.

Dorothy had a determination in her eyes and a strength that John knew he couldn't overcome.

'Get on the bus…we'll talk when you come back.'

He found himself agreeing with her.

'Talk…yes…when I get back.'

The bus driver pressed a button and the doors creaked loudly as they started to close. For a few seconds they stood and stared in silence before the driver put the vehicle into gear and pulled away.

He watched as the image of Dorothy faded into the distance. He'd never felt so hopeless, so alone. What was going through the poor girl's head? Worse, what would their respective families say? The bus took six hours to Redcar. It was the longest six hours of John's life.

Redcar was by the sea. John hadn't been aware; no one had told him. He found out later the same afternoon when an over-aggressive PT instructor took them for a five-mile run along the beach. It would be the first of many but John didn't mind; he daydreamed during those long runs trying to work things out. His head was filled with beautiful thoughts; a wedding day, a family gathering and the image of a beautiful bride. John convinced himself that everything would be fine, he loved her and she loved him and they both knew that they would marry each other and have children. They would marry; he'd do the right thing and ask her when they next met up. Okay it had come a little bit earlier than expected but so what. There was a war on, sons and daughters were being slaughtered right across Europe, it wasn't the worst thing in the world to have happened.

It took him three days to get everything clear in his head. Their love had produced an end product, a beautiful son or daughter awaited them and he'd convince Dorothy that he'd make her the happiest woman in the world. He was smiling now as his feet pounded along the beach, the heaviness in his legs had gone and he started passing his squad members as they ran the last half-mile of the BFT, the Battle Fitness Test.

It was the first of many tests and examinations John would undergo in his two months at Redcar. He won the Recruit Cadre BFT in a time just a few seconds short of that year's record. He hadn't realised he was so fit but put it down to his powerful legs and shoulders, muscle development and stamina courtesy of the cool waters of the Crook O' Lune. That and a certain girl and a forthcoming wedding that would make him the happiest man in the world. An added bonus would be that he would be able to wear his recently acquired RAF uniform. Who knows, he might even apply a little Brylcreem to give his hair a bit of shine. He'd sworn to Norman he wouldn't be seen dead with his hair 'Brylcreemed up' but after a couple of weeks at Redcar the slicked-back look was beginning to grow on him.

He knuckled down with a new vigour. Now more than ever he needed to make sure he kept his nose clean and dealt with everything the RAF could throw at him. Once he passed out he would be on the daily pay rate of a sergeant. He would have a wife and a young baby to support soon and there was no way he was going to fail. Within a couple of weeks he had commenced his flight mechanics training.

After a particularly long lecture that lasted late into Friday evening he walked the half-mile back to his lodgings in Marske Road, weary, but at the same time enjoying the pressure and the satisfaction of knowing that he'd coped well. No resits. Everyone had at least one resit he was told but not him, not yet anyway. He packed his overnight bag and prepared for his first official leave. The bus left at 7.30 sharp the following morning.

'John, what the hell have you done with your hair?'

It wasn't exactly the romantic greeting he'd hoped for. Then Dorothy smiled.

'You look a little older, Flight Engineer Holmes. RAF life is treating you well.'

He moved forward and took her in his arms. He wanted to hold on forever, he'd missed her so much. They parted and kissed passionately, oblivious to the world around them. They didn't care. It was Dorothy who broke the kiss, John would have been quite happy to linger there forever. Dorothy caught her breath and smoothed down her jacket with both hands.

'Take it easy Flight Engineer, you've already got me into enough trouble with moves like that.'

John smiled. 'I didn't hear you complaining at the time.'

'Perhaps, John, but nevertheless…'

John put a finger to her lips, stopped her in mid-sentence. 'Shh, Dorothy. Be quiet for a second. I need to tell you something.'

Dorothy remained silent but her look told John to carry on.

'We need to go and see your father.' He stuttered a little. 'I need to go and see your father, this weekend… today if possible. I, I, I… need to…' Jesus Christ, he thought to himself, why won't the words come out?

'I need to ask…'

Dorothy reached for his hands. 'What John, what is it?'

As always her hands felt so good in his. It was as if her soft touch eased the words from his mouth.

'I want to ask him…'

'Yes?'

'If I can marry you.'

All John could hear was the deafening silence that engulfed him. The moment seemed to be frozen in time as Dorothy's hands slipped from his and her mouth fell open. For a second or two he thought she might even faint.

'John, you don't have to, I –'

'I want to Dorothy, I want to marry you more than anything in the world. I need to see your father.'

'Hadn't you better ask me first? What if I refuse?'

'I know you won't Dorothy Shaw, I've known from the day I first danced with you that you'd be my wife someday.'

'Cocky little sod aren't you?'

John picked up his bag and reached out his hand.

'Well… will you marry me or not?'

Dorothy Shaw slipped her hand into his and they started walking. 'C'mon, let's go and see what Father has to say.'

'Is that a yes then?'

She kissed him gently on the cheek. 'It's as good as you're going to get. Now come on before I change my mind.'

The elation of the moment quickly disappeared as they came to the exit of Greaves Park. The colour had drained from John's cheeks.

'Are you okay?' she asked.

'I've felt better.' John walked through the door of Belle Vue Terrace cursing his knees as they knocked together, his legs heavier than the worst ever day running on Redcar beach. As they walked into the lounge John Shaw stood in his familiar position that John Holmes knew so well. Immaculately dressed as always, he was knocking his pipe out into an ashtray on the fireplace.

'Ah…young John,' he announced with a smile. 'How's it going at Redcar? Tough work I hear. Real tough going for Flight Engineers I'm told.'

'Yes Mr Shaw but I'll get through it, I'm really enjoying it and…'

John Holmes tailed off. This wasn't how he wanted it to be. He was rapidly losing the will to live, his courage deserting him at a rapid rate of knots. It was now or never. Ask him. *Ask him*, he told himself.

'Yes, John?'

Ask him. Ask him.

'C'mon boy spit it out.'

He reached for Dorothy's hand and she sidled up close. He reached deep inside his soul, pulled out everything he had and squeezed her hand tightly.

She smiled, John smiled. They looked at each other and then both of them gazed over to John Shaw as his pipe fell noisily into the fireplace.

'I would like to marry your daughter, Mr Shaw. I would like your permission please.'

John Shaw had asked Dorothy to leave the room. He'd instructed a nervous 19-year-old to take a seat and he'd joined him at the table. He wanted to talk to him man to man. He wanted to know how soon they wanted to get married.

'Next month.'

John Shaw raised his eyebrows. 'That quick?'

If John Shaw suspected his daughter was pregnant he controlled his emotion very well. He never asked and John felt it unnecessary to tell him; he would find out sooner or later. He professed his undying love for Dorothy and swore he would never leave her, and that he would protect her until the day he died. He meant every word. John Shaw saw the sincerity in every movement of John's lips. He gave his permission and called his daughter in to tell her. He pointed to the kitchen door.

'You'd better get your mother in here our lass. She's a wedding to arrange.'

CHAPTER FIVE

The Foreign Secretary Anthony Eden spoke to a hushed House of Commons. It was December 1942. The MPs who had gathered in the house could not take in what he was saying. It had taken World War Two to a new level. It appeared Hitler wanted to wipe whole nations, cultures and races from the face of the earth. It was intimated he had started gassing Jews at huge concentration camps in Germany and Poland.

Anthony Eden read out a United Nations declaration condemning 'this bestial policy'. He said news of German atrocities had been sent in by the Polish Government and the information had been confirmed as credible but it would only serve to strengthen Allied determination to fight Nazism and punish all those responsible. After his announcement the House rose and held a one-minute silence in sympathy for the victims.

Looking at John Holmes getting ready for his wedding in his small back bedroom in Ashton Drive you could have quite easily forgotten there was a war on. John positively beamed back at his reflection in the mirror that hung just to the left of his single bed as he straightened his tie. For John, life couldn't get any better. He was marrying the girl he loved, about to embark on the second part of his training with the Royal Air Force and within a few short months he would become a father. He was proud. So, so proud.

His face showed a flicker of a grimace as he remembered his wife-to-be was pregnant. He wondered if their respective families had guessed. The wedding had been rather rushed and on more than one occasion he had walked into a room and his mother and father had curtailed their conversation rather abruptly. They weren't daft. But then again it mattered not, a dozen wild horses wouldn't stop him marrying Dorothy and a hundred wild horses wouldn't prevent the birth of their child. It wasn't the *done thing* in those days, not the expected sequence of events, especially in the close-knit streets and communities of Lancaster. But then again when had John Holmes ever conformed? Going against the grain was in his nature.

He fingered a tiny speck of dust from his pristine white collar. The smile had returned to his face again. He took a step back, admired the view then *about turned* in military style and made his way downstairs.

His parents and sisters stood waiting in the kitchen. He paused in the doorway and felt everyone's eyes on him. His mother took a few steps forward, took his tie and pulled it back and forth as if it hadn't quite been one hundred per cent perfect. Her eyes were moist.

'You look gorgeous our John, she's a lucky girl is Dorothy, I hope she realises it.'

'I'm a lucky man, Mam.'

His mother nodded.

64

'C'mon,' his father said as he picked up his coat. 'We don't want to keep the vicar waiting.'

They walked the three miles to St Paul's Church in Scotforth on the other side of town.

Various members of each family had gathered on the steps of the old Victorian building. John's sisters fussed around him and he wished that his brothers could have been there too, if for no other reason than to dilute the female presence a little.

The lack of male company reminded him of the war that seemed to rage on and on. The wedding was very low key. Dorothy hadn't wanted to be married in white with a full church blessing. Nor did she want all the pomp and ceremony with organs and candles and choirboys bedecked in white, singing words that she neither knew nor understood. John was with her on exactly how their wedding day should be. John and Dorothy had also agreed that they didn't want a huge feast afterwards with relatives and friends travelling from far and wide to attend. She'd said to her parents that it didn't feel right spending so much money when there was a war on.

Reluctantly, Dorothy's mother had given in. She'd met with the officials from the church, explained her daughter's wishes and settled on a buffet in the church hall for a few friends and family. Reluctantly, after a fierce bout of persuasion they'd agreed on a three-day honeymoon to Blackpool, bought and paid for by both sets of parents. Their present to them, they'd explained.

The wedding day had been exactly how they'd wanted, close friends and immediate family. 'The special people' as Dorothy had described them to John. Nevertheless, even the quiet wedding was a huge effort for Dorothy in her condition. She was a slight woman and her pregnancy hadn't yet begun to show but by eleven o'clock as the celebrations continued she was exhausted. The newly married couple slipped away unnoticed around quarter past eleven.

It was a silly place to have booked a honeymoon but John didn't say anything. Those three precious days should have been just that… precious. A young couple joined in love, a time to forget about war and death and destruction of Coventry and service life and RAF training. But it wasn't to be. Every step he took along the promenade at Blackpool, every time his eyes fell on the huge 518 feet tower that seemed to dominate the skyline, every corner he turned, it reminded him of his induction training some months before.

The three days were still idyllic because for the first time ever it was just him and his beautiful bride.

The train to Cardiff seemed to stop at every town and village in England and Wales.

It took forever. John tried to focus on other things, good news, the news that Dorothy had disclosed at the end of their honeymoon. She had notified her employers that she was 'in the family way' and they had immediately placed her on a month's notice. Her days and nights in Coventry were numbered. Thank God for that.

At Birmingham New Street station John had been amazed at the number of troops milling around, young men on their way to battlefields in France, others bound for Southampton and Bristol on ships that would take them to South America and Asia. John Holmes just wanted to get there and get on with it. The last two hours were the worst. Why did the damned train have to stop at so many places and for so long? Abergavenny, Pontypool, Cwmbran and Newport. Surely it couldn't go on much longer? Newport was the last stop but the train waited at the station for over an hour. This was perfectly normal in war, the guard had explained, but couldn't give the exact reason why.

The train pulled into Cardiff a little after midnight and a bus met the latest forty two RAF trainee flight crew and drove them thirty miles to St Athans, on the outskirts of Barry in the Vale of Glamorgan. At the time it housed 12,594 RAF personnel and 1,376 WAAFs.

In daylight, John was astonished at the sheer scale of things. St. Athans was one of the largest stations in the Royal Air Force. As he walked around that first morning he discovered it was split into two, known as East and West Camp. The two camps were divided by the airfield runway in the centre and during a discussion that morning with another trainee who simply called himself Taffy he claimed that the perimeter of the camp was reckoned to be 27 miles.

'I kid you not my friend,' he said. 'Within the camp there are three bloody railway stations.'

John had been told to report to an office in East Camp, to 4TTS (Technical Training School.) This was where his main training would be carried out.

The office front was a hive of activity, young men jostling for position, giving out names and handing in ID. The men were anxious, keen; this office contained the key to something special. Then it dawned on him. This was where they would be handed the uniform of Her Majesty's Royal Air Force. This was where they would be 'kitted out'. Proud was a word that sprang to mind as John returned to his billet with his arms full, two of everything.

They'd been given the rest of the day off to prepare their uniform, wash, iron and make any necessary alterations. They'd need to bull up their boots, the stores clerk had advised, and make sure they wore or carried everything when they reported for duty the following morning. John laid his supplies on his bed and took a step back. He threw his standard issue life vest on the bed and reached for the emergency whistle in his pocket. A familiar voice broke the silence.

'How the bloody hell we're going to get this lot ready for tomorrow I'll never know.'

It was the man known as Taffy that he'd met early that morning. He'd crept into the barrack room quietly and stood near the bed next to John. He sauntered over.

'Taffy Stimson's the name. Looks like we're going to be getting to know each other a little better.'

'John Holmes. Err… John Holmes from Lancaster.'

Taffy Stimson and John walked out together at precisely 6.35 the following morning. It was late January 1943 and it was still dark.

'These bloody shirts and vests and bloody socks and bloody jackets itch like buggery,' Taffy announced, clawing with one hand between his legs and the other under an arm.

John laughed. 'Don't worry Taffy, it'll be okay after a few washes.'

'Don't worry boyo, this bugger's in the wash again just as soon as I get in tonight.'

Once again John thrived at RAF St Athans. The training was carried out in the East Camp while the West Camp was mainly used for general maintenance. There was only one goal and that was to pass everything and get the coveted Flight Engineer's brevet and the rank of Sergeant.

John studied airframes, more hydraulics, electrics, carburettor air-intake and fuel jettisoning controls. The instructors went into detail on cockpit heating, the electrical distribution panel for all the decisive components throughout the aircraft and the oxygen distribution too. He thought the study would never end and between him and Taffy they'd moan about it constantly. The intricacies of aircraft design and maintenance were beginning to get the men down. The officer in charge spoke.

'If you think this is bad, wait until you get assigned to your own aircraft type. Then you'll know what real study is.'

A young man in the front of the class raised his hand.

'Not sure what you mean, Sir.'

The officer took a deep breath.

'Well, Flight Engineers.' He purposely scanned the thirty or so men that sat hanging on his every word.

'Don't go getting too carried away. As you know you have a lot of exams and assessments to pass. If you succeed you'll need to make a choice on what sort of aircraft you wish to fly in.'

The officer paced slowly, side to side at the front of the class.

'As you know you have the choice of Stirlings, Halifaxes and Lancasters. Once the choice is made then you'll take more classes and more assessments and more examinations on the exact aircraft you've chosen to fly in.' He threw out a forced laugh. 'By Jesus if you thought this was hard you haven't seen anything yet.'

He turned towards the blackboard, his hands clasped behind his back, and stood for a few seconds before turning to face the class.

'Take the Lancaster for example.' He pointed at a young, dark-skinned man sitting at the front of the class.

'You, Wilson.'

'Yes Sir.'

'You like the Lancaster Bomber don't you?'

'Yes I do Sir.'

The officer nodded his head in approval and raised an eyebrow as he spoke.

'Do you know the chemical makeup of the tyres that go on the Lancaster bomber?'

'No Sir.'

'Do you know which factory they are produced in or where that factory is?'

'No Sir.'

'And do you know the name of the checkout clerk who gave his stamp of approval to that tyre, what time his last lunch break was or when he last visited the toilet?'

'No Sir.'

The officer grinned, bent forward, leaned towards the man and whispered just enough so that the rest of the class would hear.

'You will, Wilson. Cross my heart and hope to die you will and you'll even know what sort of paper he used to wipe his arse.'

John couldn't put his finger on what it was that made him choose the Stirling Bomber. The Lancaster seemed to be the most popular choice among the other airmen but to him there was something about the Stirling that he'd simply fallen for. The Short Stirling was the first four-engine British heavy bomber of the Second World War. It was far from perfect, almost like an overweight hunting dog with three legs and one eye. It was as if it cried out to be loved and John Holmes fell for it hook, line and sinker.

It had a cruising speed of 230 mph, not quick, especially when it was loaded up with a maximum bomb load of 14,000 pounds. It was rumoured in certain circles that the wingspan had been chopped to 100 feet so the aircraft would fit into existing hangars, hence all the problems on take-off. There was another theory that the wingspan limit was imposed in an attempt to ensure the Stirling's weight was kept down.

It didn't matter to John. There was just something about the aircraft he adored. Majestic. Massive. Just standing next to one of its huge wheels was enough to make him realise just how big it was. Watching the huge effort as it groaned to take off when John had stood a mere fifty yards from the runway had a strange effect on his heartbeat. It was almost human. At times as he looked on, he almost expected it to speak to him. John had made his decision. He wouldn't be swayed.

The day dawned when the official choices had to be made and not surprisingly John couldn't sleep. It was around 5.30 in the morning when he slipped from the darkened billet fully dressed, showered and shaved. He walked the mile and a half to the section of the airfield that housed the huge aircraft hangars. The ghostly apparition of a lone Stirling loomed up before him as he walked briskly through the bitterly cold, early morning air. He looked beyond the aircraft up into the sky. The early dawn light was beginning to paint the horizon a multitude of pastel colours. Already, even at that ridiculously early hour, half a dozen ground crew fussed around her undercarriage. Keeping a Stirling in the air was a 24-hour job.

It was fair to say John Holmes was in awe each time he stood within touching distance of the bomber. He walked over to the huge nose section and stood directly underneath. Just how do they lift into the air, he wondered. His thoughts were interrupted by a voice behind him. John detected a slight North American accent.

'Beautiful isn't she?'

A tall, well-built man walked around to the side of the Stirling and pointed to something John couldn't see.

'*Semper in Excreta*,' he announced with a grin.

John shrugged his shoulders. 'It sounds like Latin but I'm not sure what it means.'

'I studied Latin over in Canada. Latin and French.'

'So you're Canadian.'

'I am indeed. I'm a Canadian with enough knowledge of Latin to know what that means.'

John walked around so that he could see the insignia with the motto crudely painted underneath.

'Go on then, surprise me.'

The Canadian's shoulders heaved as he broke out into a laugh.

'*Semper in Excreta* – always in the shit!'

John couldn't help but laugh too, the Canadian's mirth was infectious and he warmed to the man immediately.

'That's me and you little buddy, we're in the shit too.'

John frowned. 'I'm err… not with you.'

'You're in the shit because like me you've chosen to fly in this bloody thing. Too heavy, too slow and badly designed as you'll find out the first time you help put her into the sky.'

'What's it doing here anyway?' John enquired. 'This is just a training school, they don't normally land here.'

'Emergency landing, I was told. Poor bastard was shot up at Brest in France, thought he could limp back home to the Midlands but ran out of fuel and had to ditch it here.'

John walked a few paces and offered his hand. 'John Holmes. Pleased to meet you, but how did you know I've chosen to fly Stirlings? I haven't officially told anyone yet.'

The Canadian took his hand and placed his left hand on the back of John's right cupping it and shaking it vigorously.

'Matthews… Lofty Matthews, they call me. I'm very pleased to meet you too. And to answer your question I can tell by the way you are looking at her that you've already made your mind up. Jesus… I swear if she had a pair of tits and a cute ass, you'd be asking her to the Saturday night dance.'

John went for breakfast with Lofty Matthews. A little later Taffy Stimson joined the table. John had known one man just over a week and the other for just a few hours but as they stood up and placed their dirty dishes onto a large table in the centre of the mess hall they walked out chatting and laughing as if they'd grown up as brothers.

Later that day John was called into the adjutant's office where he was handed a travel warrant.

'Five days' leave, Flight Engineer. Don't tell me that the RAF doesn't look after you. I think you've just about had enough studying to last you a lifetime, time to recharge the old batteries.'

John hadn't expected the leave but wished they'd given him a little warning.

'When can I leave sir?'

The officer looked at the warrant. 'It's valid from today son, there's a truck going into Cardiff in just over an hour. If you get your arse into gear you can be on it.'

The temptation was too great. His head filled with the picture of his new wife and family and he almost ran from the office.

John almost burst through the door at Belle Vue Terrace. He found Dorothy sitting in the kitchen with her mother and she nearly fell from her seat.

Dorothy's mother spoke first. 'My my, John, the RAF are very good with their leave.'

He knew it wouldn't always be like this. As soon as he was qualified and up in the air, leave periods would be in the lap of the gods and of course a little Austrian sitting in a fortified bunker somewhere in Berlin.

John sensed the atmosphere in the room immediately. Dorothy was not the same as she'd been on his other visits. She hadn't rushed to greet him. Something was wrong. It only took a few minutes before the news was out.

'Something's wrong, what is it Dot?'

He pulled a chair from the kitchen table and moved it alongside Dorothy and sat down. He put his arm around her and pulled her towards him. 'Tell me what it is?'

Dorothy buried her face into her husband's chest and the tears flowed like torrents. Sara Ellen Shaw explained. Cliff, her eldest son, had been fighting out in the Far East in Burma. He had been taken prisoner by the Japanese. John knew it was as good as a death warrant, a terrible fate. He'd heard all about the Japanese and the way they treated their prisoners. In the eyes of the Japanese a prisoner was dishonourable; surrender was not an option to the average Japanese soldier. A few RAF pilots had managed to escape from Japanese POW camps and made it back home. They painted pictures of a hell on earth, prisoners treated like animals, underfed and undernourished, beaten, tortured and some executed for the smallest of reasons like failing to bow to a Japanese officer as he walked past. It made no difference – men, women or children, they were all treated the same.

Dorothy sobbed as John tried to console her.

'At least he's alive, Dot, at least he has a chance of making it back.' John lied. 'The Japanese have to treat the prisoners well. We all do. He'll be well fed and back home just as soon as you know it.'

He wondered if she'd heard the stories filtering back, whether Sara Ellen Shaw had heard them too. Sara Ellen didn't seem too bad, probably trying to bear up, not wanting to show her daughter her true feelings.

The sobbing had subsided slightly as Dorothy drew strength from the body of her husband. When he was with her everything in the world felt better. Sara Ellen spoke.

'Maybe it's a good idea to get away for a few days, John. I

think it would do Dorothy the world of good. You need some time on your own.'

John hadn't even thought about it but suddenly had an urge to get away from it all. As much as he enjoyed life back in his home town surrounded by both families he wanted to take Dorothy away somewhere pretty, on their own so they could spend some real husband and wife time together and of course talk about the imminent birth of their new child. She needed to forget about Cliff, if only temporarily.

The honeymoon in Blackpool was good but he wanted something a little more. He took a firm stand and at first Dorothy resisted. However between him and her mother, eventually she succumbed. Eventually she agreed and he suggested she started packing a bag.

'Where will we go?'

John shrugged his shoulders.

'I haven't got a clue but we'll find somewhere.'

They'd been sitting for just over an hour when Sara Ellen Shaw made the suggestion. 'They say the Peak District is nice this time of year, a little snow on the fells and the leaves of the trees a thousand different colours.'

John and Dorothy looked at each other and both knew instinctively what the other was thinking. The Peak District was a great idea, absolutely perfect. Quiet enough and yet plenty to see and do.

Sarah Ellen had already located the railway timetable and announced that a train left for Derby at 9.37 the following morning.

They booked into a small bed and breakfast just off the main street in Whaley Bridge.

'Greta Haven' was a beautiful old house at the top of a hill just off the main street ran by a delightful elderly lady called

Olive Bryson. She couldn't do enough for them especially when John disclosed what it was he was doing in the war. Both of Mrs Bryson's sons were on active service in the RAF somewhere in the Far East.

Bed and Breakfast became Bed, Breakfast and Evening Meal as Mrs Bryson insisted on cooking for them every night. John and Dorothy weren't complaining, her cooking was superb and she insisted it was all included in the price they had agreed at the beginning of the stay. They wandered down to a few pubs in the town centre that evening and when they returned Mrs Bryson had a map of the area unfurled on the kitchen table.

'You have to make the most of your time here. Have you been to the Peak District before?'

Dorothy had been to Glossop as a young child but couldn't quite remember it and John announced this was his first trip to the area.

'You have to visit some of our beautiful lakes and try and wander up a fell or two.' She looked at Dorothy. 'It will do you good my dear... especially in your condition.'

John and Dorothy were flabbergasted. Yes, Dorothy had a bump, but the baggy winter woollies and top coat certainly wouldn't have given the game away, she was slightly built and it wasn't obvious she was pregnant.

Dorothy flushed as she spoke. 'You can tell?'

'Oh I can tell dear, don't you worry about that.'

Mrs Bryson quickly changed the subject.

'You'll need to see Ladybower Reservoir, they had to flood two of our villages to construct it but I confess it's a beautiful site and a bus leaves from the town centre every day at 10.40. You can have a nice lie in and a little cooked breakfast and be there by noon.'

The bus left on time and made its way eastwards towards the reservoir. It was a beautiful crisp sunny day and the fells burst into colour as soon as the bus hit the open road. It was nice to get away he thought as he sat holding Dorothy's hand as they both stared out of the window in awe of the beautiful countryside around them. It seemed like a different world and John promised himself he'd be back to this part of the world soon, with his son or daughter and other members of the family when they eventually came along.

Everything changed as the bus pulled into the village of Ashopton. Military police were everywhere and the road that led down to the lake was sealed off.

'What's going on John?'

He shook his head. 'I haven't got a clue.' He spotted an RAF uniform standing by the road block.

'Look there's one of our boys I'll ask him.'

John walked over and introduced himself, took out his RAF ID card and showed it to the men on the road block. By way of an introduction he said he was stationed at RAF St Athans and had a few days' leave.

'My wife and I were really hoping to see the lake today. What's going on?'

The RAF man spoke. 'Bit of a top secret exercise I'm afraid, old bean. You won't get to see the lake today, not from ground level anyway. My advice is to head out of the village and take the route to the fells. They have part of it sealed off but if you show them your ID they may let you through.' He smiled. 'After all it is an RAF exercise.'

'What type of exercise?' asked John.

'Can't tell you any more I'm afraid and to be quite honest I don't know the full ins and outs myself.'

Just then they were almost deafened as a RAF Lancaster flew

over the village at a height of no more than a few hundred feet. The man grinned.

'That should give you a clue Flight Engineer Holmes. Simulated bombing on the lake I'm led to believe and that's as much as I know.'

John thanked him and walked back out into the village.

'Where are we going John?'

He took Dorothy's hand.

'You heard Mrs Bryson, a little stroll up a fell will do you the world of good.'

The track was long but not too arduous. They took their time and after about thirty minutes they reached an opening in the forest that gave them an unrestricted view of the lake. John had counted four different Lancaster's during the time it took to climb up to around 1,000 feet.

Dorothy's cheeks were flushed red and she was breathing a little hard.

'We don't need to go any further, this will be fine.'

'Thank God for that,' she said as she loosened the buttons of her coat. 'I'm walking for two you know.'

John stood behind her and wrapped his arms around her. He pulled her tight into him, took in the smell of her perfume combined with the crisp, unpolluted air. The smell was heaven, unlike anything he had ever smelled before. They looked down onto the lake. A fine mist lay undisturbed a few feet above the calm dark water and John could just about make out a family of swans drifting with no sense of purpose in the idyllic setting. He couldn't help feeling a little envious of the swans, no war to fight, no need to kill or to fight. Just peace and quiet.

'It's beautiful John, simply beautiful.'

Before John could answer he heard the distant familiar

drones of aeroplane engines. He took a while to locate them but sure enough they were coming in from the west.

'There Dot, look there.'

The Lancasters reduced altitude as they approached the lake. They flew in formation one behind the other, no more than a hundred feet apart. The planes were almost approaching the head of the lake as they reduced their height even further. John's heart was in his mouth as the planes went lower and lower. It looked as if they were almost touching the lake.

'Jesus Christ, they're flying at no more than thirty feet, perhaps less.' He turned to Dorothy. 'That RAF chap got it wrong, they won't be dropping bombs from that height, it must just be a low level exercise. I can't understand why everything was so secretive. '

The planes flew the length of the lake, sometimes no more than twenty feet from the top of the water as if in some bizarre competition to see who could get the lowest. They climbed quickly as they approached the far side. John's attention had been taken by something at the far end of the lake. Was he seeing things? A crude yellow and black construction stood at the east end of the lakeshore. Dorothy had spotted it too.

'What is it?'

'Beats me, it just looks like a huge big wall.'

The Lancasters had turned and circled the lake. They flew out westwards once again. Within five minutes they were back to repeat the exercise.

Now John was puzzled. 'I don't understand...their bomb doors are open...'

The first Lancaster had just reached the shore of the lake flying in at fifty feet. The pilot brought the huge plane ever nearer to the water. John's heart was in his mouth as he realised it had dropped something.

79

'There, look Dot, he's dropped a…'

'Bomb?'

John shook his head. 'No it's too low…it's a…'

The dummy device hit the water and John was totally unprepared for what happened next.

'Well bugger me!'

'What's it doing John?'

'I don't believe it…it's…it's bouncing along the water like a stone skipping the waves.'

'What's bouncing, John, what is it?'

John was grinning now as he looked at the wall and saw the other Lancasters coming in dropping what looked like huge black footballs. It was clear they were aiming for the man-made structure at the far end of the lake before climbing steeply into the sky.

'I was wrong, Dot.'

'What about?'

'I said they weren't dropping bombs but they are. They're dropping *bouncing* bombs.'

Dorothy watched as another Lancaster came in for a repeat run.

'A bouncing bomb John? Bombs don't bounce, you idiot!'

'He's too low. Good God he must be touching the top of the water.'

The pilot dropped his dummy bomb from less than twenty feet. His speed was too slow and as the bomb bounced back up from the water it clipped the tail of the Lancaster. The pilot could do nothing as the whole tail section sheared off and the nose of the plane propelled into the water. The whole plane broke up and shattered on impact as if it had crashed into concrete.

Dorothy's scream pierced the silence as she buried her head into John's coat. He held her tight, unable to take his eyes from the wreckage that now littered the lake. She was inconsolable, sobbing uncontrollably. She knew instinctively that everyone on board had died. And in less than a split second she was only too well aware of just how dangerous it was to be a member of RAF aircrew.

CHAPTER SIX

B ack at St Athans the assessments and examinations went on
and on, week after week.

On 4th April 1943, John and the rest of the assembled class
awaited the results of a particularly difficult test. For two weeks
they'd had lectures on the Stirling's throttle settings, propeller
variable pitch lever positions and studied numerous pamphlets
on the very temperamental engine and oil pressure gauges
which were prone to overheating. John was fairly certain he
could recall the engine cowling gill positions in his sleep and
he knew the manuals back to front. He was confident, 100%
confident that he'd passed the tests and wouldn't need to resit.
So he wasn't too anxious when a Flying Officer interrupted
the teacher and appeared to be pointing at him. John broke the
eye contact, had a flick through one of the manuals that lay on
his desk.

'John Holmes.' John rose to his feet, stood to attention.

'Yes Sir.'

'Flight Engineer.'

'Yes Sir.'

'I'm afraid you're going back home to Lancaster.'

John shook his head in a slow motion as he felt his legs begin to give way at the knees. He was about to protest in no uncertain terms when he noticed the Flying Officer and the teacher laughing. By now some of the class were looking at him and they were smiling too. He looked around the class then back to the front.

'I...I don't understand, Sir.'

The Flying Officer broke out into raucous laughter.

'You should do Flight Engineer. You should understand very well. Get back to your billet and pack a bag. A car is waiting to take you to Cardiff. Your wife has gone into labour and you are about to become a father.'

John Holmes ran from the classroom to the cheers of his colleagues ringing in his ears.

On the train he read a letter that had been given to him. He had to report to Lancaster Royal Infirmary as soon as he could. Unusually, Dorothy hadn't had the child at home. The Lancaster Royal Infirmary had a new maternity annexe in Haverbreaks.

It was all over by the time John arrived at the hospital. Sara Ellen Shaw stood at the front gates of the hospital pacing back and forth. She'd heard the running boots of her son in law way off in the distance. John ran the whole way from the railway station and for once thanked the sadist of a RAF PT instructor for maintaining his high fitness level. Dorothy's mother had a look on her face that he'd never seen before. Sara Ellen walked over to greet him.

'Congratulations son. Congratulations.' She shook his hand warmly placing a friendly hand on his shoulder and kissed him gently on the cheek.

'What is it, where is she, is she well, is it well, what is it?' Dorothy's mother reached for the RAF standard issue bag that John held in his hands.

'Everyone's fine John, just calm down.' She pointed to a large stone built building standing on its own in the far corner of the spacious grounds. 'Your wife is in the new maternity annexe over there with your new baby and I think it should be her who answers all of your questions. I'll wait here with your bag, now get going.'

John nodded and suddenly he didn't seem to want to move so fast. Once inside he asked directions from a stern looking matron and she pointed down a long sterile white corridor.

'Keep on walking,' she announced, 'fifty yards down on the left.'

It was a big open ward with lots of beds but somehow, as if some strange power took over, his eyes fell on a bed on the far side of the room. He walked over.

Dorothy was asleep; the infant wrapped in fluffy white towelling nestled into her breast. They were both sleeping… at peace with the world. John pulled up a chair unsure of what to do next. The chair clattered off the metal bed frame and Dorothy awoke with a start. For a split second the moment was frozen in time and then Dorothy broke out into a big beaming smile. She looked radiant, happier and more content than he could ever remember. She prised the cover from the child's head, John leaned forward.

'Meet your son, John.'

John wanted to burst into tears and did his best to control himself. His eyes glazed over and his life changed in that remarkable, amazing, emotional moment. It was truly indescribable as a strange warm feeling enveloped him. He took Dorothy's hand and kissed her gently on the lips. 'I can't believe it Dorothy, he's beautiful, you look beautiful. You seem to have taken everything in your stride.' He kissed her again and whispered quietly.

'You are one truly remarkable woman, Dorothy Holmes. You've made me the happiest man on the planet.'

Dorothy stroked the side of the face.

'It's so good to see you John. You look a million dollars in that kit.'

John had forgotten. It was the first time Dorothy had seen him in uniform.

John looked down at his son again, couldn't quite believe the perfect bundle that his wife held. Who said newborn babies were like wrinkled prunes? He traced a finger gently along the baby's nose. The child stirred, reacted to its father's touch.

'I want him to wake up.'

Dorothy smiled. 'Can't be doing that John, you should never wake a sleeping baby.'

A young nurse walked over and told John he only had one hour to go, then the doctor would be making his rounds. John looked at his watch.

'We'd better get on with it Dot.'

Dorothy looked at him with a puzzled expression on her face.

'His name, Dorothy – what are we going to call him?'

Dorothy stroked at his tiny shock of dark hair.

'I've already thought of that,' she said, 'I was thinking of calling him John.'

John felt the tears welling up once more.

'After me? Fantastic, wonderful, brilliant.'

Dorothy smirked.

'Don't get too big headed and full of yourself, Mr Holmes, I was thinking about my father actually!'

John's mouth fell open as he started to laugh.

'Well I never.' He sat back down in the seat and took stock of the situation before announcing.

'Very well. If you're naming him after your father then we'll name him after mine too.'

John reached across and lifted the tiny bundle onto his lap. He gazed down as the child's eyes flickered open.

'Welcome to the world John William…welcome to the world. It's not much of a world at the moment but me and my Stirling will sort it all out for you. That's a promise'

The trip back to St Athans seemed a little quicker than the first time John made the journey but it was a hundred times harder climbing on the train to be waved off by his wife as she cradled their first born child in their arms. The long journey gave John time to think and ponder the many questions that hadn't been answered and probably never would. He was a little happier knowing that at least her and John William would be relatively safe and well cared for and fussed over by the two respective families. But why did he have to leave her and his newborn son? Why couldn't he lay his head on the pillow next to them each night? He wanted a normal marriage; he wanted to play the role of the father to the full, watch young John take his first steps, utter his first word, play with him in the park and push him in his pram and show him how beautiful the Crook O' Lune was. It wasn't to be. What a crazy world. Why did arguments over land have to be settled by warfare? Why did millions and millions of young men and women have to be slaughtered? And he wondered when the war was over would anybody learn.

John Holmes lay on his bunk the night of May 16th 1943. His thoughts were with his family, his young son and Dorothy and he wondered about the whereabouts of his brothers James and Ernie. As he dozed certain images filled his head and no matter how hard he tried he couldn't shake the strange, almost vivid recollection of the day he stood on the fell with Dorothy watching the men with the bouncing bombs. It was crystal clear, why did it suddenly seem that way, tonight of all nights?

Royal Air Force No 617 Squadron were already on the runway at RAF Scampton, five miles north of Lincoln. The operation to attack dams in the Ruhr Valley had been given to No 5 Group RAF which had recently been formed especially to undertake the mission. The squadron was led by Wing Commander Guy Gibson, a veteran of over 170 bombing and night-fighter missions. 21 bomber crews were chosen from the Group to join the new squadron using a specially developed 'bouncing bomb' invented and developed by Barnes Wallis. They had trained several weeks earlier in various locations in the UK such as the Peak District and in the sea off Margate.

The British Air Ministry had identified Germany's heavily industrialised Ruhr Valley, and especially its dams, as important strategic targets. They provided much needed hydro-electric power, essential to Germany's war production. The targets were the Möhne, Edersee and Sorpe dams. They had been repeatedly attacked before but only sustained minor damage. Dropping large bombs from high up required a degree of accuracy which was almost impossible, like trying to find a needle in a haystack according to one bomb aimer. The dams were also protected by heavy torpedo nets making an attack from the water impossible too.

The aircraft the squadron used were modified Avro Lancaster Mk IIIs. It was necessary to reduce the weight of the standard

Lancaster and much of the internal armour was removed, as was the mid-upper machine gun turret. The size of the bomb and its unusual shape also meant that the bomb-bay doors had to be removed. The bouncing bomb was part suspended below the fuselage of the aircraft. Before the bomb was released it was spun up to speed by a motor. This would ensure maximum distance, the bomb effectively bouncing up to a dozen times before hitting the dam wall. This would allow the pilots just enough time to climb over the dam wall and over the hills beyond.

The bombers flew low, less than thirty metres, as they made their approach into Germany. It would allow them to avoid radar detection. Flight Sergeant George Chalmers, radio operator on one plane looked out and was astonished to see that his pilot was flying towards the target along a forest's firebreak, below treetop level, an indication of how dangerous the whole operation was.

The first formation arrived over the Möhne Lake as Gibson's and Hopgood's aircraft prepared for the first runs. It wasn't a good start as the Germans were alert and all too aware that they had come under attack. Hopgood's aircraft was hit by flak and was caught in the blast of its own bomb. The plane was unable to recover and crashed soon afterwards when a wing disintegrated. There were only two survivors.

Gibson flew his aircraft across the dam to draw the flak away from Martin, who was up next. His aircraft was slightly damaged but nevertheless he made a successful attack on the dam. After Martin's attack, Gibson, with Young accompanying, led Shannon, Maudslay and Knight to the Eder. The Eder Valley was covered by heavy fog but not defended particularly well, however the forests and the surrounding hills made for a difficult approach. Shannon's aircraft made six runs, one after the other. Maudslay's plane then flew in but his bomb struck the top of the dam and the aircraft was severely damaged in the subsequent blast. Shannon made another run and successfully dropped his bomb. The final bomb of the formation, from Knight's aircraft finally scored a direct hit on the dam.

The Sorpe Dam was a huge earthen based dam rather than the concrete and steel ones previously attacked. Casualties had been high and only three Lancasters ultimately reached the target. Joe McCarthy's plane was on its own when it arrived at the target and he realised immediately that a direct hit was almost impossible. The flight path led over a church steeple in the village of Langscheid and gave the pilot only seconds to spare before he had to climb to avoid hitting the hillside at the other end of the dam.

McCarthy wouldn't give in. He made nine approach attempts to bomb the dam but wasn't satisfied with the combined speed, the direction and altitude. Luckily for him and his crew the Germans had believed that the dam was impossible to attack from the air and there wasn't a single anti-aircraft gun in the area.

On the tenth attack he gave the all clear to his bomb aimer. He released the bomb and the crew let out a huge cheer of relief as the bomb exploded. However when McCarthy turned the plane he was disappointed to see that the damage was minimal. The main body of the dam itself was intact.

On the way back to England, again flying at less than thirty metres, two more Lancasters were lost. One was struck by flak near Netterden in Holland and the other brought down near the Dutch coast.

There were only nine surviving bombers. They began landing at Scampton at 03:11 hours. The last of the survivors put its wheels on the ground just after six o'clock in the morning. The surviving crews were not in a jovial mood as they attended their early morning debrief. They were informed about their missing friends and colleagues. 53 men were killed, a casualty rate of 40%. They had flown to the best of their abilities but told their commanding officers of the near impossible conditions and of the technical difficulties the fog and darkness presented. In all honesty they could be no more than 'hopeful' that they had succeeded in their mission.

At 07:30 hours a Spitfire piloted by Flying Officer Frank 'Jerry' Fray took off from RAF Benson to assess the bomb damage in the Ruhr Valley. The photo-reconnaissance plane arrived over the Ruhr River just after first light. He took photographs of the breached dams. He described his experience on return to RAF Benson and his report would later be read out to the survivors of the 'Dambusters Squadron.'

> When I was about 150 miles from the Möhne Dam, I could see the industrial haze over the Ruhr area and what appeared to be a cloud to the east. On flying closer, I saw that what had seemed to be cloud was the sun shining on the floodwaters.
>
> I looked down into the deep valley which had seemed so peaceful three days before but now it was a wide torrent.
>
> The whole valley of the river was inundated with only patches of high ground and the tops of trees and church steeples showing above the flood. I was overcome by the immensity of it.

The Flight Engineer's role was a complex one and give the RAF their due, the training was intense. The Flight Engineer was responsible for a whole host of things, at times John would worry how the bloody aircraft took off in the first place.

The Flight Engineer liaised with the ground crew identifying and solving problems before they became major events. John studied the electrical, hydraulic and mechanical systems of the aircraft and took examinations that would prove he knew the aircraft inside out and back to front. Before any sortie the Flight Engineer was where the buck stopped. He was responsible for everything. He checked the electrics and hydraulics made sure the mechanics were working properly. The fuel tanks in the wings needed to be balanced and the engines double checked for temperature and oil pressure. On the outside of the aircraft the flight engineer had to make over forty checks alone on the flaps and mechanical linkages. On top of all that he needed to ensure that both his and the pilots control panels worked like clockwork.

John studied hard and passed with flying colours without the need to take any resits. He was feeling quite happy with himself until the Wing Commander officiating the exams brought him down to earth.

'Well done Holmes, you know everything there is to know before the aircraft takes off. The question is, will you be able to cope when the fucker is in the air?'

The Wing Commander threw a textbook in his direction and he caught it in mid-air. It was at least three inches thick.

'New study material, Holmes. Once you've read that back to front we can press on and teach you your other duties.'

'Other duties, Sir?' John asked rather shell shocked.

'Other duties, Holmes. The Flight Engineer looks out for flak and enemy fighters during the flight. You help the bomb aimer and the pilot too.' The Wing Commander grinned. 'And of course if the poor old pilot is shot up by a stray Messerschmitt you've failed to spot, you'll have to fly the plane.'

'But –'

'Yes Holmes, we even need to train you up as a pilot.'

John Holmes was lost for words. A few swear words came to

mind but as he closed his exercise book for the day he wondered what he had let himself in for. He walked back to the billet that evening a little disillusioned.

The following morning he was in a better mood, he put the previous day behind him and put it down to missing his family.

By mid-August all the exams and tests were over. He sat with Taffy Stimson and Lofty Matthews in the King's Head in Cowbridge, a small village a few miles from the camp. They had been given the night off. Tomorrow was the big day, tomorrow they would be handed their results.

All three were quietly confident. Many of their colleagues had been sent home at various times during the many months they'd been at St Athans but all three had made it to the final day and now it was down to percentages. The sergeant's stripes and coveted brevet would be awarded to the men achieving between 60 per cent and 70 per cent; anything above that and the trainee would become an officer. All three agreed they had no aspirations to become officers and thought it unlikely that they would achieve the necessary marks.

'Let's enjoy the moment, lads.' John Holmes raised his pint of bitter. Lofty and Taffy reached for their glasses.

'Cheers,' they announced in unison.

'Where to after this?' Taffy asked.

No one knew.

The three men had become very close but there were literally hundreds of RAF stations all over the country, however the fact they had all finished their training at the same time and had all chosen to fly the Stirling gave them a glimmer of hope that they would be sent to the same place.

It was August 16th 1943 when the three men officially became sergeants. John Holmes topped the marks on 69 per cent, narrowly missing out on becoming an officer. Taffy and

Lofty were both just a couple of marks behind. A small presentation ceremony had taken place mid-afternoon and the three men sat in the billet sewing their sergeants' stripes and their brevet onto their uniforms. They had been given five days' leave and informed a letter would be sent home advising them where they would need to report for duty.

John almost caressed the brevet as he placed it above his breast pocket and prepared to sew. His mind was in another place as he daydreamed he was stepping off the train, meeting up with Dorothy, wearing the uniform with a renewed pride. He was proud and his Dad would be so proud. He deserved it. He had worked harder than he had ever worked before and at times it was a struggle, at times he'd wanted to quit. But he hadn't. He'd battled through like he always had done, like his father had taught him.

John had moved into Belle Vue Terrace with Dorothy and her parents. It was a huge three-storey terraced house and John and Sara Ellen Shaw had allowed them to take over the top floor of their home. It was perfect, two bedrooms and a bathroom. Dorothy had already decorated the smallest of the bedrooms for baby John and a small crib stood in the corner by the window. John walked over to the crib which contained his son. He couldn't quite believe how much the child had grown.

'Does he spend his whole life sleeping Dot?'

Dorothy walked over and peered into the crib. She stroked at his hair and for a moment his eyes flickered and John thought he was going to wake up.

'Pretty much so, he's good as gold through the night too.'

John wrapped an arm around his wife and pulled her towards him. 'You're a lucky lass. A child as good as gold and Flight Engineer Holmes here for five days to pander to your every whim.'

John kissed her gently on the lips.

'Let's make the most of it, I don't care if you have to wake the little fella but do it…I need to go and see my parents. I've something I need to show Dad.'

The letter arrived first thing on Monday morning. John had to report to a place called Waterbeach in Cambridgeshire.

The airfield looked very ordinary as the bus pulled up to the main gates. An armed sentry inspected the paperwork the driver had handed to him and waved him through. The bus drove for about half a mile and ground to a halt. The driver shouted half a dozen names from a list. John Holmes was the last name called.

'Your stop, lads,' the driver bellowed down the bus. '1651 Heavy Conversion Unit.'

As the men climbed from the bus he shouted after them.

'Give Jerry hell, see you do.' The doors closed and he was off.

John felt strangely nervous, a little apprehensive. He'd spotted several planes on the short journey to his unit, more planes than he'd seen in the many months he'd been stationed at St Athans. This was it. This is what he had trained for. It was at RAF Waterbeach that John would finally fly in a Stirling. The RAF wasted no time. Within the hour he was booked in, shown his billet and issued with new essential supplies, a flying suit, a service revolver and an individual parachute. There was no turning back… now it was getting serious.

It was at breakfast in the mess hall the following morning that John met up with two old adversaries. The RAF cook had placed a final piece of bacon on his plate; he thanked him politely and turned around to look for somewhere to sit. There were forty or fifty tables in the mess hall each sitting half a dozen men. As his eyes scanned the room they were drawn to a tall man with a familiar profile. The square jawline and slightly hooked nose were unmistakeable and a sight that brought a smile to his face. Lofty Matthews crammed half a sausage into his mouth, chewed for a few seconds then turned to talk to the man sat next to him. He started to talk to Taffy Stimson.

John literally ran over. Any apprehension he'd felt the day before deserted him instantly.

'Mind if I join you, gentlemen?'

Lofty and Taffy nearly fell off their seats.

'Well bugger me, John!' Taffy announced.

'I'd rather not Taffy,' John quipped, 'if that's okay with you.'

Lofty shook his hand vigorously and Taffy ruffled at his hair like a father would with his small son. Suddenly RAF Waterbeach didn't seem such a lonely place.

Unfortunately the lectures were not over. John couldn't wait to get up in a Stirling but the RAF didn't appear to be in much of a hurry. He asked one of the lecturers last thing one night.

'When do we start flying sir?'

The officer was a man in his mid-fifties with slightly thinning hair and he looked John up and down as if he were stupid.

'Patience is a virtue my man. Don't be getting too keen.'

'But Sir, it's what I've trained for. I am keen.'

The officer stacked up a pile of papers and sunk back into his seat.

'You'll need a crew before you do anything.'

'Yes Sir I know,' said John. 'When will that happen, how is a crew selected and how…?'

The officer held up his hands.

'Whoa, soldier boy I've had a long day, remember what I said about patience. Your crew will find you soon enough.'

The remark puzzled John.

'I'm not sure what you mean, Sir… the crew will find me?'

'That's what I said didn't I?'

'But aren't crews selected? How can they find me?'

The officer had stood up and was already walking towards the door.

'I've had a busy day, Holmes. I need a bite to eat and perhaps a few pints and a good night's kip.'

'But Sir, I need to know. I —'

The officer turned around. He'd placed a finger to his lips.

'Just be patient, Holmes.' He laughed out loud. 'Be patient…that's an order. They'll find you.' He closed the door quietly and John was left on his own.

The last colours of the sunset were fading into a dusky pink as it painted the whole sky. It was an incredible sight but John was lost in his thoughts.

Taffy Stimson and Lofty Matthews had been 'found'. They told John at breakfast three days later.

'What do you mean, they just asked you?' said John.

'They asked me,' said Lofty between mouthfuls of another huge cooked breakfast.

'They asked you?'

'They asked me.'

'Me too,' said Taffy. 'Came up to me and said they needed a Flight Engineer for their crew. Said they liked the look of me. I was walking across the airfield late yesterday afternoon.'

'What did you say?'

Taffy buttered a piece of toast and looked up.

'They seemed like nice fellows so I said yes.'

John had lost his appetite and laid down his knife and fork.

'You're taking the piss aren't you? This is the RAF. Things like this just don't happen by chance. If I know the RAF, crews will be carefully selected and even tested together to see if they bond.' He directed the statement to Taffy. 'You don't get found and you don't just put your life in the hands of total strangers because they seem like nice fellows.'

Before they could take the argument any further a stranger pulled at the empty seat by their table.

'Is this seat taken, chaps?'

Lofty Matthews spoke first. 'You take it, my friend, you're welcome to join us.'

The man introduced himself as Bob Crosby, a gunner from Newcastle upon Tyne.

Henry Vanrenen instructed his crew. While he spoke they listened… always. Although a native Australian, the pilot was the personification of a sophisticated quintessential English gentlemen. If it wasn't for his slight, almost undetectable Australian accent you'd have thought he'd come straight from Eton. When he spoke he commanded a presence. Six feet tall with a shock of wavy hair and with such a supreme air of confidence the female civilian workers on the camp and the WAAFs found him irresistible. The day's instruction and lectures were over and Vanrenen wanted some action.

'We need two more crew and I want then found within the next 24 hours.'

Vanrenen and his crew had already flown in Wellingtons and were now converting to the four-engine Stirling.

'Find the right crew and we can be airborne by the end of the week.'

Len Jones was a rear gunner from Toronto, the youngest of four children whose parents had emigrated from England in search of a better life. He therefore felt strangely at home in England. Len had been an excellent student in Canada achieving very high marks, so much so that he'd been asked to stay behind in Canada to instruct the new trainees. He had declined; the lure of excitement overseas was too much. He wanted that much more, he wanted to fight the Germans.

Vanrenen was still speaking.

'I don't want any old shit. I want the best, so take your time.'

The other members of the crew looked on. Although certainly respected, Vanrenen was not well liked. He was very aloof, thought he was better than the other members of the crew, and never joined them on their frequent evenings out. The fact that he was never asked didn't help. It was very much a boss and worker situation and Vanrenen never stopped reminding them. His word was final, never questioned.

Reg Tammas somehow knew that Vanrenen would take no part in searching for the final two members of the team. That was simply below him; why have a dog and bark yourself?

Reg had been celebrating his 19th birthday when the Second World War broke out. He volunteered his services the very next day and was assigned to digging trenches along the east coast in his home county of Norfolk to repel the suspected Nazi invasion. When eventually called up, he trained as a navigator with the RAF which suited him perfectly as he was a good mathematician. He was due to be married in a couple of weeks, a source of irritation for Vanrenen as it would delay the crews training somewhat as Tammas had been granted a few days leave.

Still Vanrenen droned on about quality and valour and used words that some of the crew had never even heard of. That was Vanrenen, never one to miss an opportunity to remind the crew where they stood.

'Make sure you tell them how lucky they are to be flying with the best bloody pilot in Europe.'

The other two members of the crew were Doug Handley, the bomb aimer and Jack Chalk. They were the best of friends.

Jack was 27 years old and half French. He was the quiet man of the crew and the wireless operator. Doug leaned over and whispered to Jack.

'I bet that fucker won't be trudging round the airfield looking for a flight engineer and a gunner.'

Jack smiled and shook his head ever so slightly. Vanrenen cleared his throat.

'Okay men, you have a day off – but a day off with a little twist. You need to find me two good men.'

Len Jones asked the question on everyone's lips.

'Will you be out looking too, Sir?'

Vanrenen glared at Jones as if he'd just asked to sleep with his wife.

'Me, Jones? How absurd. No, I'll leave that menial task to you plebeians. I've far more important things to be getting on with.'

The crew would never find out exactly what was so important that Vanrenen couldn't assist with the crew selection. And yet they accepted his decision, they almost respected it and although they genuinely disliked the character of Henry Vanrenen, if asked in private they would tell you they wouldn't replace him with any other pilot in Britain.

Lofty Matthews and Taffy Stimson waxed lyrical about their new team mates.

'Great bunch of lads my lot, can't wait to get up in that Stirling next week,' said Lofty.

John Holmes was jealous now and more than a little concerned. Lofty and Taffy would be flying next week and at this rate he'd still be grounded. He'd done nothing but walk around the huge base at Waterbeach since he'd been told that a crew would 'find him' and as he turned every corner it was as if a Stirling bomber had mysteriously been placed within touching distance.

So near and yet so far.

What a stupid system, he thought to himself. There were thousands of different flight engineers and pilots and navigators and gunners on the base; why didn't the bloody RAF just put them together?

As he took a mouthful of tea he became aware of a man invading his space. The stranger leaned across him and extended a hand in the direction of Lofty Matthews. John felt like pushing it away, telling the stranger to mind his manners. He spoke. Another North American accent; too many bloody Canadians around here, John thought.

'Hi there buddy I couldn't help noticing your accent, those tones are very familiar to me.'

Lofty shook his hand warmly. 'What part of home are you from?'

'Toronto. The name's Len, Len Jones.'

'Lofty Matthews, I'm from The Beautiful Province.'

'Quebec?'

'You bet Buddy, you want to join us?'

'No thanks I've just finished my lunch, gotta get going. I've a lot to do. We've a lot to do, I mean.'

The stranger was joined by another man.

'This is my best buddy Reg, he's our navigator. I was wondering if you wanted to join us, Lofty? I see you're a flight engineer and we're in of need one. Better still you're from my neck of the woods, it would be great to have another Canadian on board.'

Lofty was quick with his reply. 'You're about two days too late Len, I'm already taken.'

'Aw that's a shame buddy.'

Lofty held up a hand. 'But fear not, it's your lucky day because I just happen to know one of the best Brit Flight

Engineers in the world. Not quite the same standard as us Canadians of course, but definitely the next best thing and he's looking for a crew.

'You do?'

Lofty nodded his head and pointed across the table to John Holmes. His brevet had been on Len Jones's blind side.

'Len meet John, John meet Len.'

The two men shook hands, and the Canadian spoke first.

'You're looking for a crew buddy?'

John nodded his head rather shyly, tried to act a little casual.

'I suppose I am. Where are your lads from?'

Len Jones pulled up a seat, Reg followed suit.

'A real mixture. Brits, a Canadian…' He poked a finger at his own chest, 'an Aussie and even half a Frenchman… a right mongrel of a crew.'

'All good lads?' John asked.

The Canadian removed his hat and sighed.

'Alas, no, my friend.' He shook his head. 'I have to tell you that our skipper is the biggest bastard under the sun.'

John looked at Reg, who was nodding too.

'He's right John, a right son of a bitch.'

John stood as if to leave. Reg and Len looked at each other as if their open admission had cost them yet another flight engineer. John smiled and extended a hand.

'Then that's good enough for me. At least there are two honest lads on board, three if you include me.'

Reg and Len stood up and embraced John Holmes. Everyone round the table grinned.

'Nice to have you on the team, John.'

Reg formerly introduced himself.

'Reg Tammas. Welcome aboard, Flight Engineer Holmes.'

'One more question, Flight Engineer,' said Len Jones.

'What's that?'

'I don't suppose you know where we'll find a spare gunner?'

Bob Crosby raised his hand rather sheepishly. 'I'm a gunner and I'm looking for a crew.'

Len looked at John and then at Reg.

'What the fucking hell did he say? I can't make out a word he said.'

John laughed. 'You'll get used to it Len, he's one of those Geordies.

'A what?'

'A Geordie. From Newcastle upon Tyne. His name's Bob Crosby.'

'Where?'

'Newcastle, up north. They're like Scotsman only with their brains kicked out.'

Len stood, looked Bob Crosby up and down.

'You're a good gunner?'

'The best, Yankee boy, simply the best.'

Len held out a hand.

'Then I'm pleased to have you aboard. Fucking hell, what a crew? Aussies, Canadians and Brits and now bloody Geordies.' He put a hand on his furrowed brow and shook his head.

'We're on borrowed time, Reg, I can tell you. I only came to this table to pick up another bloody Canadian.'

CHAPTER SEVEN

Vanrenen commanded a presence, an aura whenever he stood, sat or entered a room. John and Bob Crosby had met the rest of the team as they'd shared cups of tea and biscuits in the mess hall. It had been a warm, friendly, hand-shaking, back-slapping meeting and John had warmed instantly to his new colleagues. Just as well, as he'd place his life in their hands in a matter of days when they all took off in the 'Queen of the Skies'.

The Vanrenen welcome, if it could be construed as that, was totally different from what he'd experienced at breakfast. As the door of the mess hall opened it was as if a switch had been flicked in the room. The noise dropped and time seemed to stand still. Reg Tammas had noticed him first and elbowed Len Jones.

'Aye aye, here's the gaffer.'

Vanrenen's eyes scanned the room like a huge bird of prey seeking out a small vole or a rabbit. When he spotted his crew there was no flicker of emotion, no spark of satisfaction in his eyes. John almost expected him to shrug his shoulders and grimace. He didn't walk over, he appeared to glide. Within an instant he stood at the head of the table and John was rather surprised that he wasn't offered a seat.

Vanrenen spoke. He directed the question to Len Jones, glaring at John Holmes and Bob Crosby.

'I take it you've found me two crew members?'

John felt the urge to stand and introduce himself.

'John Holmes, Skipper, pleased to meet you.' He held out a hand and Vanrenen shook it rather weakly.

'You're Flight Engineer Holmes? You realise it's an honour to fly with me.'

John managed an astonished nod before Bob Crosby stood.

'Crosby, Sir, mid upper gunner, from Newcastle upon Tyne. God's own country.'

Vanrenen stared at Reg Tammas.

'What did he say? You've got me some fucker that can't even speak properly.'

Reg Tammas grinned, while a few of the others laughed out loud. Vanrenen remained emotionless. He looked the stunned mid upper gunner up and down as if he were a piece of meat. He had no intention of having any sort of direct conversation with Bob Crosby. Vanrenen spoke as if he wasn't there.

'Oh well it could be worse I suppose, he's the mid upper gunner so I won't need to talk to him too often.'

'Cup of tea, Skip?' asked Reg.

Again Vanrenen just stared for a few seconds as if Reg Tammas had asked him to partake in a cup of poison.

'I think not Tammas, I've more important things to do than to sit nattering with you degenerates.'

And then he was gone. He'd breezed into the room like a

hurricane, carved out his trail of destruction, left his mark and disappeared.

'Fuck me.' It was Bob Crosby who spoke first. 'You weren't kidding were you?'

The rest of the crew were laughing.

'Slightly less civil than I'm used to,' John said. 'Does he ever socialise with you, sit down and have a bite to eat or a drink?'

'Never.' said Len Jones. 'We don't think he eats; he drinks the blood of failed gunners and flight engineers and returns to his coffin each evening.'

'What about the pub?' asked John. 'Surely he must take an odd drink? Tell me he comes to the pub with you occasionally, I mean it's all about bonding, trusting your mates.'

'Never,' Len repeated, shaking his head. 'We asked him a few times when we first started flying with him and he always declined.'

'Not even politely,' interjected Jack Chalk. 'Said he wouldn't be seen dead with oiks like us. We stopped asking in the end.' Jack paused, looked around at the rest of the table before continuing. 'And yet when we're in the air or in the training room he's okay. He shows us a certain respect, seems to put up with us. Occasionally I get the impression he actually likes us.'

John was shaking his head.

'I can't accept that. Right through our training we're told how important it is to bond, to be like one big family. Surely Vanrenen has gone through that training too? It's not right.'

The conversation continued, but John was lost in his own thoughts.

'I'm going to ask him again.'

Bob Crosby agreed. 'Yeah, come on, at least give him another chance.'

The rest of the crew members wouldn't have it. They'd given

Vanrenen every chance under the sun. To a man they seemed to hate the ground he walked on. Deep down though, they respected everything he stood for when it came to flying aircraft.

John Holmes took his chance at a training lecture three days later. There was a dance in Cowbridge and the rest of the crew had agreed to meet up in the King's Head at eight that night.

Vanrenen and a RAF trainer had been instructing the crew on some of the problems associated with the Stirling. The last talk of the day referred to what was known as 'coring', a condition when engine oil became congealed as it passed through its radiator resulting in the frozen oil not circulating properly throughout the engine. Subsequently over-heating would occur. The solution to the problem, Vanrenen explained, was to promptly lower the undercarriage and flaps to reduce the air-speed passing through the radiator.

'Thereafter,' Vanrenen announced, 'the engine's RPM rate increases and rectifies the problem.' He snapped shut the huge technical manual in front of him. 'We'll try that out for real next week, gentlemen, but for today that's it. Enjoy your night out.'

Vanrenen had been courteous all day, especially animated and humorous in the afternoon. He was in a good mood, no doubt about it, thought John. Seize the moment, his Dad had once said, so he did.

John raised his hand. 'Sir?'

'Yes, Flight Engineer?'

'Sir…' John hesitated a little but plucked up the courage to continue. 'I was wondering… me and the boys are off to Cowbridge tonight, and err…'

Vanrenen remained silent. He gestured with no more than a raised eyebrow.

STEVE HOLMES

John smiled nervously. 'I was wondering, Skip, if you'd like to join us for a few pints.'

Vanrenen stood, leaning gently with his hands splayed out on the desk. A puzzled look spread across his face as his eyes took in the rest of his assembled team. Then he spoke.

'Mr Holmes, how very noble of you.'

John's smile returned. He gazed around at the other men feeling more than a little smug.

'Firstly, I have to tell you that I wouldn't raise a glass of that pig swill you British call beer anywhere near my superior Australian lips.' He twisted at the end of his carefully combed handlebar moustache before continuing.

'There again, let me think, let me imagine the sort of night we'd all have together.' He stroked at his chin with his thumb and forefinger as he gazed at the ceiling with his eyes closed. He held up a hand. 'Don't interrupt me, I'm painting the picture… it's coming to me.'

John looked around again; some of the crew had covered their eyes and were sniggering but Bob Crosby caught his stare and gave him the thumbs up.

'Yes… I've got it now I can see it all before me.'

He opened his eyes, leaned forward and placed his hands on the desk again.

'Mr Holmes. Gentlemen.' He looked around the room and frowned. 'I'd rather stick fucking pins in my eyes.'

'We told you, you silly bastard but you wouldn't have it!'

John Holmes sat rather sheepishly in the back of Len Jones's car. John wished he'd listened, wanted to turn back the clock, but of course he couldn't. It should have been a special night out, the first with his new crew but instead something told him he was in for a ribbing that would last until the early hours of the morning.

And what a way to get to Cowbridge too. Len Jones didn't just have any old car, no. He'd turned up at John's billet in a most impressive MG TB Midget convertible. It was Jonesy's pride and joy. Reg Tammas sat in the front with John Chalk already in the rear seat.

'C'mon, Johnny know-it-all,' Reg had shouted as John stood leaning on the billet at the prearranged time. He hadn't noticed his new friends from a distance, thought that the car was full of officers and had been surprised when it had slowed to a stop.

'Jump in clever clogs, you can look after us,' taunted Jonesy. 'You know best.'

John had eaten humble pie and apologised to his new team, and they'd all roared with laughter. It seemed as if it would all be forgotten but somehow he knew it would run and run.

The autumn wind was cold as they sped onto Cowbridge, Len insisting that the roof be kept off. Len loved his car and announced that he'd already made one trip dropping the others off earlier on. In no time they had walked into the King's Head and as soon as John caught up with the other members of the team it started all over again.

Bob Crosby fiddled with his breast pocket.

'Have you got any pins, John, please?'

John patted at his side pockets.

'No I haven't, sorry. Why do you want pins anyway?'

Bob Crosby could contain his laugh no longer; the whole crew were in on the joke. 'So I can stick them in my fucking eyes.'

'Very funny… very funny.' John looked at his mates, they were in hysterics. He'd walked into another one head on.

Two pints later and the last of the jokes were being squeezed out, the gentle taunting had all but finished. They needed to move onto something else.

'Nicknames!' announced Reg Tammas.

He pointed at Bob and John.

'We ain't going up in that old bird with two lads called John and Robert. No way.'

'He's right,' said Len Jones. 'You have to have a nickname. I'm Jonesy,' he pointed to each individual around the table. 'Reg here is Tam, Doug is Blondie and of course we have Chalky.'

'What about Vanrenen?' Bob Crosby chipped in, 'what's he called?'

'You can call him what you like Geordie boy, but to his face he'd better be Skipper or Sir. Nothing more, nothing less and woe betide anyone that slips up.'

'So he hasn't got a nickname?'

Len Jones shook his head.

'But you have, Geordie boy, I've just christened you Geordie.' Len Jones looked for approval around the table and got a unanimous thumbs up. 'Geordie it is then.'

He looked at John.

'That just leaves you Flight Engineer Holmes; we ain't having any ponce in our team called John.' He stood up and rested on the table. 'Any suggestions men?'

'Needles.'

'What?'

'As in needles and pins.'

The joke raised a few laughs but no thumbs up.

'The virgin.'

'The what?'

'The virgin, the bugger's never been up in a plane before.'

Then Doug Handley piped up.

'Sherlock, after Sherlock Holmes. When he takes over from Vanrenen we can call it Sherlock's Squadron.'

The crew all laughed, Bob Crosby slapped John on the back.

'Are you going to become the next Skipper, Sherlock? You know better than everyone else.'

'Just give it a rest, lads, please. Okay I mucked up but when is this going to end?'

'Look Sherlock, when you fuck up around here we never let you forget it. The theory is you will only fuck up once and when we're in the air you'll be on your best behaviour and with a little bit of luck we'll all come back home in one piece.'

Len Jones's analogy was an accurate one, one that made sense and suddenly John could see his crew mates for what they really were. The jokes were harmless, they meant nothing and at the same time the men were relaying an underlying message.

It said simply... trust us.

The village dance was somewhat frustrating for certain parties. While the rest of the crew took their chances with the pretty Welsh girls who'd come into Cowbridge in their droves, two men found it particularly frustrating having been married fairly recently. John and Reg stood at the bar nursing a pint each, both men more than content to look but not to touch.

'I've everything I need back home, Sherlock,' Reg announced. 'I'm not going to let any of these Welsh girls get me into bother.'

A girl floated past the bar, no more than eighteen years of age with a bust that looked almost out of kilter with the rest of her body. Her face was as smooth as a peach, long auburn hair cascaded and flowed behind her and she smiled at the two RAF men as they stood and gawped.

'We can look but we'd better not touch, Tam.' John was missing his beautiful young bride more than ever. His son's face was etched permanently on his mind and temptation, no matter how great, would never be able to come in between him and his perfect family. It was hard to resist a pretty face but it wasn't impossible.

'Well stacked though isn't she Sherlock?'

John laughed, feigned a puzzled look. 'Err… was she? I can't say I'd really noticed to tell you the truth.'

Reg Tammas pulled John into a headlock and rained a few pretend punches into his face. 'You're some fella you are Sherlock, I'll say. You've caused more hassle in the two seconds you've been with us than anyone I can remember.'

Reg Tammas broke the grip.

'Something tells me we're going to get along just fine.'

'We are that Tam… we are that.'

Later that evening the beers kicked in and a more melancholy mood ensued. John was always one for contemplating after the effects of alcohol kicked in and his mood deepened as he thought about the family he'd left behind, his brothers wherever it was they were and his mother and father. He had a new family now, he told himself, albeit a temporary one. His temporary family would ensure that the world would be a better place for the permanent family he'd left behind. He firmly believed in what it was he was doing.

And that night he dreamt. He dreamt about huge aircraft and bombs and factories and ships and German airfields blown to bits. But towards the end of the dream there were visions of distressed children and weeping mothers and the shock of it all woke him with a start.

Vanrenen stood with a stranger at the front of the lecture room. He introduced him as Flight Lieutenant Bill Short from Berwick upon Tweed, a pilot instructor.

Vanrenen broke the news.

'We'll be going up this afternoon. 1500 hours.' Vanrenen

smiled. 'Today, gentlemen, we will be taking our first trip in the Queen of the Skies.'

Vanrenen and Short took the morning class between them, before breaking for lunch. John's legs were like jelly as he tried to stand to leave the room and for the first time he realised he was positively petrified.

Reg noticed too.

'Look at Sherlock, Len, he's shitting himself.'

John tried to laugh it off.

'No I'm not. I'm just a little rough from last night… too many beers.'

But he was shitting himself and he knew it and so did the rest of the room. John didn't notice as he walked outside that the rest of the team were gesticulating to each other in silence behind his back. They were concocting a ruse and poor old Sherlock would be at the centre of it.

'Worst bloody plane in the RAF, the old Stirling.'

Doug Hanley drew on a cigarette as he walked down the narrow corridor that led the way outside. A large plume of smoke rose to the ceiling. John took the bait.

'It is?'

'Damn right it is, you've heard about the swing on take-off haven't you?'

'Yes I have, but…'

'And the collapsing wheels on landing?' said Chalky.

And so it went on for the ten minutes they stood and loitered outside before lunch. The entire crew tore the Stirling Bomber to pieces so skilfully that John Holmes was convinced his life expectancy had been slashed to that of a week-old kitten at the annual Cambridgeshire Fox Terriers Ball.

'You dining with us today?' asked Bob Crosby.

John shook his head and explained that he'd arranged to

meet up with Lofty Matthews and Taffy Stimson. He wanted to see how their first few flights had gone.

'Surely the Stirlings can't be as bad as what you lot are saying?'

As soon as John had made the announcement, Doug Hanley had quietly slipped away to find Lofty and Taffy. He needed to bring them in on the joke.

John took lunch in the Sergeants' Mess. He spotted Lofty and Taffy sitting with a group of other flight crew and walked over with his lunch piled high. It would be a lunch that he would not touch. Lofty and Taffy and the entire table had been 'got at'. Doug Hanley had slipped out of the mess unseen, with seconds to spare.

Taffy introduced his pilot, Henry 'Chuck' Hoystead, an Aussie, who knew Vanrenen. Although Hoystead was an officer he was the exact opposite to Vanrenen and preferred to eat with 'the boys', steering clear of the Officers' Mess whenever he could. Lofty's pilot was also there, Warrant Officer Keith Prowd, another Aussie and a navigator, Flight Sergeant Clive Westoby.

For the next hour, John asked the questions and Lofty and Taffy's crew answered them. To say they exaggerated the failings of the Stirling Bomber was the understatement of the year. Clive Westoby was particularly animated playing up the role of chief exaggerator to the full.

John was quaking in his boots as they approached the huge Stirling a few minutes before 3 pm. He was a little dismayed that he hadn't had time to pen one last letter to his wife. It looked bigger than ever, almost taunted him as he approached it, daring him to climb inside. Bill Short gave him a little wave from the cockpit that towered twenty nine feet above him.

Even climbing into the Stirling seemed fraught with danger. The most unpopular method of getting into the aircraft involved a 22-rung ladder climb direct into the cockpit which gave relatively easy access to the rest of the plane. It was not used very often but today, typical of the RAF, it was. Despite his misgivings John still had an overwhelming desire to get into the plane.

Every member of the crew had a one to one instructor with them, specialising in their own particular field. John's man was a flight engineer with three years' experience flying Stirlings. Archie Murray was an amiable guy from the Borders of Scotland and a good friend of Bill Short. Although a little shaky, John managed the ladder without a problem. Bill Short welcomed him aboard with a handshake and although Vanrenen was also on board, he had his face buried in a flight chart and neither noticed nor acknowledged the virgin Flight Engineer. Whilst the Stirling bomber was huge from the outside, the inside was a completely different story.

John tugged at his collar, feeling a little claustrophobic as he peered down the fuselage. To use a popular expression–there wasn't room to swing a cat. Archie encouraged him to take a trip down the plane to familiarise himself with the lay out. Although he felt he knew every inch of the plane through the many months of training and study nothing could prepare him for this moment, knowing that within thirty minutes or so this huge monstrosity would be bumping and shuddering down the runway at 125 miles an hour attempting to make it into the air. As John climbed into the bomb bay and imagined it crammed with nearly eight tons of bombs (today it was empty) he wondered just how accurate the assessments of his crew members really were.

Just how bad was the plane? How cumbersome and badly

designed was it, and more importantly what was the real life expectancy of the plane according to the RAF? How many sorties were a crew expected to make before they crashed or were shot down?

These were not questions he should be asking himself now, he thought, as he became aware of the first of the four huge engines sparking into life. He continued to crawl through the plane, annoyed at how cumbersome his attached parachute was becoming. The crew had been told to wear the chute at all times during the inaugural flight to get used to it. He passed the rest bed, which in theory would give a member of the crew a chance to catch forty winks on a particularly long flight. It was nonsense since no one in the crew had time to take a rest during any operation. Its true purpose was for wounded crew members, the dead or dying. The mattress itself gave the game away as it was covered with plastic sheeting to prevent blood soiling the bed.

Archie shouted through to him to take up his position.

The Flight Engineer's instrument panel was positioned about six feet behind the second pilot's seat and gave a perfect view out of the cockpit window when standing. Archie sat, making all the checks as John looked on with admiration. He worked the checks like clockwork, no notes, no manuals to help him, just an automatic routine. He made it look effortless. As the time for take-off approached John began to perspire a little. By now the crew and all instructors were in place, it felt like the black hole of Calcutta.

All four engines had been fired into life and Bill Short eased the huge plane forward as it lurched with an almost human like objection as if to say *why are you disturbing me*? The aircraft creaked and groaned and strained as it made its way towards the centre of the airfield. John felt every bump, every gap in the concrete approach road as it taxied towards the runaway. Bill heaved at the small wheel as the giant aircraft turned and as John peered over his shoulder a mile and a half of runway loomed up before him. It was the most terrifying two minute ordeal of his life as the huge Stirling thundered down the runway. The noise from the four engines was deafening as they strained to power themselves to the required take off speed. Bill Short's hands visibly vibrated on the wheel, they were almost a blur and John couldn't help but notice the determined but anxious look on his face. He closed his eyes, trying to block out everything until a swift dig from Archie Murray told him that he was here to watch and learn. He looked back over Bill's shoulder and noticed the airfield perimeter fence draw ever nearer. They would never make it.

And still the aircraft seemed to fight against the pilot and he recalled the stories of the Stirling stalling at crucial moments, of poor manoeuvrability, the sheer bulk and weight of the craft, the wingspan that was too short and the legendary swing that could occur without warning as it left the runway. His mind was in turmoil as the engine noise increased again in a final effort to lift the beast into the air. And then the Stirling was airborne.

In an instant, in a split second, all of John's anxieties had disappeared into thin air. The wheels and flaps came up, the engine noise died a little and as the ground disappeared beneath them the Stirling came to life. John felt an uncontrollable smile pull across his face. He lifted himself from the seat and gazed out of the window as if in a trance.

A cheer came from behind him. His wireless operator, navigator and bomb aimer had watched the terrified individual transform into a man without a care in the world; a man who'd just experienced one of life's great wonders, how 46 tons of metal could defy gravity. And at that moment he realised that his colleagues had been winding him up, putting him to the test because he was, as Chalky had commented in the King's Head in Cowbridge, a flight virgin.

But he was a virgin no longer and still the smile wouldn't leave his face as he slowly fell in love with the noise and movement, even the smell of the Stirling Bomber. Archie Murray shook his head and grinned. He'd given up on his trainee flight engineer who had no hope of learning anything on his first flight. It was why the RAF sent up an individual instructor with every crew member, because flight engineers like John 'Sherlock' Holmes were absolutely useless and besotted with the Stirling, reduced to the stature of a schoolboy with a huge crush on the sexiest and most glamorous teacher in the school.

CHAPTER EIGHT

It would have been hard to describe John Holmes's state of mind as the Stirling climbed to around 5000 feet. It was another world, but a world that he was more than comfortable with. He tried hard to tear himself away from the view outside as the aircraft climbed ever higher. It was a perfectly clear day and the English countryside looked like a huge patchwork quilt beneath him. Bill Short pointed out various landmarks during the short flight. They flew out over Newmarket and John marvelled at the miles and miles of gallops that had been used to exercise racehorses from the early 1800s. He spotted what he thought was a string of racehorses moving quickly against the contrasted green background. They looked just like ants. Bill Short flew the Stirling south over Ipswich and followed a line along the Orwell Estuary out into the North Sea. He banked the huge plane and followed a line along the coast before announcing to the crew that they were heading back towards Waterbeach and the airstrip.

It was what was known as circuit and bump training. They would take off, land and taxi back to the huge hangers. They'd repeat every check verbatim then prepare to take off again. The Stirling would be airborne for no more than an hour, circuit and bump, circuit and bump and circuit and bump again. John Holmes's confidence in the aircraft grew and grew and by the end of the day he loved every single second of flying time. He loved every bump, every rattle, every turn the Queen of the Skies took and it had manoeuvrability in the air that John couldn't quite comprehend. He couldn't quite believe how something so heavy, so clumsy and big on the ground stayed up there, let alone fly like it did once in the air. Archie grinned at him and shouted above the noise.

'Beautiful isn't she?'

John simply nodded.

Everyone agreed that they had to celebrate John's first ever flight and the rest of the crew's first trip in a Stirling bomber. They went to the King's Head in Cowbridge; that is everyone except Vanrenen.

'She's like a big, clumsy old woman on the ground,' said Reg, 'but Jesus Christ when those wheels lift off she's as elegant as anything I've ever flown in.'

'Incredible turning circle I'm told, don't think Bill put her through her paces today.'

Doug looked at his flight engineer.

'Didn't want you shitting your pants on the first trip Sherlock… wouldn't be good for morale if the virgin crapped himself would it?'

The rest of the crew laughed. John didn't care. The jokes would continue but eventually die away. He felt part of the crew now, couldn't wait to get back up in the air if the truth were told and couldn't wait until they ditched their instructors and flew solo. But there was a lot to do before then. Reg explained that the next two weeks would be only circuit and bump, no real height or any night flying. Once the instructors were happy with the crew they'd let them go solo and they'd practice again and again and again.

After ten days the instructors deemed the crew competent and allowed them to fly solo for the first time. John admitted to feeling a little nervous but completed his pre-flight checks with ease. For the first time Vanrenen took the controls while Bill Short stood on the ground and watched. Vanrenen was supremely confident and handled the Stirling as if he'd been flying it for a hundred years. John couldn't help but look on with admiration as he put the plane through a series of tight turns. Vanrenen shrieked with joy from the cockpit in an uncharacteristic show of emotion.

'This ugly brute will out turn a bloody glider.'

John had the proof of the pudding. Reg had told him that the Stirling could outmanoeuvre a Bf 110 Night Fighter. He'd doubted him at first but now he knew the truth. As the plane climbed higher than they'd ever climbed before, Vanrenen announced they were flying cross country. He'd take the plane up to around 16,000 feet and they'd need their oxygen masks for the very first time. They would be in the air for over four hours.

They flew over Norwich and up the east coast past Grimsby and Newcastle upon Tyne. Vanrenen announced on the radio they'd turned due west and were following a line along Hadrian's Wall out past Carlisle and into The Irish Sea. It was a beautifully languid sunny morning and the sun flitted in and out of the sparse cloud cover casting shadows on the swell of the sea below. Before long they were over the water and Vanrenen pointed out The Isle of Man in the distance. Before they reached the island the giant craft turned again and headed back towards land. Within the hour they had started their descent into Waterbeach. Vanrenen brought the Stirling down near perfectly. As far as John Holmes was concerned it was over far too quick. It was a beautiful perfect day and John had to remind himself there was a war on.

As they disembarked from the plane and walked towards the mess hall John laughed and joked with the rest of the crew looking and feeling every bit as confident as the rest of them. He showed no sign of nerves anymore, no butterflies in the stomach or dry throat or nausea. He was 100% at ease with the Queen of the Skies.

John was brought back down to earth two days later when for the first time he experienced the notorious take off swing of the Stirling. The day had started like any other, another cross country trip but today would be a little different. It was a little gusty as they approached the plane but John didn't give it much thought. He remembered thinking to himself that it would take a wind of hurricane force proportions to move the beast he was about to climb into.

How wrong he was.

The crew all climbed in through the rear door and made their way up the plane. Vanrenen was already in place as John took up his position behind him. John completed his checks as did Vanrenen and the rest of the crew and the Skipper took the Stirling onto the runway.

The cross wind could have been described as moderate… no more. Vanrenen had trained for the swing and trained well. As he brought the Stirling to a stop and looked at the trees dancing to the tune of the wind on the edge of the perimeter fence he somehow sensed that this was the day his training would be called into question. It was only a matter of time and as the other pilots had told him, the first one was always the worst, the first swing most likely to end in disaster. It happened during the transitional period between the tail wheels leaving the ground and the tail up position on take-off. If the pilot didn't correct the swing immediately the aircraft would lurch and veer out of control causing the tall undercarriage to collapse and send the Stirling skidding into the grass at around 80 miles per hour. The wind felt stronger out in the middle of the airfield and for the first time John noticed the Stirling buffering as it prepared to take off.

'Winds a bit strong today, Sherlock.' It was Reg Tammas as he stood up and peered out of the cockpit window.

Vanrenen announced to the crew he was on his way.

John Holmes loved every second he was in the Stirling, even on take-off when some crew members quite understandably got a little apprehensive or nervous. Some men admitted in the mess hall that they were positively terrified on take-off and landing and there were more than a dozen aircrew who could tell a story of being in a Stirling as it was written off.

The first John knew of a problem was when he was slammed back in his seat with a jolt and an increase in engine noise.

Reg Tammas cursed. 'It's fucking swinging Sherlock, hang on to your hat.'

Vanrenen's training kicked in as he anticipated immediately the direction of swing and opened up the starboard throttles and at the same time partially closing the port side. Within a couple of seconds Vanrenen had regained the rudder control and brought the tail up. The engines balanced out and he increased the speed of the plane. John's heart was in his mouth but eventually Vanrenen eased the plane into the air. He felt compelled to offer a little congratulations.

'Well done Skip... well done.'

Vanrenen looked over his shoulder. 'It's a bloody plane Holmes, it catches the wind occasionally and the pilot must counteract that. Luckily you chaps have the cream of the crop flying you around so you've absolutely nothing to worry about.'

John didn't reply and suppressed a smile. That's Vanrenen for you, he thought as he returned to his instrument panel and completed the next series of checks. A little while later Vanrenen announced he would be taking the Stirling down again. He landed without incident. The wind on the ground had increased and John suspected Vanrenen may call it a day. It was not to be. Vanrenen announced he wanted to practice take off and landings in strong winds. He took the aircraft up and down six times, the wind grew stronger and stronger. The Stirling swung every time both on take off and on landing and Vanrenen mastered each one perfectly. At the end of the day's exercises the crew ended up in the King's Head. Vanrenen was conspicuous by his absence. He had better things to do but unknown to him his crew raised a glass to a very special pilot.

'The very best,' said Bob Crosby with his glass held high in the air. 'But don't ever tell the bastard to his face, his head's big enough as it is!'

John and the rest of the crew laughed but he couldn't help thinking that Vanrenen had every right to be proud of his achievements. He remembered reading a quotation somewhere that summed Vanrenen up perfectly.

'Pride is the recognition of the fact that you are your own highest value and, like all of man's values, it has to be earned.'

Perfect… thought John, *absolutely bloody perfect. I just wish I could remember who said it and where I read it.*

Two days later they were back in the air again, this time on low flying exercises. John found this part of the training exhilarating and spent most of the time standing looking out of the cockpit window as he finished the series of checks and calculations. Vanrenen called him into the cockpit for the first time.

'You can sit here for the rest of the flight, Holmes. Watch and learn. If anything happens to me you'll need to fly the bloody thing.'

John sat in awe as Vanrenen threw the aircraft round like a balsa wood boat. At times John would have sworn that his pilot was showing off, even trying to frighten the crew as he skirted the tops of trees. He flew out over the sea and followed the contours of the beach at such a low level John could almost make out the grains of sand on the beach. The Stirling handled like a dream. That night, back in the King's Head, John likened it to a white knuckle fairground ride that pumped the adrenaline around his body. He'd loved every minute of it.

From October 13th to November 15th 1943, Vanrenen's crew trained over twenty days in the air. Some days they would go up two or even three times, they circuit and bumped, flew cross country and on October 20th commenced night flying.

Flying at night was a whole different ball game as the entire country was blacked out. They relied on the skill of the navigator, Reg, picking out points on a map, rivers and canals that would reflect the light of the moon and give an indication of where the plane was. Reg had flown night flights before but his face was still a picture of extreme concentration as Stirling N6128 pulled onto the runway. The navigator was king on a night flight; he gave the instructions to the Skipper who obeyed without question.

Lofty Matthews and Taffy Stimson had already experienced several night flights and John recalled the stories in the Sergeants' Mess of a navigator or two getting it wrong. Senior flight engineers and gunners were more than happy to admit being a little scared taking off and landing in a sea of blackness.

As the Stirling lifted off, John fully related to the stories as a mild panic overcame him and he wondered how Vanrenen would bring the plane safely down to earth in the dead of night on an unlit runway. The moonlight was good that night, cloud cover sparse. They shouldn't have too many problems following a pre-planned route that Vanrenen had given the navigator earlier in the day. His thoughts wandered into the future, above Germany perhaps, on a bombing raid to Berlin or Dusseldorf. What happened if there was no moonlight, if the cloud cover came in thick? What then? Would they make it back home? Of course they would.

Reg placed his faith in his flight engineer and so the flight engineer would place his faith in his navigator the same way he had utmost faith in his pilot, his gunners and his bomb aimer. They were a magnificent crew and each trip they took in their beautiful elegant lady he loved and respected them even more.

John had completed all of his checks and notified Vanrenen. Reg confirmed the route once again, informed Vanrenen he expected a trouble free flight with good visibility from the moonlight and very light cloud. This time they were heading south, down into Kent, skirting the outskirts of Dover creeping a few miles into the English Channel before heading back home. The exercise was primarily for the navigator. Vanrenen had informed the crew they would be doing a series of circuit and bump night runs over the next few nights and then resume low level flying exercises again. The engine noise increased telling the crew that Vanrenen was just a few seconds away from preparing for take-off. Vanrenen powered the aircraft down the runway into the big black void. John stood and the engines screamed as they reached their maximum torque. There was nothing to see, no trees, no perimeter fence just blackness. John had counted down the seconds until the Stirling lifted from the runway and as always he'd calculated it just about right as the plane gave one final groan and heaved into the air.

John was quite surprised just how much he could see on the ground despite the fact the total country was in darkness. Nature was a powerful thing, the light from the moon stronger than he had ever expected. It was low in the sky, it almost seemed to be drifting above the pine trees, silhouetted on the horizon as they left the airfield far behind.

Reg pointed out the marks he had made along the way, relaying the instructions to Vanrenen each time he changed his course. Bob came across the radio after about fifteen minutes. 'You're going the wrong way navigator, that's the Tyne Bridge down there.'

Vanrenen was quick to admonish him.

'This is a serious exercise gunner, no one jokes about anything on any of my flights especially when it comes to navigation.'

Crosby apologised to the skipper and promised to remain quiet for the rest of the flight. John looked out of the window, pinpointed the bridge Crosby had been referring too but confessed it looked nothing like the Tyne Bridge.

The flight lasted just under two hours and despite the pitch blackness of Waterbeach Airbase and the surrounding countryside, Vanrenen brought the Stirling down onto the runway with barely a bump. As the crew alighted from the plane Vanrenen even congratulated the navigator on a job well done.

'Now I'm getting worried,' said Reg as the crew piled into the Sergeants' Mess for a quick pint before bedtime, 'Vanrenen never praises the crew, he just expects perfection every time.'

'Fairs fair though.' It was Len's turn to offer a pat on the back. 'I don't know how you do it, Tam. Map reading's hard enough during the day but in the dark... Jesus it must take some concentration.'

'Tonight was easy, lads, believe me, no cloud and plenty of moonlight and flying over a country I'm very familiar with. A cloudy Germany will be a different kettle of fish.'

Bob Crosby slammed his pint glass onto the table.

'Oh brilliant,' he announced in mock consternation. 'Our navigator here has just admitted he's going to get us lost over Germany.'

Reg refused to rise to the bait.

'I'll get better, that's all I'm saying Bob. Tonight was a piece of cake, a few more night flights and I promise you I'll bring you back home safe and sound every time.'

John slapped him on the shoulder. 'We know you will Tam, we know you will.'

Vanrenen's crew undertook more night flying and more than their fair share of low level flying. On 11th and 12th November they practiced simulated bombing runs. They hit the mock target area every time. They celebrated with a heavy night out at The King's Head.

'More low flying tomorrow, Vanrenen told me,' said John.

'And next week apparently,' Reg commented. He continued. 'A little bit too much low flying if you ask me. You don't drop bombs from less than a hundred feet.'

John laughed 'Can't you handle it Tam? Vanrenen make you a little nervous as he clips the tops of those trees?'

Reg had taken a mouthful of beer, returned his glass to the table before wiping the froth from his lips.

'Not at all Sherlock, I'm with you on the adrenalin trip, I love it but you must have heard the rumours?'

'Rumours?'

'Yeah, the rumours about the Stirling not going bombing.'

'What?' John Holmes looked at his navigator incredulously. 'Not going bombing?'

Len chipped in.

'I've heard them too. It's been whispered quietly in the Sergeants' Mess, the officers won't have it but I confess some of the other Stirling crews reckon all they're doing is low level stuff, dropping loads and paratroopers and you don't drop bombs from the tops of trees.'

'But we've been bombing today,' said John. 'I accept we might have to do a troop drop occasionally but surely bombing's what these big buggers are designed for. They can take three times the load a Wellington can.'

Len Jones shrugged his shoulders and reached for his pint.

'Guess we'll just have to wait and see my friend.'

Although John and his crew didn't know it at the time the rumours were more than that. The powers at the top had already decided that the Stirling Bomber's role was about to change. The Air ministry had decided that the Stirling lacked the potential for development as a bomber. The Stirling would be redeployed as a glider tug and paratrooper transporter, hence the regular low level flying exercises. In April of 1943 trials had already begun towing loaded Horsa Gliders and the Stirling's manoeuvrability and tight turning circle was proving more than adequate for the job.

Vanrenen made the announcement in the Sergeants' Mess on the evening of 13th November. It was a rare excursion for Vanrenen and as John spotted him walking through the door he had an inclination that something wasn't quite right. Vanrenen had ordered some drinks at the bar and casually strolled over to the table with a tray full of beers and placed them in the middle of the table but didn't stand on ceremony. He placed a beer in front of each crew member and a large whisky in front of Bob. He announced that the Stirling Bomber had been redefined as a troop carrier and that already it was being converted for that sole purpose. He placed a hand on Bob's shoulder.

'I'm afraid we're losing our mid upper gunner.'

Bob Crosby frowned. 'You're getting rid of me?'

Vanrenen smiled. It was a sympathetic smile, the first John had ever seen from him. It showed a little emotion, a little sadness and a great deal of respect. Bob had worked well with the crew and his shooting results were up there with the best of them.

'Not through choice Mr Crosby, I can assure you, but you're going somewhere a little special, almost like a promotion really.'

'I don't understand Skip.'

Vanrenen feigned a smile as if the news he was about to deliver would somehow lessen the blow.

'You're off to 617 Squadron.'

'617, Skipper... the Dambusters?'

Vanrenen nodded. 'There's no place for a mid upper gunner in the Stirling, they're ripping the front and mid upper turret out.'

'What for?'

'Don't ask me, I would suppose it's to do with load capacity, they need to open up the fuselage for more paratroopers, maybe even something to do with the tow ropes.'

'Tow ropes?'

'Yes, for the Horsa Glider.'

Doug Handley piped in. 'We're going to be towing those bloody glider things?'

'Absolutely.'

'No bombing?'

'None whatsoever.'

The whole crew sat in silence for a minute or two. Vanrenen for once was lost for words.

'But I want to go bombing, Skip,' said Len. 'It's what I came here for. I could have stayed in Canada teaching if I'd wanted a cushy number. I want to be in the thick of the action.'

Vanrenen eased back in his chair and almost laughed.

'Oh we'll be in the thick of the action, Jones, don't you worry about that. We'll be flying at less than 3,000 feet when we enter into the drop zone, a sitting duck for Jerry.'

The enormity of Vanrenen's statement hit John Holmes like a sledgehammer. Vanrenen continued.

'I'd love to be bombing Germany too, love to be dropping our eggs on the Huns at 16,000 feet; at least we'd have a little bit of a chance.'

It was the eerie silence that ensued that sent a shiver up John's spine. Perhaps Vanrenen hadn't meant to say what he'd just said but now it was out. John looked across the table at his stunned colleagues as Vanrenen's statement sunk in.

They weren't going bombing; the Stirling had been redefined as a troop carrier, that's why they'd been doing so much low level flying. They'd be dropping troops and supplies into enemy territory, flying over the tops of the trees with German soldiers hanging from every branch. If Flight Engineer John Holmes thought it couldn't get any more dangerous than dropping bombs over Berlin, then he'd just had a rethink of epic proportions.

CHAPTER NINE

Towards the end of January 1944 the RAF dropped an incredible 2,300 tons of bombs on the city of Berlin. Berlin's western and southern districts were hit in the most concentrated attack of the period and its war industries were decimated. It was the largest raid by the RAF on Berlin and gave an indication to the failing defences of Germany's most important city. The raids on Berlin would continue until March. The devastation and loss of life was huge. The regular raids killed hundreds of people every night destroying countless thousands of homes, factories and businesses. The Berliners, however, dug deep and despite the devastation and the fact that much of their city lay in ruins, civilian morale did not break.

The raids on Berlin cost the RAF 500 aircraft, with their crews killed or captured, Bomber Command lost 2,690 men over Berlin and nearly 1,000 more became prisoners of war. It was not the result the RAF was looking for.

Later that same month the RAF used a massive 12,000 pound bomb nicknamed 'Tall-Boy' in a raid on the Gnôme-et-Rhône works in Limoges, not far from the village of Oradour-sur-Glane.

John Holmes lay awake on his bunk. Sleep was hard to come by.

He felt more than a little cheated by the men from the ministry of defence. He'd fallen in love with the Stirling Bomber, and that's what it was… a bomber. That's what it was designed for and that's what it should have been used for, but overnight it was as if someone had removed the toys from his pram.

He reached down and tugged at the laces of his boots, loosened them, eased them off and dropped them to the floor. He lay back on the bunk and let out a long sigh. *Thick of the action,* Vanrenen had said, *at least at 16,000 feet we'd have a chance,* he'd said.

John closed his eyes, tried to envisage all those low flying exercises and how skilfully Vanrenen had flirted with the tops of the hills, the trees, landmarks like water towers and windmills and although he didn't like it there was nothing he could do about it. As he drifted off to sleep he consoled himself that he and his crew really were flying with the top man and if anyone could get them out of the mess they were in then it was Vanrenen.

The RAF had made their decision and wasted no time in appointing John Holmes and his crew to 196 Squadron in Leicester. They were officially released from Bomber Command along with many other squadrons and joined the recently formed 38 Group. There, reality sank in as they spent the first three weeks towing Horsa Gliders during the day and on night exercises. The Horsa Glider carried up to 30 troops and in addition could carry a jeep or a 6 pounder anti-tank gun. Notoriously unpredictable, their safety record was pretty poor and because of their flimsy construction it was not uncommon for them to break up on landing. They were looked upon by the troops and air crew who towed them as rather unlucky. Indeed on the Horsas' very first operational flight on the night of 19th November 1942, two gliders were cast loose over the German Heavy Water Plant in Rjukan, Norway. The two gliders, each carrying 15 sappers, crashed in Norway due to bad weather. All 23 survivors from the gliders were executed on the order of Hitler.

That first mission set an unenviable precedent that would be hard to shake off.

After six weeks' training at Leicester East, the crew were sent to Tarrant Rushton in Dorset on the south coast of England, a mere stone's throw from the English Channel, a perfect launching pad for their sorties into France and beyond.

The crew of ZO U, which signified their squadron (ZO) and Vanrenen's crew (U), sat in the briefing room of RAF Tarrant Rushton on 4th February 1944. The officer in command almost seemed to be giving a lecture on the French Resistance, such was his praise for the freedom fighters who continued to battle against their Nazi occupiers. The officer had told the three assembled crews that the 2nd Panzer Division had been stationed north of Toulouse in the Central West region of France and the resistance had managed to wreak havoc in the area taking out many of the bridges crossing the River Glane, which in effect kept the Panzer Division pinned down. This had frustrated the Germans, stopping them from advancing northwards. As always the resistance wanted more weapons and of course the essential materials to construct and make shells and explosive devices.

'Bloody French chaps are doing a super job, but they need more kit and that's where we come in.'

The officer pointed to a huge map hanging on the wall.

'This is Oradour-sur-Glane, and this,' he pointed with a shiny wooden stick, 'is the bridge that the Nazis have tried to repair again and again.' The officer was almost smiling now. 'The thing is, each time the bridge is repaired the French chaps manage to blow the bugger up again.'

He walked around to the front of the table to the assembled crews. He handed each of the navigators a slip of paper.

'These are your map references. You'll be flying in tomorrow night, leaving at 22.15 and the good news is that you won't be towing any of those bloody wooden gliders. All we need to get out there will be three panniers lodged in each plane.' He looked towards the pilot of ZO U.

'Vanrenen, your boys will take the lead. You'll be flying plane EA 874.'

Vanrenen simply nodded to the officer in charge.

John Holmes sat at the rear of the briefing room with Reg Tammas on his right hand side. He breathed a sigh of relief; what was it about those Horsas that he didn't like? Reg was studying his coordinates and John couldn't help but gauge his reaction. Reg didn't seem too phased and was already making notes in his log book. A flight engineer from another crew raised his hand.

'What's in the panniers, Sir?'

The officer smiled.

'I'm afraid, Flight Engineer, that's of no concern to you. You just get them dropped and, God willing, about turn and head back to dear old Blighty.'

The officer informed them to report to the Sergeants' Mess where a late supper had been laid on for them. It was a chance to get to know the other two crews who would be flying with them. John sat next to a young man from Chiswick as they tucked into corned beef and onion sandwiches and chips with plenty of salt. John bonded instantly with the Londoner, Mark Azouz, and took an instant liking to him as they counteracted the effect of the salt with several pints of bitter the RAF had kindly supplied.

'Free beer, Sherlock,' said Azouz, 'and a feed too. Good old RAF,' he grinned. 'I only hope it isn't our last supper.'

He slapped John Holmes on the back and roared with laughter. The frivolity lasted into the early hours of the morning, the theory being that the crews would enjoy a long lie in the following day, ideal preparation for the mission that lay ahead.

At around 2.30 in the morning each crew member lined up a small whisky and gave a personal toast to something they dearly wanted to set eyes on again. John raised his glass to the Crook O' Lune and Len Jones recited a six verse poem about the Canadian Rockies and the mist that covered their peaks. When he finished everyone stood and applauded. When it was Mark Azouz's turn he simply raised the glass to Ralph and Esta… his parents. It was a fitting tribute and one that John could relate to but one he didn't need reminding of. For some strange reason he was trying to block out the images of his parents, brothers and sisters but above all that of his wife and his infant son… if only for a day or two.

As John left the mess hall and walked back to the billet he became aware of a small black and white dog following him. He bent down to stroke it.

'Hello little fella, who do you belong to?'

It was a cold night and John wondered what it was doing out so late. As he opened the door the dog made a desperate lunge to get inside. John put his foot across the gap.

'No you don't boy, no dogs allowed in this hut.'

It was another restless night on John's bunk. The beer had not had the desired affect and the memories and pictures of his beloved family could not be dispelled by alcohol. On a full stomach he prayed that sleep would come quickly but it was no good, too many cogs were turning in his subconscious.

This flight would be different to every one he'd ever flown. This time it was for real and this time the anti-aircraft guns and fighter planes of the Third Reich would be doing their level best to blow them to bits over the night skies of France.

Vanrenen's face was a picture of concentration as he eased the plane up into the blackness, turned immediately to starboard and headed towards the English Channel. Within twenty minutes Tammas had indicated to the crew that they were flying over Nazi occupied France and into enemy territory. The normal banter and high spirits were non-existent, the entire crew on high alert on the lookout for enemy aircraft. There were another two crewmen flying with them tonight, two army dispatch men responsible for throwing the panniers from the plane. Conditions however were on their side; thick cloud cover would hide the Stirling from the anti-aircraft guns below. With a little luck they would drop their cargo at the designated spot outside the village of Oradour-sur-Glane without too many problems.

John had come to terms with the kind of missions they would be flying, almost a little relieved that he wouldn't be part and parcel of a crew destined to drop thousands of tons of bombs on the innocent citizens of cities, towns and villages. He'd viewed the Pathé news reels at the cinema, the bombing of Coventry and in particular the London blitz. He wondered if the German crews had any regrets or feelings of compassion as they released the deadly loads on the innocent men, women and children below. For 76 consecutive nights during the spring of 1941 they'd rained bombs on England's capital. Over 25,000 civilians had been killed and more than a million houses destroyed.

He'd felt for them, he really had, as he'd mumbled *poor bastards* to himself over and over again in the darkened cinema. His head was full of the images from the cinema screen, young children and the elderly weeping for their loved ones buried dead or alive in the tons of masonry that had been blown apart. Were their tears any different from the German civilians in Berlin, Dusseldorf and Dresden?

They were now nearly three hours into the flight and Tammas announced that the cloud cover was breaking up as they neared the drop zone.

'Fifteen minutes to DZ,' he announced. John signalled to the two army dispatchers who sat in the fuselage. One of them crawled up towards him.

'What is it Sarge?'

'Fifteen minutes to the drop zone, are you two lads ready?'

'We will be,' he replied. 'Ready as we'll ever be, Sarge.'

The French Resistance were ready and waiting to carry out the operation with military precision. Three sections of men stood by each truck ready to go to work as soon as the containers were dropped. Pierre-Henri Poutaraud, Louis-Leonard Chapelot and Henri-Pierre Raynaud were in charge of their respective teams. Henri Pierre spoke.

'What time do you have Louis, how long is it until our friends arrive?'

Louis-Leonard Chapelot checked his watch.

'A little over four minutes. Tell the men to get ready.'

Henri Pierre signalled to the man standing by the haystack.

He removed the cap from a small tin of petrol.

Vanrenen had brought the Stirling below the clouds and listened to Reg as he called out the decreasing altitude level every twenty seconds. The adrenalin was coursing through John's veins and he positively tingled as he sat in the second pilot's seat and looked below. Gradually the shape of the French countryside unfolded before him. Vanrenen glanced to his right.

'See it yet Flight Engineer?'

'Not yet Skip.'

'What about you Bomb Aimer?'

Doug Handley lay flat on his stomach in the front turret.

'Negative, Skipper.'

'Shouldn't be too difficult to spot, the terrain's fairly flat. Keep your eyes peeled.'

'Will do, Skipper.'

Vanrenen spoke into the radio. 'I'm opening up the doors Bomb Aimer.'

John heard the hydraulics of the hinges grind into action. Len Jones, the rear gunner confirmed that the other two Stirlings were following suit and all three were lined up like three geese crossing a lake.

'I hear them Pierre, I hear the planes.'

The resistance fighter assigned to the petrol can had heard it too and didn't need any prompting as he poured the fuel onto the haystack and struck a match. The haystack exploded into a ball of flames that lit up the night sky.

Louis-Leonard clasped his hands together and prayed that the men from the RAF were as anxious as they were to complete the mission and get out of there as quickly as possible.

Top: An official RAF photograph of 'Sherlock's Crew' circa 1944. (*Top row, left to right*) Chalk, Crosby, Holmes, Jones. (*Bottom row, left to right*) Tammas, Vanrenen, Handley.

Middle left: John Holmes 1945. Patch is looking out of the window.

Above: Sherlock and friends relaxing outside their billet. (*From left to right*) Holmes, Chalk, Jones. (*Seated*) Handley with Patch and Tammas.

Left: Chalk, Holmes and Tammas at Shepherds Grove only a few hours before their doomed final flight.

Henry Poleman Vanrenen

Len Jones

Reg Tammas

Len Jones

'Jack' Chalk with Patch

Top left: Henry Poleman Vanrenen, much has been written about the pilot who flew 'Sherlock's Crew.' A fiercely proud man, at times outspoken and aloof, occasionally downright rude, But his crew would not have swapped him with any other pilot in the world and owed their lives to his skill and judgement on that final doomed flight when their Stirling bomber crashed near Overloon in Holland.

Centre: Len Jones with his beloved convertible and an unknown member of the ground crew.

Doug Handley

Mark Azouz

George Tickner

Keith Prowd

Lofty Matthews

LJ 979 WHICH CRASH LANDED NEAR
OVERLOON HOLLAND
L-R. HANDLEY TAMMAS

LJ 979 WHICH CRASH LANDED NEAR
OVERLOON HOLLAND
L-R. TAMMAS HOLMES JONES HANDLEY

Top: Original crash photographs taken by the villagers of Overloon 1945.

Above: Chuck Hoystead and crew. 1944. (*Left to right*) Ray Owen, Taffy Stimson, Chuck Hoystead, Jack Hooker, John Barker. Kneeling; Bill Garretts.

Right: (*Back row left to right*) John Caldwell, Rolf Mann, George Humphrey, Eric Quirk. (front row left to right) George Tickner, Joseph Stevenson.

John was the first to spot it.

'There Skip, there it is,' he shouted with excitement as he signalled to a faint glow two or three miles to the west.

Vanrenen had already banked the plane to the port side and threw it into a steep dive. Once again John Holmes marvelled at the manoeuvrability of the Stirling but in particular the skill of Vanrenen who within a few seconds had levelled the plane out and reduced the speed so much that it convinced him it would simply drop out of the sky.

'Bomb Aimer, you take over from here, make sure you're ready to tell those chaps when to push.'

'Ready and waiting, Skipper.'

John could see the lights of the truck now; the French Resistance fighters had turned the vehicles to light up the drop zone.

'I reckon about ten seconds bomb aimer…nine, eight, seven.'

The Stirling was almost touching the tops of the trees as Vanrenen continued the countdown, Doug Handley was ready to push the button that would light up a signal box a foot or two away from where the army men stood.

The lone German sentry at the Chateau Marmont at the end of Rue de la Lande in Oradour-sur-Glane had noticed the change in the contrast of the night sky. The chateau housed the 2nd Waffen SS Panzer Division. The sentry was already on the radio and a truck load of German soldiers had been scrambled. The driver was already at the wheel of the truck as the sentry opened the gates to the street outside.

'Probably just a barn fire,' one of the soldiers said, complaining as he ran alongside his colleague while fastening the buttons of his jacket. 'I thought we were supposed to be the best fighting soldiers in the world, not fucking peasant firemen.'

As they climbed into the truck another soldier reminded him that the French resistance fighters were very much alive and kicking in this part of France.

'We need to make an example of these fucking pig dogs when we catch them. Line the bastards up against the wall and shoot them in front of the whole village, that's what I say Hans.'

'Go, go, go!'

The Stirling was less than fifty feet from the ground when Doug Handley pushed the button and screamed at the top of his voice. One by one the panniers almost seemed to float through the night sky before crashing onto the muddy ground the French resistance fighters had soaked earlier that day. The panniers landed perfectly, skidding through the quagmire before coming to a halt. The other two Stirlings flew in behind Vanrenen and his crew and repeated the drill faultlessly.

Len Jones' excited voice came over the radio.

'Nine boxes on the ground Skipper. Mission accomplished.'

John couldn't help thinking that Len was being a little premature. After all they had to get back home and one thing was for certain, the fire that shone like a beacon and the noise of three Stirling Bombers less than 50 feet from the ground had awoken every German within a 20-mile radius. Vanrenen had already started climbing and gave the orders to the other two Stirlings to head for home. John's heart was in his mouth at what he'd noticed just over a mile to the east of the drop zone.

'Headlights Skipper, at nine o'clock, looks like someone's in a hurry to see what's in those boxes.'

Vanrenen cursed. He looked over to the headlights of the vehicle getting ever nearer.

'Shit, shit, shit, they'll never make it. Jerry will be on top of them in two or three minutes.' Vanrenen spoke into the radio. He told the other two crews he was heading back into the drop zone. The other planes had noticed the rapidly approaching truck too and Mark Azouz who flew the second plane asked the lead pilot if he wanted assistance. Vanrenen declined.

'We'll lend a little hand to the Frenchmen; I've a good rear gunner on board, no use putting anyone else in danger.'

The other two navigators charted their course for home and Vanrenen swung the Stirling to port side as he pushed her into a dive and lowered the speed.

'Flight Engineer, get yourself to the back of the plane, make sure the rear gunner is well supplied with ammunition.'

'Yes Skipper.'

John Holmes knew exactly what the order meant. The rear gunner was a sitting duck at this level of operation, life expectancy low. Vanrenen had ordered his replacement to the rear of the plane.

'Rear Gunner!'

'Yes Skipper.'

'You'll only get one chance at this. The area will be crawling with Huns soon. I don't want to hang around here too long, but if we don't do something to help, the operation fails.'

John made his way down the plane and crouched behind Len in the rear turret, which gave a bird's eye view of the world. Len gripped the handles of the gun and trained the sights on to the ground.

John peered out of the turret too, desperately looking for the headlights of the German truck.

'There,' he shouted. 'There Jonesy, there they are.'

Len nodded, twisted in his seat a little and concentrated hard.

He opened up his fingers and closed them half a dozen times

then returned them to the gun. He had turned one hundred and eighty degrees in his seat and faced his flight engineer. He looked up and gave John a little wink.

'I've got them, Sherlock. I've got the bastards in my crosswire.'

'Slow down a little, Skip,' he called into the radio. Vanrenen eased back on the throttle so much that John felt sure the giant aircraft was about to stall. By now the truck and the helmets of the Waffen SS were clearly visible.

'Rear Gunner, don't be tempted to take out those Jerry bastards, aim for the underside of the truck, that's where the gas tank is.'

'Roger, Skipper.'

The German truck was now less than half a mile from the field where the French Resistance fighters were loading the panniers into the trucks. They only suspected something was wrong when the Stirling flew over the tops of their heads. A split second later they heard the sound of gunfire.

The truck had slowed to almost a stop as the German soldiers stood up shooting at the fast disappearing Stirling. Bullets rained down in the direction of the truck and tracer fire lit up the night sky. Two bullets ripped into the fuselage and out the other side narrowly missing the head of Reg. He screamed into the radio.

'C'mon Jonesy, save my fucking life, the bastards are out to get me.'

Vanrenen had taken the Stirling down to less than a hundred feet as they flew over the vehicle. By now Len's fingers were permanently fixed on the triggers as the Browning machine guns pumped out bullets at the rate of 1,200 rounds a minute. It took less than ten seconds before half a dozen bullets raked into the tank beneath the truck.

One solitary round of tracer ignited the full tank of fuel in a deafening explosion as the flames leapt thirty feet into the air. The soldiers of the Waffen SS never stood a chance with their single shot rifles as they tried to compete with the Browning guns of the Stirling. A huge ball of flames engulfed them and their guns fell silent.

Reg was back on the radio whooping and cheering.

'You fucking beauties, the beers are on me when we get back home!'

John smiled at the reaction of his navigator but it was also a smile of relief. He'd been exposed in that turret with Len Jones, he could almost smell the German bullets as they'd flown just whiskers from the Perspex dome and they had ridden their luck... of that there was no doubt. Another three or four seconds at the most and a German round or two would have found its target.

Back at Tarrant Rushton there were more than a few anxious airmen training their eyes on the southern night sky. The two crews of the other Stirlings had landed thirty minutes ago.

'They should have been back by now,' whispered Mark Azouz to his navigator. 'Even if they'd had a ten-minute skirmish they should have been back by now.'

Azouz bent down to stroke the small black and white dog that had mysteriously appeared by his side.

'Whose dog is this, what's his name?'

The navigator shrugged his shoulders.

'I think it might be Sherlock's, Skipper. It was with him last night as he left the mess.'

Azouz stroked at the back of the dogs neck.

'You looking for Sherlock, little fella? Coming back to see you, is he?'

Just then the dog's ears pricked up and his nose pointed up into the sky. He barked twice and looked up at Mark Azouz.

'What is it boy? What can you hear?'

The navigator spoke.

'He hears something Skip.'

Mark cocked his head and strained to hear above the noise of the wind. Two or three seconds passed and then his face broke out into a broad smile as he slapped his navigator on the back.

'I hear it too. Four bloody engines. I'd recognise that sound from a million bloody miles. They've made it.'

As Mark finished talking the silhouette of Stirling EA 874 loomed up like a ghostly apparition and the dozen or so men let out a huge cheer. The dog ran around in a circle barking excitedly. Mark Azouz bent down and picked it up.

'Don't worry son… Sherlock's coming home.'

The plane landed and taxied towards the assembled men. John was the first to climb down from the rear hatch, quickly followed by the rest of the crew. Mark walked over and offered his hand.

'Where the hell have you guys been? You should have been back ages ago.'

John shook his hand warmly and Azouz embraced him.

'The Skipper thought it best to fly west out to sea. He said that every German anti-aircraft gun between Limoges and La Havre would have been waiting for us on the way back so he got Reg to draw up another route home.'

'Makes sense I suppose.'

John grinned. 'I can't argue with his logic, after all we're back home in one piece.'

Vanrenen breezed past them aware of their conversation.

'Head for thinking, Flight Engineer, feet for dancing. We Australians are taught that from quite a young age.'

All three squads attended a debriefing in the Officers Mess and the RAF had woken a barman to pull a few pints. The small Jack Russell had followed them in and no one seemed to mind as it squeezed under the table and lay at the feet of John. He leaned across to Mark and whispered.

'By the way Mark, what's your dog called?'

'My dog? It isn't my dog, Sherlock, I thought it was yours.'

CHAPTER TEN

Keevil Airfield was located four miles east of Trowbridge in Wiltshire. It was 16th March 1944 and Sherlock's Squadron were on the move yet again. John Holmes had walked the leather from his boots in a vain attempt to find out who owned the black and white Jack Russell who had followed him around for three days. He'd kept back a few sausages from breakfast time as had Len and Reg and Doug had even poured some sweet tea into his water bottle so that the dog would enjoy a hot drink that morning.

John was determined to find the owner, though the rest of the crew weren't so sure. They'd been relayed the story of how the dog was the first to hear their Stirling as it flew in late from Oradour-sur-Glane and it instantly became a good luck charm.

Len sat proudly at the wheel of his MG TB Midget convertible, the roof off, despite the cold temperature of a particularly freezing spring morning. He was berating his flight engineer.

'Just get in the fucking car Sherlock and bring that stupid dog with you. I'm telling you no one owns it… it's yours, it's ours.'

The rest of the crew had left for Keevil by bus some time ago. Len said that John could travel with him.

'No way Jonesy, it must belong to someone. It would be like stealing.'

The unnamed dog sat patiently by the car cocking its head in different directions as the conversation progressed. John watched it.

'I swear that dog is the nearest thing to a human I've ever met, it knows everything we are saying.'

Len looked at his watch for dramatic effect.

'Listen mate I love you like a brother but if we don't get going we'll miss dinner and supper and more importantly a night out at the local boozer too. I can handle missing a couple of meals but not a couple of pints of England's finest bitter.'

John looked at the dog, then Len Jones, who had started up the engine.

'Last chance mate, climb in or you're walking.'

'You wouldn't?'

'I would.'

John pleaded with Len Jones. 'Look, Jonesy just give me another half an hour and I'm sure his owner will turn up.'

Len Jones was shaking his head.

'Thirty seconds.'

'Look mate, I…'

'…29…28…27…26.'

John realised he had pushed Len's patience to the limit. He picked up his kit bag and threw it into the back of the car.

Len slapped at his forehead.

'At last.'

John bent down and the dog came towards him.

'I'll miss you little fella but you need to stay here.' The dog cocked his head again, listening as if trying to understand what John Holmes was saying. 'Your dad will be back soon, I'm sure he will.'

John lifted his head upwards and planted a lingering kiss on its head.

'You stay there boy, I'm sure we'll see you again.'

'In the car, Sherlock, spare me the emotion.'

John opened the door and climbed into the seat. Len Jones revved the engine and put the car into gear.

'You sure you want to leave him?'

John nodded, felt a lump forming in his throat.

'Okay Sherlock, your decision.'

He lifted his foot from the clutch and the car lurched forward.

'Don't look back Sherlock; you'll regret it for the rest of your life.'

'I won't Jonesy… I won't.'

And he didn't. John kept his eyes firmly fixed on the three long concrete runways as they drove past them. He kept his eyes on the sentries as they drove through the gates and locked them onto the tarmac as they hit the open road.

John and Len were silent for the best part of five minutes. It was Len who broke the ice.

'You should have brought him with you, you're going to pine for the rest of the month you silly bastard.'

John remained silent, lost in his thoughts.

'Oh fucking great, what an exciting trip this is going to be.'

Silence.

'So Sherlock, where do you fancy tonight? Know any good boozers in Wiltshire?'

Len Jones kept up his sarcastic comments for over fifteen minutes.

'I've heard Trowbridge is quite nice in the spring.'

And on it went until suddenly John Holmes exploded.

'For fuck's sake Jonesy, can't you shut up for one minute?'

Len Jones turned to face him.

'Ooh, it has life, master…it speaks.'

John Holmes suppressed a smile; he knew he was out of order, knew he shouldn't be acting this way. It was only a dog… someone else's dog for that matter.

'And one other thing.' John said.

'Speak to me, Sherlock.'

'Turn the fucking car round and let's go and get Patch.'

'Patch! Who the hell is Patch?'

'That daft dog we left in Leicester.'

Len Jones brought the car to an abrupt halt as the tyres bit into the road with a screech.

'You want me to turn back?'

John nodded. 'Yes I want you to turn back… I'm sorry.'

'Sorry? Fucking sorry…' He shook his head incredulously then gripped the steering wheel as if he was going to rip it from the steering column. He turned to face John. 'And anyway, since when was he called Patch?'

'About two minutes ago mate… that's when I named him.'

Len opened the door, walked around to the passenger side and stared John Holmes in the face.

'I can't believe I'm hearing this, don't you know there's a war on? Petrol's in short supply.'

'I'm sorry, I'll reimburse you. I'll get you a few gallons.'

Len walked back to the open door, climbed in and slapped the dashboard hard. 'Jesus Christ.'

John looked at him nervously. 'Well?'

'Well what?'

'What are you doing? Are we going back or not?'

Len tapped at the fuel gauge on the dashboard. The needle hovered just above half full. His face broke into a beaming smile.

'You bet we are buddy, you bet we are.'

Patch hadn't strayed an inch from the spot where they had left him. The little dog's tail started wagging as soon as he had heard the familiar sound of the engine as it had approached the gates of the airfield. John simply opened the passenger door and he had jumped on his lap, licked him once on the face and then turned around several times as he made himself comfortable. Len Jones reached across and opened the glove compartment and pulled out a bar of chocolate. He broke off two squares and pushed them gently towards his mouth. The dog took the gift gratefully, chewed on it then closed his eyes as the car moved off.

'Bloody chocolate on ration too Sherlock, you gonna reimburse me for that?'

John smiled, reached over into the back seat into his kit bag and pulled out his RAF-issue sweater. He wrapped it around the dog to protect it from the cold. The dog slept like a baby until the car pulled into RAF Keevil.

Reg and Chalky were standing at the gatehouse as they pulled up to the barrier and the two sentries brought the car to a halt.

'Jesus Christ where have you two been?' asked Reg.

Len Jones shook his head.

'Don't ask Reg… don't ask.'

By now Patch had woken and stood up. He arched his back and let out a long yawn. Reg and Chalky spotted him and broke out into broad beaming smiles.

Chalky spoke. 'You brought the dog, Sherlock.'

'That I did, Chalky. Now stop standing around and go and get the poor bugger something to eat.'

The sentry who had been inspecting John's paperwork reached across and stroked him.

'Lovely little chap isn't he.' He handed John his documentation back. 'Everything in order, there's just one thing not quite right, Sergeant Holmes. Wait here a second will you.'

The sentry walked quickly back to the gatehouse and disappeared inside. John looked at Reg and Chalky, shrugged his shoulders. Two minutes later the sentry reappeared with a small package, stood beside the door of the car and reached inside.

'Can't be having the little fella saying RAF Keevil doesn't feed him.' He pulled out a sandwich. 'Corned beef, I'm sure he'll approve. Welcome to RAF Keevil gentlemen, please enjoy your stay. And you too, err…'

'Patch,' said John, 'his name is Patch.'

Just before they drove away the sentry called over again.

'Sergeant Holmes, I almost forgot. You have a letter postmarked Lancaster.' He handed the letter over. 'It came redirected about two hours ago along with a dozen others that came into Leicester early this morning.'

John tore at the seal with vigour.

'I know what this is. My sister is pregnant, due any day now.'

The rest of the crew watched patiently as John quickly scanned the letter. The important information was at the bottom of the first page.

'I'm an uncle, an uncle to twins no less!' He turned the page over and continued to read. 'Margaret and Lillian, two little girls.'

Reg Tammas grinned broadly.

'That's great news, we're wetting the babies' heads tonight, don't you worry about that. C'mon Uncle Sherlock, let's go and find you your bed because you're going to need it tonight.'

Reg and Chalky stood on the running boards of the car as they guided them towards their accommodation. They explained that they had booked the whole crew into their new billet. Everyone, that is, except Vanrenen who had somehow wangled something a little better. They were lodging with another crew headed up by a pilot from Australia called George Tickner.

Reg explained.

'It's much better accommodation, just a small dormitory with about 25 beds and three big bathrooms.'

They pulled up outside and the two men jumped from the running boards as John, and Len opened the doors of the car and walked towards the building. Patch jumped down from the car and fell in behind John taking time to urinate on the tyre of the car and then the doorstep before they all went in.

Six or seven men lazed around on the beds. One of the men stood up and walked towards the door. John noticed from his uniform that he was a pilot. He introduced himself.

'George Tickner, gentlemen. Pleased to make your acquaintance.'

John shook his hand as did Len. Tickner introduced them to the rest of his Australian crew and one RAF Flight Engineer George Humphrey.

Len was in his element.

'Well bugger me Sherlock, now the foreigners outnumber the Brits in this hut. Something tells me we are going to have a great time. Who knows, we might even win the war.'

George Tickner and the rest of the Australian crew were all

STEVE HOLMES

laughing. George Humphrey strolled across and shook John Holmes's hand.

'That may be the case, Sergeant Holmes, but not one of those bloody Johnny foreigners is clever enough to be a flight engineer.'

John grinned broadly; something told him he was going to get along just fine with his new colleagues.

All occupants of billet number 78, RAF Keevil, climbed into a four-ton lorry laid on by the RAF and drove the four miles into Trowbridge. Patch sat up front in the cab with the driver, John and George Tickner. The driver proceeded to tell them where the best pubs were in Trowbridge and dropped them by the railway station on Boundary Walk. It was another RAF bonding session and one that John and his crew appreciated.

'You've got four hours,' said the driver, 'and I'll be back to pick you up. If you're not here then you're walking back and you might find yourself on a charge.'

'We'll be here,' said John. 'Don't you worry about that.'

They visited the pubs on Stallard Street and an old fashioned Inn on Wicker Hill where the ale flowed like there was no tomorrow. By the end of the evening the Australians and the Brits were like long-lost brothers. John struggled to stay awake on the way home. By the time he crashed onto his bed and his head hit the pillow he was sleeping like a baby. Patch curled up at the foot of the bed and followed suit.

At a meeting the following day, The RAF announced eight days leave for the crew men of Billet 78. They were told to report back on April 3rd. The men queued up for their travel warrants in the Adjutant's Office two hours later. The line was full of friendly banter as they spoke of where they were going and what they were going to do. The Australians had requested warrants to London and talked about the West End shows and the pretty Cockney girls they would meet up with. Those who had families requested train warrants to their home town station.

'Home station, Sergeant?'

'Lancaster Green Ayre, Sir,' John Holmes stated as the officer looked up.

'And is that where you wish to go sergeant or are you heading for the bright lights of London too?'

'No Sir, Lancaster please, I'm off to see the family, you can keep London for me.'

'Me too.' It was Len Jones who had spoken behind him.

John turned around. 'You're not off to London Jonesy?'

'I don't know Sherlock… I suppose I have to, I mean where else is there to go? I'm not staying here for eight days.'

John addressed the officer. 'Lancaster Green Ayre Sir, Jones is travelling to Lancaster.'

'What?' Len looked at his friend incredulously.

'You're coming back home with me mate, back to sunny Lancaster where the sun always shines and the Crook O' Lune always sparkles.'

'What? But Sherlock, I…'

'That's final, you're coming back to Lancaster with me and Patch.'

Len was nodding as a smile crept across his face.

'Lancaster… with you and Patch, are you sure, buddy?'

The officer at the desk looked up.

'Slight problem there gentlemen,' he said as his finger traced a line down the long list of names. 'I can't see a Sergeant Patch, there's no way I can issue a warrant.'

As the two friends walked away laughing, with two travel warrants to Lancaster, Len turned to John.

'One question, Sherlock.'

'Yes?'

'Just what the hell is the Crook O' Lune?'

The train stopped at London King's Cross as the two men gazed out of the window. Hundreds of bodies lined the station almost fighting to get on and off the train.

Len Jones spoke.

'Jesus Sherlock, I can't say I'm too unhappy about leaving this spot behind, I don't think I've ever seen so many people in one place. I mean, where's the pleasure in this?'

The LNER Thomson class B1 loco pulled into Lancaster Green Ayre Station a little after 2 pm. John Holmes felt a little conspicuous as they stepped from the train in their full uniform which was a condition of travel. A head or two turned on the platform as they walked towards the entrance, Patch ran alongside, head held high as he breathed in the noticeably cooler Lancashire air. They took a cab to Belle Vue Terrace and were greeted on the doorstep by Dorothy's father.

'Good God John, we weren't expecting you.'

'I'm sorry Mr Shaw, we were just told yesterday. I didn't have time to get a letter off.'

John Shaw removed his pipe from his mouth and shouted into the hallway. 'Sara Ellen, look who's here, go and fetch our Dorothy.'

John introduced Len Jones.

'A crew mate of mine John, Len Jones, is it okay for him…'

'…to stay here? Of course it is. We've a spare room and you're more than welcome.'

Len shook him by the hand warmly as Dorothy's mother almost ran down the passageway to greet John and the stranger.

'Len lives in Canada, Sara Ellen; it's a long way to go for a few days.'

Sara Ellen had taken Len by the hand and was leading him towards the kitchen.

'You need a nice cup of tea Leonard and a warm by the stove. It's bitter out there today.' Sara Ellen almost pushed the Canadian airman into the kitchen then she turned to her son in law. She pointed up the long flight of stairs.

'And you, Flight Engineer, had better go on up those stairs and say hello to your wife and son.'

John called on his parents later that evening. He'd left Len in the same position in the kitchen as he revelled on the attention Sara Ellen and John Shaw lavished upon him. He'd eaten more sandwiches and drunk more cups of tea than had been healthy for him.

John's mother had burst into tears when she'd seen him on the doorstep and disappeared upstairs for a good ten minutes whilst he chatted with his dad. It unnerved John slightly; he'd expected surprise, even a few tears, but nothing had prepared him for that sort of reaction. He wondered if anything was wrong. They sat in the kitchen until nearly midnight talking about old times, the war and of course family members in Lancaster and beyond stretching as far as Canada.

Just before he left for Belle Vue Terrace, John's father suggested a day out at the pub the following day.

'It's what Sunday afternoons were made for,' he said, 'a few pints. Perhaps John Shaw might want to come along?'

It was settled. They'd go to The Royal Oak in Skerton for opening time then head back home for Sunday lunch in Ashton Drive.

'That's not like you, Dad. You were never a pub man before I went away.'

William shook his head. 'You're right son I wasn't. But then again I had more than enough sons and daughters to keep me busy.'

John's mother spoke. 'It's a big house John, it seems a little empty with everyone away. Your Dad doesn't like too much peace and quiet, the lack of activity drives him daft.'

William just sat and shook his head, didn't contradict his wife because he knew it was true.

'So our John, what do you say? You and the Yank?'

'He's from Canada, Dad, not a Yank, his name's Len. But yes... that sounds great.'

William Holmes knocked on the door of number one Belle Vue Terrace at exactly quarter to eleven the following day. John Shaw answered the door and took him into the kitchen and without being able to refuse, Sara Ellen had pushed a cup of strong tea into his hands

John came in a few minutes later, immaculately dressed in a two piece suit, shirt and tie with patent leather black shoes. William Holmes became immediately agitated. John noticed it and Mr and Mrs Shaw noticed it too. For a few minutes the atmosphere could have been cut with a knife, William's face was a picture of disappointment. *Just what was wrong with Dad,* thought John, *what have I done*? But then he seemed to mellow slightly, the moment had passed. Whatever it was, John needed to know. He took his chance as they walked out into the hallway and headed outside. John shouted up the stairs.

'C'mon Len, time to go.'

He heard Len mumble a reply from a far off room somewhere in the huge house. John Shaw apologised as he said he couldn't find his pipe and walked back through to the kitchen. It left John and his father alone on the front step. His father gazed up the street with no real purpose. John placed two hands on his shoulders and turned him around so that they were facing each other, barely a few inches apart.

'Do you want to tell me what's wrong, Dad?'

William Holmes tried to break the gaze, mumbled a few denials, said he didn't know what his son was talking about.

'Dad, I saw your face as I walked into the kitchen, what's wrong?'

'Nothing's wrong, now come on let's get to the Oak, the beer's getting warm.'

William Holmes turned to walk away but John held him tight. 'What is it, Dad? Why did you look so disappointed?'

William Holmes's face changed. He looked sorry, almost apologetic and the lines around his eyes and his mouth seemed to soften as he shook his head.

'Disappointed…? No John, I wasn't disappointed. You couldn't be further from the truth.'

John felt his father's defences crumble; the word he'd used had broken down the barriers. John stayed silent, his father had to explain. He was ready to explain.

'It's just…'

John dropped his hands to his side, raised his eyebrows.

'I just thought you'd be in uniform, that's all.'

John's jaw dropped. 'Dad, I've been in that bloody uniform for months, day in, day out. Why would I want to wear it when I'm on leave?'

Now it was William's turn to lay his hands on his son's shoulders. He smiled and the tears welled up in his eyes as he spoke.

'For me John… just for me. Because I'm a sad old man and a proud father. Lads from these parts don't join the Royal Air Force, fly Stirling Bombers. Lads round here join the army or work in the mills, nowt else. I was disappointed that you weren't in uniform that's all. I wanted to show you off to my mates like the silly old bugger that I am.'

John burst out laughing. 'You wanted to show me off?'

William nodded, a tear trickling down his cheek.

'That's all, son. I wanted them to see my boy the RAF man, my son in his uniform with his brevet that tells everyone he's an integral member of the air crew.'

William edged a little closer.

'I'm so proud of you John… so immensely proud you couldn't ever begin to measure it. You'll never realise how proud I am and I'm just a little upset that it's taken me this long to tell you.'

William took another step and embraced his son as the tears flowed. It was a defining moment. John's father had never expressed his emotions like this…never. And he was wrong. At that moment John knew exactly how proud his father was.

A few minutes later John Shaw appeared smoking his pipe and Len came out just behind him. William had just about managed to compose himself. The four men stood in the street as John Shaw leaned over to pull at the handle of the door.

'Are we ready then gentlemen?' he asked.

John spoke. 'Not quite Mr Shaw, I need to have a quick word with Jonesy here. He's not suitably attired for a Sunday afternoon in an English country pub.'

Len looked down at the suit he was wearing, then at his three drinking partners who appeared to have dressed in similar fashion. He looked a little embarrassed, as if he'd made an obvious error, but the harder he looked he just couldn't put his finger on it. John took him by the sleeve and turned him round to face the house.

'Come with me mate, it'll only take five minutes.'

John Shaw and William Holmes passed the time of day on

the front step. It was a crisp and cold frosty morning and they could see their breath.

'What's wrong with those two silly buggers, Bill? They looked fine to me.'

John Shaw shrugged his shoulders and gazed up to the front bedrooms.

'Don't know my friend but I hope they hurry up. I'm getting cold.'

Soon after, John and Len reappeared in the full uniform of the Royal Air Force. The four men got in the waiting cab that would take them to the Royal Oak in Skerton.

William Holmes was the proudest and happiest man in Lancashire, England and beyond. Words could not describe the pride that oozed through his body, so much so he positively tingled. As they'd walked into the bar of the Royal Oak, it was almost as if the place had fallen silent, not unlike when a stranger walks into the saloon in those western movies he had watched at the Roxy. He wouldn't have wanted it any other way, he wanted them to sit up and take notice, wanted them to say 'Who are those Brylcreem Boys with?'

And he told them... everyone who asked.

'That's my son John, and his friend from Canada,' he proudly boasted.

He'd tell his friends they weren't just ground crew, oh no, they flew in Stirling Bombers – but he couldn't tell them any more. Top secret, you understand.

William wouldn't allow the two RAF men to buy a single pint and more than one of his friends sent a drink over for 'the boys' who were helping to turn the tide against the Nazis. William stood at the end of the bar and looked on, he looked at his son as he chatted to his friend as they enjoyed more than their fair share of free beer. John was a man, a mature man. He'd waved off a young boy the day he commenced his training in Redcar and the RAF had turned him into a man. He recalled the moment when his wife had burst into tears and ran from the room. He'd questioned her about her tears later that evening. She'd said it was because that was the day she realised her little boy had gone and a man had taken his place.

William walked over and ordered another round of drinks. He told John he had another surprise for him – that his sister Mary, her husband Gilbert and the newly born twins were taking a little Sunday lunch at Ashton Drive.

John turned to Len.

'You'd better drink up, Jonesy – we've a big afternoon ahead of us. Knowing my Mam there'll be enough food to feed the 5,000.'

CHAPTER ELEVEN

John, Len and Patch returned to RAF Keevil on 3rd May. For the early part of May they flew more equipment over to France and then engaged in dozens of exercises towing Horsa Gliders. It was clear that the RAF were gearing up for something big and the rumours were rife. John lay on his bed in billet 78 talking to George Tickner as he stroked the dog, who had snuggled under the blankets, his head resting on the pillow. George Tickner's crew had been training with the Horsa Gliders too.

'I tell you Sherlock they aren't giving us all this training for nothing. Why would they have us bloody training when there's so much work to do? No one's flown anything over to France for at least a week; those poor resistance chaps will think we're ignoring them.'

It was all very frustrating and John couldn't help thinking there was some logic in George Tickner's theory. With the amount of equipment they'd dropped into France they had to be making some sort of a difference and apart from a little light anti-aircraft flak they'd encountered on one sortie, the skies over France were relatively quiet. He'd also been aware of the ground crew painting up the three big white stripes on the fuselage of every aircraft on the base. He asked the air crew what they were doing and why but no one claimed they knew. They were simply obeying orders they said. One aircraft mechanic however claimed it was fairly obvious.

'They're the invasion stripes,' he'd said. 'There will be so many bloody planes flying to France the Allied lads will need to be able to distinguish which is which.'

The aircraft mechanic was deadly serious and John had to admit it did all seem to make sense.

Dare he believe the rumours that France was about to be liberated by the Allies. Was the time right for an invasion of Northern Europe and were the Germans really on the back foot?

Adolf Hitler sat at a huge Austrian pine table surrounded by his generals as he studied a large map of France, Belgium and Holland. It was June 3rd 1944. During the early years of the war Hitler had been content to rely on the advice of his trusted generals and played no part in the decisive victory over Poland and the occupation of Holland, Belgium and Norway. However, thereafter, Hitler took an increasingly active part in the direction of the Third Reich's military operations. One of his big regrets in the battle of France was to rely on the advice of Field Commander Rundstedt, who advised Hitler to halt the Panzers outside Dunkirk in 1940.

The war had reached a critical point and German intelligence had warned of a massive imminent Allied invasion of France, the only question was, where? Brauchitsch, Halder,

Blomberg, Keitel and Hasso von Manteuffel, the general of Panzer Troops, all offered advice to Adolf Hitler who would ultimately take the decision on where to deploy the majority of his troops. The majority of the generals and Hitler had expected an invasion of Normandy and had committed most of their forces in the area. However German intelligence gathered and painted an altogether different picture.

Hasso von Manteuffel spoke. 'Herr Fuhrer, look at these images taken only yesterday from one of our reconnaissance planes.'

Hasso von Manteuffel spread a series of photographs on the desk in front of him and arranged them so that he could study them carefully.

'This one is taken at Folkestone and this one at Deal in Kent.'

The pictures needed no further explanation. The beaches on the south coast of England appeared to be saturated with tanks, trucks and other military hardware.

'And these pictures too, Herr Fuhrer, Dover and Ramsgate and literally thousands of boats and ships either already anchored up or on their way en masse.'

Hitler massaged at his temple with his forefinger and thumb as he drew a circle around the perimeter of Calais, placed a couple of crosses on the beaches either side. He looked up.

'So what are you telling me, General?'

Hasso von Manteuffel spoke with a renewed confidence now. His Fuhrer was listening to him… asking his advice.

'Herr Fuhrer, if the British and the Americans wanted to land in Normandy they would have assembled around Dorset and Hampshire, the docks and harbours in Portsmouth and Southampton are almost deserted.'

Brauchitsch stood up and pointed to another huge map pinned to the wall. Hasso von Manteuffel smiled; he knew he had the full support of everyone seated around the table but it was still nice for someone else to back up his suggestions.

'The British bombers have bombed the Pas-de-Calais beach area and the railway sidings surrounding the town and even the road signs around Calais have been changed to English. We have recovered almost fifty Horsa Gliders and boxes and containers all dropped within a fifty mile radius of Calais, Dunkirk and Boulogne.'

Brauchitsch frowned, almost apologised.

'I'm afraid they were all empty Herr Fuhrer. Whatever troops and supplies the British have dropped have long since gone. We believe upwards of a thousand British paratroopers are hiding in the woods and forest areas surrounding Calais.'

Adolf Hitler trained his eyes on the map laid out in front of him. He held a pencil between both thumbs so tightly it snapped in two. Hasso von Manteuffel delivered his pièce de résistance that would convince Hitler to once again rely on intelligence and of course the expertise and intuition of his generals.

'We have evidence of troop movements heading towards south eastern England. Americans, Canadians, New Zealanders and Australians. Pas-de-Calais is the point on the French coast closest to England. It makes sense that they will start the invasion from there. We have agents who have even managed to steal the plans.'

Hasso von Manteuffel looked briefly at Brauchitsch and the rest of the generals before delivering his final statement to his Fuhrer.

'We are led to believe that the invasion will begin on the evening of 5th June.'

On the south coast of England at RAF Keevil at almost exactly the same time as Hitler spoke with his generals, 196 Squadron were being briefed by Wing Commander Baker. 23 crews sat in the converted gymnasium viewing almost identical photographs to those that were being studied by Hitler and his generals.

The Wing Commander held up each photograph with two hands above his head and paced up and down an aisle between the aircrews giving the men time to digest each photograph.

'Thousands of tanks, gentlemen; tanks and trucks, jeeps and motorcycles ready and waiting to make the short journey over the English Channel to Calais, Dunkirk and Boulogne.'

John couldn't help feeling that Wing Commander Baker was almost about to break out into a smile at any moment. Here he was addressing his crews about the biggest and possibly the most dangerous military invasion in history and he was almost laughing. He wasn't imagining it, the tell-tale lines at the side of his mouth and his eyes were beginning to form into a smile. He was sure of it.

Wing Commander Baker continued. 'Your colleagues from 167 Squadron in West Malling have been mighty busy over the last twenty four hours taking Horsas over the channel and letting them loose a few miles from the coast. We're fairly sure the vast majority have made it onto French soil. The Germans must be in no doubt that an invasion is almost imminent.'

And then he let it out. Wing Commander Baker broke out into a huge smile and started to laugh uncontrollably and twenty three crews of 196 Squadron, pilots, navigators, gunners, flight engineers and bomb aimers wondered if he had lost his mind.

Blomberg and Keitel had moved around to the other side of the desk and stood either side of Hitler pointing out the positions of every Motorized infantry and Panzer Division in France, Belgium and Holland. Each division was marked with a red counter.

'We have fifteen divisions already in the area Fuhrer but I recommend we deploy more,' suggested Keitel. 'We have ten Divisions in and around Normandy and the 21st, 22nd, 23rd and 24th Panzer Division just north of Paris.'

Blomberg took over, pointing at central France with half of the pencil that Hitler had broken.

'We have at least a dozen light infantry divisions...'

Hitler looked up and glared at Blomberg. His stare stopped him in his tracks.

'Don't guess, Herr Blomberg, the time for guessing is not now. I want to know exactly how many light infantry divisions we have there and how quickly they can get to Calais.'

Hitler had unnerved Blomberg. Beads of perspiration had appeared on his brow as he quickly calculated his numbers and spoke.

'Fourteen, Fuhrer. Fourteen light infantry divisions in and around Central France, they can be in the area within twenty four hours.'

Adolf Hitler picked up the half pencil and began to take notes, scribbling down the number and names of each division. The generals remained passive and stood in stony silence for at least five minutes. At last Hitler gave his instructions.

'I want these divisions to head immediately for Calais and Boulogne, these divisions to Dunkirk to provide support for our men who are already there.' He tore off a small piece of paper.

'21st, 22nd, 23rd and 24th Panzer Division are to head for Arras and wait for further instructions.' Hitler traced his finger further down the map.

'And this division here, which division is this?'

His finger lingered over the Limoges region of Western France. Blomberg looked down and checked on a notepad he held in his hand.

'That, Fuhrer, is the 2nd SS Panzer Division stationed at a place called Oradour-sur-Glane.'

Hitler nodded... tapped his finger on the map.

'Then mobilise them, send them to Arras with immediate effect.'

Some of the air crew were also laughing now but not sure why. Wing Commander Baker's laugh was of the infectious type but almost as suddenly as he'd started he'd stopped again. He looked around the room.

'Any questions, gentlemen?' he grinned.

John Holmes raised his hand; he was smiling too but also a little confused.

'Sir...' He hesitated, unsure of whether to ask the question.

He swallowed hard and spoke.

'I'm just not sure what's so funny, Sir?'

Wing Commander Baker clapped his hands together and shrieked. 'Ha! At last someone brave enough to ask the question.'

The Wing Commander walked back to the desk and picked up one of the larger images. It showed a huge concentration of tanks pointing towards the sea on the long flat beach at Deal in Kent.

'Do you recall this photograph, gentlemen? That's what I'm laughing at; I'm laughing because these tanks don't exist.'

He's lost his head thought John, *I can see them with my own eyes... they do exist, they're there in black and white.*

Wing Commander Baker held the picture to his chest and pointed to a group of tanks on the photograph.

'These tanks here are made of rubber.' He moved his finger. 'And these trucks and jeeps are made from balsa wood. They are what are commonly known as decoys.'

There was a collective gasp from the assembled men, a few murmurs, one or two even started clapping before the Wing Commander lifted his hand and signalled for silence once more.

'But from the air or from a Jerry U-boat out in the English Channel they pass for the real thing.' He placed the photograph on the desk and began to pace the front of the room. 'We have these dummies in place right across south eastern England. We've sent phoney wireless signals to Calais that have been intercepted by the Germans, even sent men into the town to change the road signs and blasted the rail lines to pieces.'

George Tickner raised his hand to ask a question.

'Yes, Flying Officer.'

'Sir, you mentioned earlier on that 167 Squadron had been busy dropping panniers and containers, I assume the Horsas were full of men too.'

The Wing Commander shook his head.

'Empty Sergeant. Empty boxes and empty planes dropped in an area where we know the Germans will stumble across them. And when Jerry do find them they'll put two and two together and make five and automatically assume that the area is awash with Allied troops, weapons and mortars.'

John Holmes was stunned. He'd covered his open mouth with his fist as the magnitude of the hoax gradually sank in.

Quicksilver, as it was named, was the brainchild of Colonel David Strangeways, Montgomery's deception officer, and carried out under his supervision. The operation was intended to show military units and hardware massing in south-eastern England. He'd also put together false reports which he allowed to fall into a German double agent's hands. The alleged stolen documents described the closely guarded invasion plan of Calais, Boulogne and Dunkirk but were carefully constructed so as not to arouse suspicion. In actual fact the real tanks and military hardware were already in place further along the coast, carefully concealed in the forests of Sussex, Dorset and Hampshire together with over 150,000 troops. A flotilla of nearly 5,000 boats, ships and small craft had also been instructed to head for various locations on the south coast.

Mark Azouz raised his hand in the air and asked Wing Commander Baker if there was going to be an invasion of France and if so where and when. The Wing Commander simply gathered his paperwork together and made an elegant but hasty exit towards the doors at the rear of the gym. As he walked past the puzzled and astonished men he was prompted again, this time by Lofty Matthews.

'You'll know soon enough chaps,' he said. 'You'll know soon enough.'

On June 4th in Oradour-sur-Glane, Henri-Pierre Raynaud and Pierre-Henri Poutaraud had made their way under the cover of darkness to the house of their good friend, Louis-Leonard Chapelot. A meeting had been hastily arranged early that afternoon.

'What is it that is so urgent?' asked Henri-Pierre as he walked into the small kitchen of Monsieur Chapelot's house.

'Be patient Henri-Pierre, let us take a coffee, perhaps something a little stronger. We have much work to do.'

Louis-Leonard Chapelot spoke about the recent developments and the reports from the other side of the channel that had filtered through to the key personnel in the French Resistance. He explained to his two grinning colleagues that the invasion of France by the Allies was only a few days away. He'd also had his sleepers report to him that the 2nd SS Panzer Division based in the village appeared to be getting ready to move out.

'They are preparing to head north my friends, they are on their way to the beaches of the north.'

'And good riddance I say,' said Pierre, 'fuck the lot of them. I hope they get cut to ribbons with our friends' bullets and shells.'

Chapelot wagged his finger.

'No, no, no my friend, you do not understand, we must keep them here, pin them down. The less Panzer Divisions that make it to the beaches of northern France the better.'

'So we keep them here, we keep that scum in our village?'

'Yes.'

'For how long?'

'For as long as it takes for our Allies to establish a foothold. The Germans are already in disarray, they are fighting on too many fronts. Can you not feel their anger as you walk past them in the village?'

Pierre-Henri Poutaraud picked up a glass of the red wine that his host had poured out for the three of them. He took a drink and spoke.

'Yes I feel it. I feel it every time I encounter them and I feel we are fighting a desperate enemy. But if the reports filtering through are correct it will not be too long before our country is free once more.'

'That may be the case but we must continue to inflict more damage.'

Henri-Pierre Chapelot stood up and walked from the room. A little later he returned with a roughly sketched map of the area. He laid it flat on the kitchen table.

'Gentlemen if you look at this map you will see where we are and also the road to Limoges. The blue crosses marked on the map indicate the six German Battalions stationed within a hundred mile radius.' He let out a sigh.

'But it is the red cross marked approximately seventeen kilometres from Limoges just off the main road we must concentrate on.' He looked up from the map. 'We must take it out.'

The two men waited patiently for more details.

'It's a German fuel dump,' Chapelot continued, 'and if our information is correct then this fuel dump services not only the 2nd SS Panzer Division but also most of the other battalions too.'

Chapelot drained the last of his wine and proceeded to replenish the three glasses.

'And after we have set fire to every litre of fuel in that dump we need to disable the bridges here,' he pointed to the map, 'and here. If we succeed there'll be no way that the 2nd SS Panzer Division will ever make it anywhere near our northern beaches.'

Henri-Pierre Chapelot's men were pleasantly surprised during the course of the hours they had studied the movements of the half dozen German sentries who patrolled the perimeter fence of the fuel dump north of Limoges. For once the Germans appeared lackadaisical and even casual in the application of their duties. They relied on the rather remote location of the farm they had taken over in 1941. It had never once been attacked and they assumed it simply hadn't been discovered. It lay at the end of a single track road facing east which was always patrolled by two guards. Chapelot's men went in from the West side across several acres of vineyards. The vines were well on their way to producing that year's crop, perfect cover to get within a few metres of the fence. The fencing was neither alarmed nor electrified; two men opened up a gap with hand held bolt clippers and were through within a few minutes. After they'd gone, Chapelot and another man closed up the gap with wire and slipped back in between the vines.

The men worked quickly and located the main supply of fuel, ten huge tanks with taps fitted and surrounded by large drums. Two metres away lay more manageable containers. The depot seemed to be in darkness, most of the guards fast asleep inside the converted farmhouse. They waited until two of the guards had drifted aimlessly by on the other side of the fence then opened up all the taps. The fuel spilled noisily onto the dusty ground. They then opened up two of the smaller containers, held them in their arms and began walking backwards to the damaged fence laying a trail of petrol in their wake.

As they approached the fence they stopped, whistled to simulate the hoot of an owl. A few seconds later the signal was returned and they knew it was safe to move. They breached the fence once again and continued to pour the line of fuel deep into the vineyard.

The night was silent and calm and Chapelot peered over the top of the vines.

'All clear,' he said to the young man ready to strike the match. 'Go.'

The young man grinned as he lit the match and threw it to the floor. They watched on in amazement as the fuel took hold and all of a sudden a line of fire burst through the vineyard and surged towards the fence. Chapelot signalled.

'Come, let's go, all hell will break loose in two seconds flat.'

Chapelot had miscalculated slightly. It took about thirty

seconds before the first tank exploded. By this time the small group of men were already out of the first vineyard and racing towards the forest beyond. One by one the huge tanks exploded; the intense heat blew up the drums and the containers too and balls of burning oil and fuel fell onto the barracks that housed the so called protectors of the depot. Within the hour there wasn't a single drop of fuel anywhere within the compound.

At 02.30 Pierre-Henri Poutaraud's men disabled the bridge on the outskirts of Oradour-sur-Glane and forty minutes later a team led by Henri-Pierre Raynaud blew up the bridge at Saint-Junien. The 2nd Waffen SS Panzer Division was effectively stranded.

CHAPTER TWELVE

George Tickner walked with John across the airfield towards the Sergeants' Mess. Patch walked dutifully behind, never more than a few yards from the heels of his new master. John pointed ahead.

'Isn't that Lofty Matthews, George?'

'I do believe it is. Give him a shout, he must be on his way to breakfast too.'

The men shouted after him and Lofty turned around to acknowledge them. He waited until they caught up.

'Morning Lofty.'

'Morning chaps, not a bad morning for England but what bloody time of day is this to have breakfast?'

The RAF had moved breakfast on 5th June 1944. It was now more of a brunch, 11am, with plenty of fried food and more coffee pots than tea urns. It meant only one thing.

'Night exercises, I bloody hate them,' said Lofty Matthews. 'It buggers up the whole body clock, don't know when to eat, when to sleep or even what time to shit.'

The other two men laughed.

'It's true, it buggers your whole system up for days. It's not natural to be nocturnal.'

The sight that greeted the three friends in the mess hall rendered them speechless at least for a few seconds.

A RAF corporal stood at the front of the big dining hall trying to monitor the mass of bodies and retain some sort of order. He looked at the three men as they walked in.

'It'll be another ten minutes, chaps, before I can get you a seat, is that okay?'

John nodded. Lofty let out a gasp. The large dining facility was never very full even on a busy day at the peak of the breakfast rush, 100, perhaps 120 dining at any one time. Today the dining room was crowded with men, packed to the gunnels.

'Jesus fucking Christ when did this lot arrive?'

The corporal grinned. 'Through the night when you lot were fast asleep.'

'What's going on?' asked Tickner. 'I haven't seen this many paratroopers in my life.'

The corporal checked his watch.

'You've a briefing at noon, we should have you out of here by then… just. What crew are you chaps with?' The corporal picked up a clipboard and studied the list of the crews.

'Vanrenen, Tickner, Prowd.' The men answered individually in turn.

The corporal scanned the sheets with a pencil as he located each pilot.

'You crews are altogether, 23 of you in the north gym. 12 noon, don't be late.'

John Holmes didn't feel too much like a hearty breakfast; the sheer scale of the operation became apparent as paratroopers poured through the double doors of the dining room as they ate. Patch sat under the table, more than happy with the extra food coming his way. When they finished and walked outside at least another 500 stood patiently in a queue and thousands of them walked around aimlessly with no apparent purpose. Sure enough some of them confirmed they'd been brought in during the cover of darkness, another described army and police road blocks outside the base and the town of Trowbridge had been effectively sealed off.

Twenty three crews sat in the same converted gym that they'd sat in two days prior and the briefing commenced. Again, it was the same Wing Commander who'd relayed information about rubber tanks and wooden trucks two days before. This time there were no smiles, no humour. His face was stern; he could not have been more serious as he described the scale of the operation and the role 196 Squadron would play. The Wing Commander spoke.

'Operation Overlord is one that will go down in history.' He leaned forward and placed his hands on the desk. 'Gentlemen… I am honoured that 196 Squadron will play a major role. In fact if you chaps fuck up then we're done for.'

'No pressure then,' called out one man from the back which brought a peal of laughter from the assembled men.

'Gentlemen… prepare yourself for the longest day of your lives. We commence the Allied invasion of France with the first part of Operation Overlord. We've about 2,500 paratroopers of the British Army stationed on or around the vicinity of this airfield and our job is to drop them safely inside enemy territory about five miles from the French coastline.'

Wing Commander Baker reached up with a hooked stick and placed the hook in a brass ring suspended from the ceiling. He pulled down and a large map unfurled. He let the men of 196 Squadron take it in for a moment.

John studied the imagery, they were flying into Normandy. He looked at the places marked on the map, he saw places called Cherbourg and Caen and something marked in heavy black pencil called Sword Beach. At the bottom of the map marked in red it said *Operation Tonga*.

Wing Commander Baker braced himself and prepared for the briefing speech of his life.

'Men… The name of the airborne part of the operation is called Operation Tonga. We will be landing troops in Normandy. Each crew will be flying two or even three night time missions and we will commence our first flights at around midnight. It is imperative that we get our troops on the ground before first light.'

John Holmes couldn't quite believe what he was hearing. *Two or three ops in a row, Jesus*, he thought, *this is big.*

'We will be landing men on the eastern flank of the invasion area, near to the city of Caen. The paratroopers' prime objective is to secure this bridge.' He pointed to the centre of the map and a thin grey line over the Caen Canal.

'The Germans think we are landing in and around Calais but they will quickly discover they've been duped. But you can rest assured that the Hun will try and hot foot it over to Normandy just as soon as they can. The men that we are dropping will stop them but it's important that we have as many of them as possible on the ground so they can dig in and secure bridges of strategic importance, bridges like the Caen canal and here… on the Orne River.'

Wing Commander Baker asked if there were any questions and Lofty raised his hand.

'How many paratroopers are we dropping, Sir?'

Wing Commander Baker raised an eyebrow but nevertheless decided to answer the question. It wasn't the time to keep the men in the dark. They needed to know the scale of the operation and they needed to be aware of exactly how important their task was.

'I've already said we will be responsible for 2,500 men.' Baker took a deep breath. 'Another ten squadrons will be taking part in Operation Tonga… we will be dropping around 24,000 men.'

John nearly fell from his seat. Before he could take in the numbers Baker continued.

'Our paratroopers will also be responsible for assaulting and destroying the Merville Gun Battery, an artillery battery that Allied intelligence believe houses a number of heavy artillery pieces, the only one in the area if the intelligence reports are right. They have the range to bombard Sword Beach and inflict heavy casualties on our troops and of course they will be doing their best to shoot you poor bastards out of the sky. I want you men to think Sword Beach for 24 hours; we must buy time for the thousands of men who'll be stepping onto Sword Beach at first light. We must ensure that the seaborne troops cannot be attacked during those critical first few hours when they are at their most vulnerable.'

Wing Commander Baker smiled.

'Oh…I nearly forgot. Once you've dropped the paratroopers during the hour of darkness your work will continue.'

He looked at his watch.

'196 Squadron will be dropping supplies on Sword Beach throughout the day from six in the morning until at least midnight again.'

Wing Commander Baker ran through the feeding arrangements for the day and told them there would be a never ending supply of coffee on the ground and flasks to take up in the air.

'It will be a long day chaps…the longest day ever, of that I'm sure. Nevertheless we'll get there if we all pull together. I suggest you relax for a few hours, take a long walk and perhaps a nap later this afternoon.'

Baker reached across the desk for his cap and placed it firmly on his head.

'That will be all gentlemen. The very best of British to you all.'

A walk sounded like a good idea to John Holmes.

'Walkies, Patch?'

The little dog started wagging his tail at the sound of the familiar word. John reached down and patted his head. He looked over to his assembled crew.

'Anyone fancy a wander round the airfield? We've a fair amount of time to kill.'

Taffy Stimson called to him from a few rows back.

'I'll have a nice little stroll with you Sherlock; my skipper Chuck will have a walk too.'

They were joined by Lofty and Flight Lieutenant Fred Gribble and his navigator, Len Jones and Reg Tammas and other people who John had met in and around the briefing room and the mess hall. It seemed that the idea of an afternoon stroll appealed to everyone. Patch had never been happier; he had at least a dozen masters to walk him round the base.

John walked up front with Chuck Hoystead as Patch led the way. Chuck was another Australian pilot that John got on particularly well with. They were all good down to earth men, they were all like brothers to him and he wondered how many would make it back from their next mission, the Allied Invasion of France. And what about the next mission, and the next mission after that? What about at the end of the war, how many would make it through to the end?

'I had a wee dog like that back home Sherlock, a right little bastard he was,' said Fred.

John laughed as he bent down to give Patch a stroke. 'Can't say that about this fella Sir, he's a little gem and he waits for our plane to come back every time we take off.'

'So I hear mate, so I hear, the whole bloody camp knows about this little man.'

The men walked the full perimeter of the airfield, it took almost two hours. Afterwards they went into the mess hall where a continuous supply of pies, sandwiches and cakes had been laid on the whole day. Soon after five o'clock John returned to his billet where he tried to catch forty winks.

It was no good, too many thoughts were running around his mind.

CHAPTER THIRTEEN

The grass adjacent to runway number two was in darkness. Until Vanrenen eased Stirling LK510 alongside the paratroopers no one would have imagined that the darkened airbase was awash with troops and equipment. The paratroopers were well drilled and they filed into the aircraft with their personal kit one by one in a perfectly executed exercise that took no more than a minute. Already in the hold of the Stirling was a motorcycle and nine containers of equipment.

The twenty three aircraft took off one after the other at forty second intervals. They were to fly in formation, in groups of six, the last group up numbering only five. It was no more than ten minutes before each of the Stirlings adopted their correct positions. Reg came over the radio.

'Fifteen minutes until the drop zone, Skipper. Flying in formation, all aircraft present and correct.'

John peered out into the night sky. He could just about make out the shape of the aircraft flying alongside him. Stirling LK510 was on the extreme left of the group, the other planes flown by Mark Azouz, George Tickner, Fred Gribble, Chuck Hoystead and Keith Proud close by. It seemed noisier than the normal sorties they flew. It was noisier; it was a still night and twenty four engines made a lot of noise. John prayed to a God he didn't believe in that they'd all be back very soon safe and sound, enjoying a pint of best English bitter in Trowbridge. Vanrenen's voice broke into his thoughts.

'Keep it together chaps. Flight Engineers and Gunners keep your eyes peeled.'

There was a slight pause then Vanrenen announced they were beginning their descent to drop zone N. John studied the altitude needle as it began to fall. They'd be dropping the troops and equipment at exactly 1,500 feet.

There was barely a sound from the packed fuselage where twenty men and equipment sat waiting for the signal to go, ready to drop into enemy territory. *Just what was going through their minds*, wondered John.

A sergeant stood up and began to address the men. His face was painted black and brown, striped like a tiger. A face shines in the dark; no use giving Jerry a target. The sergeant spoke well as his men listened. He told them they were heroes, the saviour of the French people and he smiled as he told them they would be the first troops to liberate a French village since the German occupation. He mentioned the village name – Ranville. John recalled seeing it highlighted on the map in the briefing room earlier that day.

The altitude needle read 2,000 feet. John signalled to the sergeant that they needed to get ready and the sergeant nodded and inched back down the plane. The paratroopers who had sat so still and so quiet began to stir and gradually their voices increased as they wished each other well and began to gather their kit.

'1750' came across the radio for all to hear.

'16'

The bomb doors opened and the paratroopers lined up. A blast of cold air whistled through the plane. There was no hesitation, no noise; it was a well-oiled, disciplined machine. The nine large panniers and the motorcycle were heaved out into the black void and the paratroopers leapt out into the unknown. John looked down and could barely make out the chutes opening one by one. Mark Azouz and George Tickner's Stirlings had dropped their men too. Fred announced he was clear and seconds later Chuck and Keith followed suit.

'Head for home chaps,' Vanrenen announced and John Holmes breathed a sigh of relief that the first part of the operation was over. As the Stirling aircraft banked to starboard the anti-aircraft fire began.

'Holy fucking shit that was a bit close!' screamed Len on the rear gun as the whole aircraft seemed to shudder.

He was more exposed than most and had a bird's eye view of the shells exploding all around as they lit up the sky. John could see most of the Stirlings around him now as the shells illuminated the area. The German battery firing from down below became more and more accurate and John sensed the shells getting nearer.

'We need to get out of here, Skip,' he called into the radio before realising the stupidity of the statement. He wanted to bite his tongue, somehow take it back but it was too late.

Vanrenen latched onto the comment sarcastically. 'You don't say, Flight Engineer, I was going to hang around a bit, see what Normandy is like in daylight, might nip over for next summer's vacation.'

The rest of the crew were laughing and it was a much needed light hearted moment as more and more shells exploded around them.

'We're hit… we're hit, Jesus fucking Christ we're hit, engine on fire.'

For a split second John wasn't sure where the voice had come from until he looked out the port side of his aircraft. The flames were coming from a Stirling fifty yards below them, the whole starboard wing was on fire and a black plume of smoke trailed behind it.

'Bail out, bail out!' the pilot screamed into the radio and it was at that point John recognised the voice. His heart almost skipped a beat as he felt a sour bile rise from his stomach and sting the back of his throat.

'Who is it?' screamed Vanrenen. 'How bad is it? I can't see from up here.'

Reg turned to John. 'It's those bastards from the Merville Battery; let's hope our Paras sort them out sooner rather than later, Sherlock. We've God knows how many trips to go, we can't be flying through this shit every time.'

The Stirling was losing altitude, the flames rapidly spreading along the fuselage. John wanted to say it was minor damage, they'd make it back but as the nose of the aircraft dipped and it went into a dive he feared the worst. It was an awful sound as the Queen of the Skies let out a stricken wail. Loud at first but then as it lost height the noise receded. John wanted to put his fingers in his ears to block it out, he wanted to close his eyes but couldn't tear his gaze away from the aircraft plummeting towards the earth, hoping that somehow it would recover, that the flames would recede and it would level up again.

John's mouth was dry as he tried hard to swallow. He had a huge lump in his throat as he recalled the conversation earlier that day as the group of friends walked around the airbase. He relived the words as if he was watching a film at the local picture house. *I had a wee dog like that back home Sherlock.*

'It's Gribble Sir… Fred Gribble. Flight Lieutenant Fred Gribble.'

'You're sure, Flight Engineer?'

'I'm sure, Sir.'

'C'mon Fred, come on-n-n,' he mumbled to himself. 'C'mon-n-n Fred, do something.'

He was oblivious to the 88mm shells exploding around his own aircraft as Vanrenen battled to steady the plane, oblivious of the flames shooting out from the guns on the ground as they found their range. He spotted two chutes opening just above the burning flames.

'C'mon Fred, c'mon'.

He was on his feet now trying hard to keep the plane in view, the flames were still visible and he anticipated the explosion any second. His heart pounded inside the wall of his chest.

The plane was no more than three hundred feet from the ground when John's very existence was plunged into darkness. The explosion was immense as a huge ball of flames erupted below them. He saw no more chutes. Flight Lieutenant Fred Gribble and his crew had gone. He remembered the faces of the crew, the bomb aimer, the gunner and of course the flight engineer.

'We're hit Skipper, we're hit.'

The familiar voice brought John back from his thoughts. It was Doug Handley.

'Starboard first engine on fire, Sir!' he cried out.

Another German shell had torn into Stirling LK510.

The ground crew were trying to calm the dog down.

'Behave little fella or we'll put you outside.'

Patch sat at the door of the mess hall while the ground crew took advantage of the late night bacon sandwiches the RAF had laid on.

'They won't be back for at least half an hour; you'll get to see Sherlock then.'

The little dog howled at the door, turning in little tight circles, listening carefully then howling again.

'He's like a little fucking werewolf. What's wrong with him?'

'He's missing Sherlock that's what's wrong; he can't bear to be without him.'

'It's more than that mate. Something's wrong, something's happened to Sherlock.'

Patch was now scratching at the door, barking loudly.

'He wants to be out. Let him out.'

The flight mechanic walked towards the door, opened it and the dog ran out yelping as it disappeared into the darkness of the night.

John Holmes had hardly registered the impact as the shell had torn through the wing leaving a gaping hole. His thoughts were for Fred Gribble and his crew. He was almost in a daze.

'Flight Engineer, feather it! Feather the starboard engine Flight Engineer!'

It was Vanrenen.

'Feather it, Flight Engineer, feather it!'

The urgency in Vanrenen's voice snapped him out of his almost hypnotic state and he went into action closing down the lines of fuel to the starboard engine. He watched, almost willing the flames to die out, as Vanrenen changed direction and pushed the plane into a steep dive so that the flames licked up into the night sky and not along the fuselage of the aircraft.

The whole wing seemed to be ablaze but gradually the flames died away and Vanrenen levelled the plane out. The wing was a smouldering blackened mess but miraculously it remained intact. Vanrenen brought the Stirling back up to 2,000 feet. John couldn't take his eyes off the wing, convinced the flames would burst into life again, or worse the fragile wing would break off and disappear into the blackness.

Vanrenen headed higher and turned for home. The Stirling almost groaned against the effort it took for the three engines to lift the huge plane higher into the sky.

'Air speed dangerously low, Skipper,' John said into the radio and yet he somehow knew that Vanrenen was well aware just how near the Stirling was to stalling in mid-air.

'I'm taking it up as high as it will let me Flight Engineer, we'll need a little more height to ride out these shells.'

John looked out below. The shells were few and far between and those that were fired exploded harmlessly, five hundred feet beneath them.

'Anyone else hit?' asked Vanrenen, 'or is it just Gribble?'

John asked the other crews to report in. It was an agonising wait but one by one Azouz, Tickner, Hoystead and Keith Prowd's crews radioed in confirming their positions. Only Chuck Hoystead's plane had suffered a little light damage. All of them were safely over the channel, an hour and twenty minutes from RAF Keevil.

They'd been flying over the channel for well over an hour. John tapped at the dial with his finger. It wasn't what a Flight Engineer wanted to see. John's instruments were showing that the other starboard engine was overheating. He reported the matter to Vanrenen who ordered him to close it down.

'Probably sprung an oil leak, Sir,' John said as he closed off the fuel supply quickly.

As always, Vanrenen's voice seemed unruffled as his dulcet tones reassured everyone in the plane.

'Don't worry chaps, we'll make it no problem, the Queen can fly on one engine at a push so the fact we have two is a bonus.'

John wasn't so sure and was acutely aware that the aircraft was losing altitude. He wondered what other damage had been done by the shells that had been exploding nonstop all around them. What if the hydraulics had been damaged and the undercarriage failed? He would soon find out.

A little while later Reg announced they were approaching the English coast.

'Seventeen or eighteen minutes till we land boys, we'll make it don't you worry.'

The other aircraft had all landed safely and both the air and ground crews were inspecting the Stirlings for any sign of damage. Patch sniffed around their feet on the lookout for familiar smells. Mark noticed him and wandered over. He picked him up and ruffled the hair on his head.

'Don't worry little man, Sherlock's okay, he's just took a hit from one of those Jerry shells. He's hurt but he's limping home, he shouldn't be too long.'

Mark Azouz tried to convince himself but he hoped that that was all that was wrong with the plane. He couldn't prevent the stark image of the burning wing from entering his head.

The little dog cocked his head back and forth as his ears pricked up and he hung on to every word.

'Jesus little fella, I swear you understand every word I say.'

Patch struggled to get down as he wriggled loose and Azouz placed him gently on the tarmac. His nose pointed up in the air again and his tail started to wag back and forth. Azouz took off his flying helmet and scratched his head.

'Hey lads,' he shouted, 'I don't believe it – he hears Vanrenen's plane again!'

One or two of the men stopped what they were doing and listened. They listened for about thirty seconds.

One of the men spoke. 'Impossible. If that dog had heard something we'd be seeing them by now.'

Azouz looked down. *Do dogs smile?* he thought to himself, because as he concentrated on the face of the Jack Russell he would swear that a big beaming smile had crept across its face.

For once the night wasn't still and other Stirlings were firing up their engines ready for sortie number two.

'C'mon Vanrenen... where are you?' Azouz whispered to himself.

'There's one I think,' said George Tickner. 'Over there, look...'

'I see it too,' said Azouz. 'Yes, it's definitely a plane.'

'Is it Vanrenen?'

The men watched as the shape of the Stirling came clearly into range.

'She doesn't sound too clever.'

One of the flight mechanics spoke. 'She's flying on two engines.'

'Shit!'

'Don't worry lads, she can fly on two no problem,' the flight mechanic said anxiously. 'I just wish her landing gear had dropped that's all. These girls don't like it too much when they land on their bellies.'

The hydraulics hadn't engaged the front landing gear and they were less than 200 feet from the ground. John Holmes didn't understand; the instrument panel indicated no hydraulic problems.

'Give it another go Skipper, there's no reason why it shouldn't be working.'

Reg sat alongside his Flight Engineer.

'Probably a bit of tiny shrapnel somewhere fucking everything up.'

Just as John was about to answer there was a loud grinding noise beneath them. They looked at each other and grinned as the hydraulics kicked in and the huge wheels swung out from the underside of the plane.

'Engaged Skipper. Wheels in place.'

Reg slapped him on the back.

'Go, Sherlock go, that's my boy. We've made it. I confess I'd almost given up.'

John Holmes grinned. 'Yeah… only another five or six to go. I hope those Paras have sorted those fucking Jerry guns out by the time we get over there again.'

The combination of bad weather and poor visibility meant that many of the airborne troops had been dropped inaccurately throughout the divisional operational area. The casualties had been high, many picked off by German rifles before they had even hit the ground. The battalion assigned to the task of destroying the Merville Artillery Battery had been heavily depleted and was only able to gather up a fraction of its strength before it went into action. The German troops had dug in well and were well prepared as the Allied Battalion threw everything they had at the enemy. Casualties were high on both sides but after a battle lasting several hours the Allied troops were successful and the guns inside the battery were disabled. The continuous fighting in and around the Merville Battery also meant a reprieve for the RAF, the Stirlings and their crews as the troops of the German artillery division diverted their attention from the air to the land. More airborne troops had poured into the surrounding villages and a bridgehead had been formed by the division as it successfully repelled a number of German counter-attacks. The enemy were led by the Wehrmacht formations stationed in the area around Caen and the River Orne. The actions of the Allied division severely limited the ability of the German defenders to repel the RAF planes as they flew into France in waves. The troops who had flown with Vanrenen's crew were part of the force that would liberate the first French village of Ranville.

CHAPTER FOURTEEN

Holmes, Vanrenen and the rest of the crew stared up at the underside of the damaged wing. Half a dozen members of the ground crew had swarmed over the plane like bees. One of them shouted down.

'It's fucked, chaps, you won't be playing games with this little lady for a few weeks.'

A Wing Commander had mysteriously appeared and stood next to Vanrenen.

'Don't worry; we have another one for you. Grab yourselves a cup of tea and a bite to eat and you can be on your way again.'

The mess hall was full of air crew. The talk was all about Fred Gribble and his men, the only plane from 23 to have been lost.

John Holmes sat in silence, acutely aware that it could so easily have been their plane. They were lucky to be alive and Tammas and even Vanrenen had praised him on his quick and efficient actions when he'd feathered the engine and effectively saved the plane. He shrugged it off.

'Any other casualties?' he asked.

Chuck Hoystead spoke. 'Unfortunately mate... Wing Commander Baker's plane was badly hit and the Navigator and Bomb Aimer bailed out.'

'Who were they?'

'Fairhill and Evans, last seen floating towards the German lines. Incredibly, though, Baker managed to get the plane back. A shell hit the fuselage right where Fairhill sat. He was badly hurt but managed to get out through the hole in the plane, convinced she was going down. Evans followed him out and Baker was just about to give the command for everyone to get out when he asked the Flight Engineer to check his panel. The Flight Engineer was Harry Morgan, said that two of the engines were fine and Baker decided to try and make it back to Blighty.'

Chuck Hoystead took another mouthful of tea and John Holmes raised his eyebrows as if to say 'come on, finish the story'.

Right on cue Chuck Hoystead spoke. 'They crash landed at Ford. The Stirling broke in two on impact but they all survived. Lacerations and a few broken bones but otherwise they're okay.'

'But Fairhill and Evans are missing.' He stroked Patch who sat on his knee fast asleep.

'Missing in action Sherlock, I'm afraid. The new Winco has stood the whole crew down, they won't be going anywhere for a while.'

As if by magic the Wing Commander he was referring to appeared at the table. He spoke to Vanrenen.

'LJ 949 is ready and waiting Vanrenen, the troops and supplies are already on board, ready when you are.'

He told them to finish their tea and report to the new plane.

He spoke to Reg. 'Same co-ordinates navigator, better luck this time.'

Within fifteen minutes they were in the air and heading for France once again, but this time flying in a formation of only five. John wondered how the Allied airborne troops were doing and if they'd managed to have any effect on the Merville Battery on the ground. He couldn't help but play with the figures. They'd lost one of their formation on one sortie with at least another two or three to complete. The odds weren't stacked in their favour. John gazed out into the night skies. He pointed above them as he spoke to his navigator.

'Look Reg, there's a couple of mosquitoes.'

'On the lookout for Hun fighters, no doubt. They'll know what's happening by now. They'll be on their way from every air base in France.'

John was well aware of the fact. Even though the Paras would do their level best to take out the Merville Battery, the Luftwaffe would now be mobilised and on their way.

Towards the east around Calais and Boulogne the 'dummy invasion' was also well underway. Operation Glimmer and Titanic consisted of six Stirling Bombers of 218 Squadron who conducted a window dropping operation to simulate an invasion convoy approaching Boulogne. They'd fly over the area and then appear to head for home only to about turn; ten miles out to sea and return to the area again and again. To the German troops on the ground and military intelligence it would appear that wave after wave of planes were dropping paratroopers and their equipment. The Stirlings were among a force of 40 aeroplanes, Hudsons and Halifaxes but they were only dropping dummy parachutists. The dummy parachutists were crude cloth representations of a human figure to give the impression of a parachutist. They were equipped with a device that would explode on impact and set the cloth and figure on fire, which suggested that the man had burnt the parachute and lay hidden ready for action and sabotage. Two SAS teams were also simulating airborne landings away from the real invasion area. The SAS even allowed some of the enemy to escape to spread alarm by reporting landings by hundreds of parachutists. The deception worked well, so much so that when the Germans discovered the second invasion in Normandy they assumed that it was the 'decoy' invasion and although they sent a few divisions to the west they concentrated most of their men and equipment in and around Calais.

The first Messerschmitt loomed out of the darkness and began firing indiscriminately at the formation of Stirlings. A mild panic set in within the confines of plane LJ 949.

Tammas screamed; John was taken completely by surprise but Len Jones on the rear gun had already released a burst of fire in the direction of the enemy craft. The Messerschmitt dived and John looked around at the other Stirlings checking for tell-tale signs to see if any them had been hit; wisps of smoke, or worse flames.

'Where is he, where is he?' Came the shout and for a few seconds there was only silence as every crew member watched the skies.

'There! There! There! Eight o'clock, he's coming in at eight o'clock.'

Before Reg had finished his sentence six or seven rounds had burst through the fuselage. The damage was minimal as most of the bullets continued through the plane and out the other side as the Messerschmitt flew on to attack the other planes. The Mosquito had followed in pursuit and John watched the initial engagement before they flew off into the darkness.

'Eight minutes to drop zone.'

It was Reg who miraculously had retained his composure and focused on his duties despite what was going on around him.

The Messerschmitt appeared out of nowhere, directly in front of them heading straight for the cockpit. John braced himself and waited for the hail of bullets that would surely come. Just then the mosquito powered in from behind them and the Messerschmitt turned to face up to its aggressor. For no more than a few seconds the sky was alight with tracer fire and John noticed a wisp of smoke coming from an engine of the Messerschmitt. That sound again, the sound that signified that the aircraft was in trouble, that same sound that he'd heard from the Stirling piloted by Fred Gribble.

Len Jones was cheering from the Perspex bubble of the rear gun. 'We got the bastard, we got him.'

John couldn't believe how quickly things happened. The Messerschmitt went into a dive as flames took hold. He was out of control and the radio waves were filled with the sound of the other crews cheering and rejoicing as the stricken plane hurtled towards the ground. Every member of the crew who could see out of a window watched the flight of the German plane as it continued downwards and hit the ground in a ball of flames that lit up the whole of the area.

'Four minutes to drop zone.'

Reg's voice brought them back to the present.

'Paratroopers ready.'

It was no more than a slight commotion in the body of the aircraft but almost immediately John sensed something was amiss.

His colleagues of the 6th Airborne Division had assumed he had simply dozed off but as they tried to wake Sergeant Roger Hill they realised he was dead. A bullet had passed through his heart and he had died instantly, without a murmur.

His body was left in the plane. John had insisted they laid him out on the crew sick bed. They covered his face with a towel as one by one his former colleagues leapt out into the abyss.

The five crews of Vanrenen, Azouz, Tickner, Hoystead and Prowd all made it back to base just before daybreak. Prowd and Tickner's planes suffered a little light flak damage but there were no major incidents. Their final night flight landed back at RAF Keevil at around 5.30 in the morning. They were told to eat and grab an hour's sleep. They would be taking off again at 7.00, thirty minutes after the first Allied troops had landed on the beaches of Normandy.

The operation was the largest amphibious invasion ever undertaken, with over 160,000 troops destined to land on the beaches codenamed Sword, Juno, Gold, Omaha and Utah. There were more than 5,000 ships involved. The assault took place along a 50 mile stretch of the Normandy coast.

'Come on Sherlock, wake up we've work to do.'

John had slept like a baby, albeit for less than an hour. Patch was curled up on the pillow beside him.

'Jesus, Lofty. Let me sleep won't you; I need my eight hours just like the next man.'

Lofty pulled at the blanket that covered John, dragged it from him and rolled it up in a ball before throwing it onto the bottom of his bed.

'Eight hours' flying perhaps, my friend. No time to sleep, we've a war to win.'

Lofty nudged Patch.

'You too my little friend, up you get, where do you think you are the bloody Ritz?'

It was 0734 when they took off. Within ten minutes John was looking down on the flotilla of boats, small craft and ships crossing the channel. He wouldn't have believed it if he hadn't seen it with his own eyes. For once the aircraft was silent, a combined stunned silence from the crew of LJ 949. John stood looking down onto the English Channel alongside Reg. Eventually he spoke.

'I can't believe what I'm seeing, mate. I didn't think there were that many boats in the world.'

'Awesome Sherlock, absolutely bloody awesome.'

They were flying relatively low. John could make out a flock of Canada geese flying in a V shape in the opposite direction. They were majestic, their wings beating in a kind of ghostly slow motion and John wondered if they realised how free they were.

Ships, boats, tankers, cruisers, yachts and barges. It appeared that every craft in England had heeded the call as they ferried the fighting men across the English Channel to the beaches of Normandy. John turned to the section leader in charge of the paratroopers sitting patiently in the hold of the plane.

'Sergeant, do you want to come up here and take a look?'

The sergeant rose and made his way through the assembled men, standing between Tammas and John. His jaw fell open as the sight registered with him. He turned and shook his head. Tears were in his eyes as he tried to speak. Eventually the words came.

'How can we possibly lose this war, Flight Engineer?'

'My thoughts exactly,' said John. He looked at his watch. 'We have time enough for every one of your lads to come up here and see this incredible sight. It'll give them a boost if nothing else.'

The sergeant placed a hand on John's shoulder. 'You bet it will Flight Engineer, you bet it will.'

The Paratroopers filed up in pairs and looked down into the

English Channel. To a man they returned back to their seats with a renewed confidence, with inspiration and adrenalin coursing through their bodies. John felt he had done his bit, somehow contributed to the assault on Sword Beach even though he wouldn't ever set foot on it. The paratroopers would run faster, fight harder and hopefully come through the day unscathed. Some wouldn't make it, he knew that, but those that did would remember what he had showed them till their dying day. All around Stirlings, Hudsons and Lancasters, some towing Horsa Gliders, while Mosquitos and Spitfires were patrolling the sky on the lookout for enemy fighters. John made a vain attempt to estimate how many planes he could see from the window above his seat.

It was impossible. There were thousands above, below and to each side.

Adolf Hitler sat in a big leather armchair as his generals looked on nervously. He seethed with anger, it was written all over his face. He knew the news was grim, he could tell by the reactions of his generals, the body language. Every picture tells a story. Brauchitsch stepped forward; the side of his mouth flicked an involuntary twitch. There were no twitches at their last meeting as he confidently warned of an invasion centred on Calais. Halder and Blomberg looked on.

Hitler spoke. 'Tell me the news, Brauchitsch. Have they fooled us?'

Brauchitsch shuffled his papers as he sat down opposite Hitler at the huge table. He tried to look at Hitler directly but as the Fuhrer's ice cold eyes bored through him he glanced down at the papers as if studying the information.

He had been handed the intelligence report only thirty minutes earlier. It was the stuff of nightmares. Only a few days before, he'd sat there with Keitel, Halder, Blomberg and Hasso von Manteuffel and they'd assured their Fuhrer that the invasion would land in Calais and the surrounding area. Hitler had ordered a massive offensive to meet them.

'There are two invasions, Herr Fuhrer.'

It was a weak opening and Hitler saw right through it.

He stood up and spoke sarcastically as he walked around the Austrian pine table.

'Two invasions Herr Brauchitsch, two invasions you say.' He folded his hands behind his back and gazed up into space. 'Two invasions... very interesting analogy. And tell me, Herr Brauchitsch, where are the bulk of our forces and what ratio have we split them into?'

Brauchitsch was being led into a trap. Hitler had already been informed of the scale of the Normandy invasion, well aware that the bulk of his forces were positioned around Calais.

Brauchitsch referred to the map in front of him. He spoke, he almost stuttered, as he pointed a shaking finger to the cross on the map at Calais.

'Our troops are in position here... and here.'

His finger hovered over Cherbourg as he looked up at Hitler for some sort of approval. Hitler stopped and leaned on the desk. He pointed at the map.

'Here and... here you say Herr Brauchitsch.'

'Yes Fuhrer.'

'And tell me Herr Brauchitsch, where are the troops concentrated? Is it here or... here?'

'Herr Fuhrer the bulk of our troops are massed around Calais as we believed...'

Hitler slammed his fist on the table. 'We, Herr Brauchitsch? We?'

Hitler raised his voice a decibel or two. He pointed to the

generals sitting around the table. 'You believed, not me, I let you guide me and my sources tell me we have been fucking fooled.'

Hitler was shouting now, little drops of spittle had gathered at the side of his mouth and as he grew angrier and screamed ever louder the small droplets flew across the room and onto the uniforms of his terrified generals.

'We have twenty motorised Panzer divisions and twenty five light infantry divisions in place here.' He jabbed his finger at the map.

'My sources tell me they have found empty boxes and dummy parachutes, there is no invasion here, the real invasion has begun in Normandy.'

Hitler fell back into a seat. Still he bellowed at the men.

'Why did I listen to your fucking shit?' He shook his head before composing himself slightly. He spoke almost in a whisper, he spoke slowly and deliberately.

'The British and American troops have dug in around Caen... they have concentrated their fire on the Merville Battery... as we speak they are securing the bridges from Ouistreham to Caen. Their troops are landing on the beaches almost unopposed.' He laughed out loud and looked up. 'We cannot get our troops across the fucking river to help them.'

'Herr Fuhrer we have mobilised the Luftwaffe and the divisions in Normandy are holding their own, we are inflicting heavy casualties on the troops that are landing.'

Herr Brauchitsch waited for the Fuhrers reaction to his positive outlook on events.

Hitler rose again. He opened up a file on the desk and took out a sketch.

'Herr Brauchitsch, this was given to me less than an hour ago.' He positioned the diagram on the desk and turned it to face Brauchitsch and the other generals. 'See here, this is an estimate of the boats and ships that are crossing the English Channel as we speak. They are heading for Normandy... not Calais.'

He leaned forward in his chair, and Herr Brauchitsch could smell his sour breath.

'Within twelve hours it is estimated that 150,000 enemy troops will have landed on the beaches and we are powerless to stop them. You told me that the poor weather conditions meant an invasion would not be possible for several days. I've ordered some troops to stand down, and many of my senior officers are away for the weekend.' Hitler wiped at his brow and frowned. 'Even fucking Field Marshal Rommel is away for a few days leave to celebrate his wife's birthday.'

Hitler looked up and glared at his generals one by one.

'I am surrounded by incompetence.'

His right hand massaged his temples with his index finger and his thumb as his palm covered his eyes.

'Get out of my sight... you useless fucking bastards.'

CHAPTER FIFTEEN

It was a well-deserved night off as the men sat in the Queen Victoria public house in Trowbridge. The talk was of D Day, as it had now been named, the biggest sea invasion in history, and cinema news reels across the country played back over and over again the pictures and moving footage of the incredible efforts by Allied civilians, troops, airmen and naval personnel.

There were a lot of men from 196 Squadron out that night, only too aware that they were lucky to have made it. Vanrenen's crew were luckier than most. More than one man cherished and appreciated the sweet taste of the ale, well aware some of their friends would never savour the moment again. They'd never spend another night in a pub, never laugh and joke the night away as the survivors were doing at that precise moment in time.

'You have to hand it to the Aussie bugger,' said John. 'He absolutely mastered that plane flying on only two engines.'

John sat next to Len with Patch fast asleep on the seat between them.

'Yeah Sherlock, he might be a stuck-up prat but he's our prat and I wouldn't swap him for the world. I think we were more than a little lucky too.'

Mark Azouz looked over at John and Len.

'Hey guys, you need to concentrate more on the beer and less on what might have been. Tonight's the night for letting our hair down, celebrating the fact that we were part of the biggest assault in history.'

John and Len raised their glasses in the direction of their friend.

'Cheers Mark, I'll get another round in,' John stood. 'Who's for another beer?'

The hands flew up around the table, Lofty Matthews, Tammas, Taffy, Tickner, Handley and many others. Their mood was one of forced joviality as if they were determined to celebrate in some way and yet more than aware that one of their crew would never make it home.

John called the round in, paid for it and the barmaid wandered over a few minutes later with a beer for everyone. As had been the protocol all evening long they stood and toasted absent friends. John hoped the deaths of the men would not be in vain. They had made a difference he reassured himself, the great deception had worked and the Allied troops were slowly but surely liberating France.

They staggered out of the bar not long after one in the morning. For once the landlord hadn't imposed drinking up time and for once the drivers of the four-ton lorries didn't mind waiting. It was as if everybody knew that D Day had been a success, as if a major celebration was long overdue. Surely the war would be over by Christmas?

John woke with the hangover from hell as he staggered into the bathrooms to ease his aching bladder. He stood and peed forever. George Humphrey came and joined him as he stood at the urinal. The air was permeated by the smell of stale beer.

'I'm never drinking again, mate,' said John.

'Me neither Sherlock, I've a mouth like the bottom of a dirty budgie cage.'

John laughed and immediately regretted his lapse of concentration as a thumping pain shot across his temples.

'Oh shit… I haven't felt like this in a long while.'

After they'd finished they walked gingerly to the hand basins and poured copious amounts of water into their mouths.

John turned to his friend as the water ran down his cheeks.

'Good night though, wasn't it?'

'You can say that again Sherlock, you can say that again.'

Just then the bathroom door flew open and Lofty Matthews stood with a beaming smile on his face. John looked across in amazement; he appeared fresh as a daisy.

'Bacon and eggs,' he announced with a grin. 'Scrambled eggs and black pudding, perhaps a sausage or two but definitely, definitely, *definitely* fried bread and tomatoes.'

He strode over with purpose. George Humphrey had already started turning green.

'Or how about some nice kippers? That'll sort the old hangover out boys.'

It was too much for George as he ran into the nearest cubicle and fell to his knees with his head suspended over the toilet bowl.

John turned to face Lofty.

'You're a right bastard sometimes, Lofty, do you know that?'

Lofty grinned. 'Absolutely, now get yourself ready. I'm starving.'

George never made breakfast; he lay on his bed most of the morning. Lofty sat with Len and John at breakfast as they discussed their next sorties.

'We're due up tomorrow by all accounts, we have the day off today,' said Lofty. 'I've already had a look at the duty sheets and we're both up on Operation Mallard, briefing at 0700.'

'Any idea where we're heading?' asked Len.

Lofty spoke between mouthfuls of the biggest breakfast John had ever seen anyone tackle.

'Ain't got a clue mate but I suspect it's somewhere around Normandy, that's where the action is.'

Len spoke. 'I've heard it's going well, the Germans are in disarray. They fell for the decoy invasion hook, line and sinker. There are a lot of the bastards left in France of course but I've heard they're at sixes and sevens.'

The breakfast lasted for hours as they were joined by Azouz and Tickner, Doug Handley and Tammas. Even Vanrenen put in an appearance to make sure everyone had made it back from Trowbridge. At one point John even thought he was about to sit down and take breakfast with them but as a plate was pushed in front of him he made his excuses and left.

'What is wrong with that fucker, Sherlock?' asked George Tickner. 'He might be a good pilot but Jesus he can hardly pass the time of day with you guys. He's not like one of us Aussies. At times I'm almost afraid to call myself an Australian.'

Len looked at John and they grinned.

'But we wouldn't swap him for the world Sherlock, would we?'

John shook his head.

'Not likely.' He grinned at George Tickner. 'It's just the way he is. Sometimes I wonder if it's all an act.'

'Well it's not right,' said Tickner. 'He should at least show his appreciation; you're a good bunch of lads. He may be a good pilot but you lot are good at what you do too.'

John took a long drink from his tea cup.

'It gets worse.'

Tickner slapped at his forehead.

'How come? How can it get any worse? Tell me.'

John continued. 'You know when you write a letter back home you have to leave the envelope unsealed so that some bugger in authority can read it and make sure you aren't divulging sensitive information?'

'Yes.'

'Well, guess who the reader in authority is?'

George Tickner looked around for a second and then the penny dropped.

'No... tell me no... not Vanrenen?'

Len Jones spoke up. 'Absolutely correct my friend. So you guys are fine if you want to bend the missus's ear and sound off about some bastard who rubs you up the wrong way, but us lot,' he pointed to John, 'we can't say Jack Shit because Vanrenen will be reading every bloody word.'

George was shaking his head.

'You can't be serious?'

The second phase of Operation Mallard never took place as all Stirlings were recalled halfway across the channel. 100 per cent cloud cover at the drop zone, they'd been told. LJ949 was beginning to be a bit of a favourite with Vanrenen as he put the Stirling through its paces on the way back throwing the aircraft into a series of steep dives and performing ridiculously tight turning circles.

He spoke to John and Doug as they disembarked on landing, looking at the plane as they walked away.

'This is the girl for me, chaps. It doesn't make any logical sense but she handles better than any other Stirling I've ever flown, she has a nice feel to her.'

'That's what you want Skip, a girl with a nice feel to her.'

Doug's little joke was lost on Vanrenen or at least he refused to acknowledge it, let alone react with a smile.

'You men make sure we are assigned this plane every time, don't let any other bastards get their hands on it.'

'How the hell are we going to do that, Skipper?' asked John Holmes.

Vanrenen furrowed his brow. 'I'm not sure Flight Engineer, but I'm sure you'll think of something… have a word with ops.'

At 0715 on the morning of 10th June 1944, 196 Squadron were briefed on Operation Rob Roy, which would fly out at midnight. It was another French Resistance drop in the Limoges area of France and would involve eight crews.

The 2nd SS Panzer Division was on the move. They'd received their instructions and were ordered to make their way up country to stop the Allied advance. The French Resistance fighters however were doing everything in their power to stop them. They had been well supplied in recent weeks by 196 Squadron of the British Royal Air Force. Their attacks had been concentrated in the countryside around the Limousin villages of Oradour-sur-Vayres and Oradour-sur-Glane. They had tormented the 2nd SS Panzer Division who wanted to head north and help their fellow countrymen. There was little tactical importance being pinned down in that particular part of France.

Louis-Leonard Chapelot and Henri-Pierre Raynaud sat in the small cafe in Oradour-sur-Glane, more than pleased with their recent skirmishes with the occupying forces. They shared a cognac together, toasting the fact that they'd taken out a strategic rail link and blown a huge crater in the road outside the Chateaux that housed the 2nd SS Panzer Division and for a few days, effectively confined the whole SS Division to barracks.

Early on the morning of 10th June 1944, Adolf Diekmann, commanding the first battalion of the 4th Waffen-SS Panzer-Grenadier Regiment, sat with Sturmbannführer Otto Weidinger at regional headquarters in Limousin. They shared a coffee together but Diekmann had grave news. Not only had the 2nd SS Panzer Division been stopped in their tracks yet again but a rumour was now circulating that a Waffen SS Officer was being held by the French Resistance in Oradour-sur-Vayres, a nearby village. The captured German was Helmut Kämpfe, commander of the 2nd SS Panzer Division.

Weidenger confirmed that the officer was indeed missing. At first it had been presumed that he'd gone absent without leave. Now Diekman and Weidenger knew the truth.

'We must make an example of these French peasants once and for all, Otto; they are getting too big for their boots.'

On 10th June, Diekmann's battalion sealed off the town of Oradour-sur-Glane. Incredibly he had confused it with nearby Oradour-sur-Vayres, where the German officer was rumoured to be held. It mattered not where the town was, Diekman was on a mission to show the French exactly how the soldiers of The Third Reich dealt with such insubordination. He ordered all the townspeople – and anyone who happened to be in or near the town – to assemble in the village square. It was a ruse; the villagers were told to assemble there simply to have their identity papers examined.

Once he was satisfied that every man, woman and child in the village were there he read the riot act to them and demanded that they disclose the whereabouts of the missing officer. He was met with a wall of silence that infuriated him even more.

He ordered all of the women and children into the local church where they were locked in. The soldiers of the SS then searched and looted the village looking for the missing officer. He was not located and Diekman ordered the French men into six barns on the outskirts of the village advising them they were to be locked up until Kämpfe was found.

It was a lie.

An hour earlier Diekman had ordered his machine-gunners to take up strategic hidden positions in the dark recesses of each barn. As they lined the men up the machine gun nests were revealed and the soldiers began shooting at them. They had been ordered to shoot them in the legs so that they would die more slowly. It was absolute carnage; each barn resembled a lake of red as the femoral arteries of the victims pumped the blood onto the dusty ground. Only a few men had died but the rest were unable to move or escape as they begged for mercy. The Waffen SS 2nd Panzer Division showed none.

They covered the stricken bodies with fuel, walked outside and set the barns on fire.

Only six men escaped. One of them was chased down a road heading to the cemetery leaving a trail of blood in his wake. When the SS caught up with him he was beaten to a pulp and executed on the spot.

190 men died in the six barns, among them Pierre-Henri Poutaraud, Louis-Leonard Chapelot and Henri-Pierre Raynaud. But the worst was yet to come.

After they'd massacred the men of the village the soldiers proceeded to the church. They locked the doors of the 17th century building and boarded up the windows. Petrol was poured through the gaps in the windows until the wooden church floor was awash. The women and children were crying and screaming, begging to be set free, only too aware of what was about to happen to them. The church was set on fire.

After it was ignited, some of the women and children managed to break gaps in the windows but they were met with machine-gun fire as they made their escape. A total of 247 women and 205 children died in the carnage. Two women and one child survived; one was 47-year-old Marguerite Rouffanche. She had managed to slip out of a window. Soon after a young woman and child followed her through. They escaped into the rear of the church gardens but were quickly apprehended when the screams of the child alerted two SS soldiers. They were lined up against the back of the church wall and shot.

The young woman and child died instantly. Marguerite Rouffanche slumped to the floor but miraculously she survived. She played dead. After the German soldiers disappeared she managed to crawl into the undergrowth behind the church where she remained overnight, bleeding heavily, flirting with death. The Germans were determined to extinguish all forms of life and to hide any evidence of their atrocity as best they could. That night, every house and building in the village was set on fire. The church burned for two days and two nights, the heat so fierce and the flames so intense it melted the huge church bells in the belfry.

A group of about 20 villagers had fled Oradour-sur-Glane as the German soldiers had appeared. The following morning some of them returned and rescued Marguerite Rouffanche, taking her to a nearby hospital where she was treated for gunshot wounds and burns. A few days later, villagers from a nearby town were ordered to bury the dead. 642 inhabitants of Oradour-sur-Glane had been murdered in a matter of hours. Incredibly Adolf Diekmann would later claim that it was a just retaliation for recent French Resistance activity and of course for the kidnap of Helmut Kämpfe.

Everyone heard the instruction from RAF Keevil as it came through the radio. The eight crews were flying south of Paris.

'Return to base, 196 Squadron, all eight crews. Repeat, return to RAF Keevil immediately.'

'Awwww bloody hell,' shouted Chalky, 'I wish they'd stop bloody doing this to us – that's two in a row. We'll never win the war at this rate.'

Vanrenen was frustrated too, and although he knew that there was a very good reason for any recall and 38 Group would not be persuaded to change their mind, he asked the question regardless.

'Vanrenen here Sir, LJ949. Any particular reason, Sir? The weather looks ideal where we are at the minute.'

The reply came in a second or two later.

'Weather ideal Vanrenen, that's not the problem. Apparently the French resistance chaps won't be there to intercept us. As simple as that. Return to base, repeat return to base.'

'Roger Sir. Over and out.'

CHAPTER SIXTEEN

July and August were frustrating times for 196 Squadron. Everyone wanted the war to be over by Christmas and all the reports were good. They wanted to do their bit to help bring the war to a swift conclusion and the reports and briefings all seemed positive. They'd heard that Caen had been taken by the Allies. All over France there were almost daily reports of towns, villages and cities liberated as the Allies pushed the German troops back ever further and on the other side of the world the defeats on the Japanese military forces continued to mount.

Listening to the reports John wondered what effect it would have on Allied prisoners of war. There had been no letters from Dorothy's brother Cliff in Burma; just how would the Japanese respond if defeat looked imminent?

The news for Hitler appeared bleak and information about an attempted assassination filtered back to London. The plotters in the bomb plot against him were hanged in Berlin on August

8th, their bodies suspended on meat hooks and pictures circulated around the world.

Wing Commander Baker smiled as he delivered even more positive news.

'The French Resistance has begun an uprising in Paris gentlemen. They've been inspired by our approach of the River Seine. Jerry's on the run men, there's no doubt about it.'

Mark Azouz raised his hand.

'Yes, Warrant Officer, what is it?'

'It all seems good news, Sir, but why can't we be a part of it? We haven't been up for over a week now and when we do get up and on our way we are recalled halfway there. Surely the French Resistance could do with a little help?'

Wing Commander Baker hung his head. His face took on a strange look, a little worry perhaps but sympathy too. Then it seemed to change to anger.

'I understand how you feel men but there are very good reasons why an op is recalled. You chaps who were on your way to France on 10th June were recalled because the French Resistance were massacred on the ground. After the war is over you will read about a village called Oradour-sur-Glane.'

The name of the village rang a bell with John. It came to him. They'd dropped supplies near the village several times; the French Resistance were very active in the area.

'The Boche will get what's coming to them, don't you worry about that. They are animals, fucking animals.'

There was almost a collective reverberation of shock. Wing Commander Baker had never uttered that word during any of the briefings before and John wondered what had happened in the French village to make him so angry. He turned to face Mark.

'You might have a handful of missions to France in the coming weeks, Warrant Officer, but I'm pleased to tell you that the Hun is almost defeated over there. Intelligence suggests that Paris will be liberated within two weeks. Then it's all but over in France.'

Wing Commander Baker had composed himself once again. He strode slowly but purposely back and forward in front of the huge map of Europe.

'196 will be needed further afield.' He pointed to the map with a gold-tipped cane. 'Here in Norway, and here in Holland.' He took in a deep breath and stuck out his chest. 'We have them on the back foot in France but they are still a bloody nuisance elsewhere. We must hit them on every front. The Russians have the situation well under control in the east and as we speak are preparing to march on Berlin.'

'It's true,' whispered John Holmes under his breath. 'It really is true... this damned war will be over by Christmas.'

The end of August 1944 was a good one for the Allies. John lay on his bunk with a copy of the *Sunday Express*. He called over to Lofty as he read the reports.

'It's all good news Lofty, if these newspaper reports are anything to go by.'

Lofty lay with a book, killing time.

'Don't be believing everything in those bloody Brit papers Sherlock. I bet they don't even mention the Canadians in there, anyone reading that would think that the Brits were winning the war single handed.'

John studied the paper, focused on a particular paragraph.

'Listen up Lofty, that's where you're wrong. It says here the Japanese are now in total retreat from India, the Canadians have been making inroads but then the 6th British Airborne Division flew in to show them how it's done.'

The words took a little while to sink in and then Lofty realised John had made the whole paragraph up.

'It doesn't say that at all, you little northern country bumpkin.'

Lofty leapt over to John's bed and upended the mattress onto the floor. John lay in a heap with Patch, who wondered what had happened. John was holding his stomach, laughing harder than he'd laughed in weeks.

'And touchy too,' he managed to say before Lofty snatched the paper off him.

John picked Patch up and gave him a hug.

'Poor Canadian's a bully isn't he Patch, my little lad.'

Lofty studied the headlines and then turned to the inside cover.

'Bloody hell Sherlock, you weren't kidding were you? Paris has been liberated. There's a picture of De Gaulle and the Free French Parade marching down the Champs-Élysées. They're even suggesting here that the German military disobeyed Hitler's orders to burn the city.'

John spoke as he rearranged the sheets and blankets on the bed.

'Yes… he's in the shit now if his own men are disobeying orders. If you read further down the page you'll see that we've captured most of the south of France, as far up as Grenoble and Avignon.

Lofty whistled as he read. 'And they've surrendered at Toulon and Marseilles as well.'

He turned to page three.

'Patton's tanks have crossed the Marne and there's an anti-German uprising in Czechoslovakia.' Lofty gave a little cheer. 'There you go; we do get a mention after all! Here, look.' Lofty pointed to a paragraph half way down the page. 'American and Canadian forces turn over the government of France to Free French troops.' Lofty grinned.

Sherlock's Squadron flew three operations to France in early September and two more to Norway where they dropped spies into German occupied land. They were all successful.

John set off on the morning of 16th September 1944 to walk around the airfield with Patch. It had become a regular occurrence on mornings when he didn't need to attend briefings or wasn't away on an operation. It all seemed quiet as they set out at first light. As they approached the far end of the airfield John walked over to the perimeter fence. He spotted the guards positioned every 20 yards. As he approached one of them he spoke to a young man a couple of years younger than himself.

'Morning soldier boy, what's going on?'

The young man looked a little nervous and looked for the rank of the man he was about to address.

'I thought you'd be used to this by now, Sergeant; I was here the last time they sealed off your base for D Day. I dare say you were too.'

'They've sealed off the camp again?'

'They have Sergeant. No one's allowed in or out, including your little dog there.'

John whistled for Patch who was sniffing at the wire fence.

'Do you know why'

The private pulled at his chin strap holding his tin helmet in place.

'I think you are likely to know more than me, Sergeant.'

John shook his head and held up his hands.

'Not me my friend, as usual I know bugger all.'

John bid the young man goodbye and decided to check on the postings over by the notice board by the Sergeants' Mess.

Sure enough a prominent notice announced a twelve noon

briefing. As John headed back towards the billet the first of the buses swept into the camp. Bus after bus drove in quietly, the men of the British 1st Airborne Division sitting patiently looking forward to a hearty breakfast and news of their next engagement.

It was déjà vu for John, another huge operation – and looking at the numerous buses pouring into RAF Keevil, every bit as big as D Day had been three months earlier. *Perhaps this was it*, he thought, as he found a spring in his step, *the last big push before Christmas… the end of the war…*

Wing Commander Baker was a familiar sight, as was the converted gym and the faces of the men he had flown into action with so many times now. John sat between George Tickner and Lofty.

The map was different this time, though, even if the Wing Commander did still hold the same gold-tipped stick. His tone was bullish, his manner calm and confident.

He said he was about to deliver some news that would make the squadron proud. Mark visibly shrank into his seat.

'You chaps weren't to know but our very own Warrant Officer Azouz flew out over the Brest Peninsula on Operation Horace a few days ago. His crew were on the run-in to the target when their aircraft was hit by anti-aircraft fire.'

Baker pushed his hands behind his back as he took a deep breath.

'Their propeller and reduction gear of the starboard outer engine were shot away. Anyone else would have turned tail for home but not our man.'

The focus of attention was now on Mark as several of the men turned to face him.

'The old Stirling was pretty well buggered up but he took the decision to push on to the target. The flak continued and other parts of the aircraft were struck by fragments of shell. Despite all this, Warrant Officer Azouz successfully completed his mission and returned safely to base. He has set a fine example of gallantry to us all.'

A ripple of applause circulated around the room as Baker announced Azouz had been nominated for the DFC, the Distinguished Flying Cross, and Baker asked the men for three cheers. It was the perfect introduction to what was to follow.

Wing Commander Baker walked over to Azouz and patted him on the shoulder like a son would a father. He returned to his position at the front of the room and almost immediately changed his face to match the message he was about to deliver.

'Operation Market Garden chaps, Operation Market being the air assault and the Garden part of the operation the land assault. We are poised to enter Holland. France and Belgium are under our control. Our American chums, the United States First Army, have already crossed the Rhine near Cologne and Bonn and the United States Third Army have crossed it here and here.' The Wing Commander paused for a second, as he guided the stick along the River Rhine hovering along the points where the Allies had breached the biggest river in Germany.

'The problem with the bloody Hun,' he continued, 'is that he keeps blowing the bloody bridges up when he's on the retreat and we can't catch up with him to give his big fat square arse the kicking it deserves.'

He spoke well, allowing a pause for the men of 196 Squadron to have a little laugh at the German's expense. Then he turned serious once more.

Wing Commander Baker pointed up at the huge map.

'We need to secure these three bridges here, here and here which will allow our boys from the west to cross them and push the Hun deeper into Holland. In a nutshell we need to have full command of the countryside surrounding Arnhem here, Oosterbeek here and Wolfheze and Driel here and here.'

John looked at the map that hung on the wall. It may have been no accident that the map was on a small scale which enabled the surrounding countries to be viewed. France and Belgium were emblazoned with small Union Jack and Stars and Stripes stickers and the Russian flags were prominent in Poland and Czechoslovakia. As Wing Commander Baker spoke he placed more American and British stickers on the continent.

Lofty nudged John and whispered. 'See what I mean buddy, not a fucking Maple Leaf in sight.'

Nevertheless the map was of great comfort to Lofty and the men of 196 Squadron. It was clear that the Germans were losing their grip on a continent they'd terrorised for nearly five years.

'Our squadron will be pushing the airborne divisions in on Horsas and they'll secure bridges across the Nederrijn within two to three days. From there in we'll have the perfect position for an assault on Germany. We'll advance rapidly northwards and turn right into the lowlands of Germany. The plan is to avoid the Siegfried line which as you are all aware is the primary German defence line.'

Then Wing Commander Baker uttered the final sentence, one that every man in the room wanted to hear.

'If everything goes to plan, gentlemen, the war should be over by Christmas.'

Wing Commander Baker smiled as he finished the briefing.

What could be simpler than that? A group of quietly confident men walked the short distance to the mess hall for an early lunch. Chalky sounded off to John.

'Bloody Horsas, what's the bloody point of those damned

gliders; they're neither use nor ornament. Why can't we just take the lads over in the Stirlings?' Mark Azouz walked alongside.

'More room Chalky, as simple as that. The Horsas can take a jeep on board, something we can't get in a Stirling. And anyway we'll be dropping the boys in from quite high up; it's an easy op for us. It's the boys landing them things who are going to take the shit that the Bosch throw at them.'

The comment wasn't lost on John. It was bad enough flying in and dropping paratroopers at 1,500 feet but the lower the aircraft went, the more chance of a direct hit. The poor souls in the Horsa Gliders had to land in enemy territory… it seemed crazy. The Horsas were flimsy. They offered no protection and it seemed that half of them broke up on impact with the ground. They were badly designed, God help the poor wretches that flew in them.

The paratroopers weren't much better off. If the Germans knew where they were flying into they had a good chance of picking them off. In day light the huge chutes were easy to spot. And what exactly went through the men's mind as they floated down into enemy territory as bullets flew around their ears? It wasn't exactly risk free taking a Stirling over hostile terrain but John would take his chances. It was the men he now talked to as they stood and queued for lunch that he felt sorry for.

The Horsas were hooked up to the Stirlings just before dawn on the morning of 17th September 1944.

It was a five-hour round trip; they'd leave in formation at 1130 hours, 25 Stirlings headed by Wing Commander Baker and his crew. Of the 25 planes that took off from RAF Keevil 21 missions were successful. Four tow ropes broke but three of the Horsa Gliders made successful landings; one glider had to ditch in the English Channel but the crew were safely picked up by Air Sea Rescue.

The mood back at RAF Keevil was one of euphoria; the operation couldn't have gone any better, could it? What no one knew at that particular time was that the 1st Airborne Division had met with fierce and unexpected resistance from the 9th SS and 10th SS Panzer divisions. Only a small force was able to reach the Arnhem road bridge, with the rest of the division pinned back on the outskirts of the city.

Back in RAF Keevil on 18th September the squadron were told they were going up later that day and again the day after.

'Three nights in a row,' whispered Len Jones to John. 'Doesn't look so happy today, old Winco, does he, Sherlock?'

It was a sound observation, John had noticed it too. Wing Commander Baker definitely looked a little ruffled, not as supremely confident as he had been the day before. Outside the briefing room Lofty ribbed Len and John.

'We've a day off on the nineteenth so we're planning a big night in town.' He ruffled John's hair. 'Wish you could come with us, Sherlock old mate, but you lot have Jerry to fight.'

Len looked at John.

'Don't worry mate we'll get a day off too. I don't think they'll send us up three in a row.'

22 crews went up on 18th September 1944. It was another successful sortie with only one Horsa failing to make it to the drop zone. As Vanrenen let loose the glider he banked and turned for home. John was aware of a little light flak that was exploding below them but it was well out of range of the Stirlings climbing ever higher. John feared for the men and the gliders below, the Germans' anti-aircraft guns concentrating their fire on them.

On the ground the British XXX Corps were unable to advance northwards as quickly as planned and were unable to relieve the airborne troops at the bridge. Unknown to Vanrenen, John and the other air crews in 196 Squadron, thousands of Allied paratroopers had been massacred as they floated to the ground.

It meant only a small British force made it to the bridge as the rest of the division became trapped in a small pocket north of the river.

The order from the ground to Bomber Command was simple. They wanted more reinforcements and they wanted them quickly. Most of the Horsa Gliders dropped by 196 Squadron were shot up before they landed; the paratroopers dropped by other squadrons of the RAF were butchered like lambs to the slaughter, the Allied generals severely underestimating the axis troops on the ground.

Back at RAF Keevil on 19th September the mood in the converted gym was sombre and tense. Although the powers at the top hadn't told the pilots and air crew of the devastation on the ground at Arnhem it was impossible not to read their faces. Wing Commander Baker was a shadow of his former self, pale, haggard looking, a million miles away from the rosy-cheeked confident man who had addressed his troops just a few days before.

John looked across the room and was a little surprised to see Lofty, Keith and the other members of their crew. He shrugged it off; *probably just want to know what's going on*, he thought to himself.

The briefing was quick. Same map, same towns, same drop zone and yet more troops of the British 1st Airborne Division dropped in on Horsa Gliders.

John caught up with Lofty half way across the parade ground.

'Hey mate, what are you up to? Off out on the town later on are you?

Lofty forced a smile.

'Not us mate, we're coming with you to Arnhem. They've decided they need some Canadians up there to show you lot what to do.'

John Holmes punched him playfully on the shoulder.

'C'mon... seriously, you're not coming with us are you? I thought you'd been stood down.'

Matthews shook his head.

'No. It seems they need as many gliders as they can in there and there's something wrong with another plane. We're coming with you. Now let's go and get a bite to eat and catch a few hours' rest before we get the call.

John looked out over the starboard wing. The two Stirlings were a little closer than he would have wished but nevertheless he could clearly see the face of Lofty waving as he caught his stare. John gave a little wave back. As always he hoped with all of his heart that they'd all be back home soon and sharing a pint at the Queen Victoria in Trowbridge. He looked to the cockpit and could just make out the shape of Keith; he couldn't see his face but instinctively knew it would be a picture of concentration.

Reg announced they would be flying over German-occupied Arnhem very soon. By now the crew knew that that meant they had to be extra vigilant. Within minutes of the navigator's announcement the anti-aircraft flak started.

John couldn't prevent the adrenalin surging through his body, he was used to it by now and it was an involuntary reaction that happened every time the explosions started. A direct hit could bring the aircraft down and they'd be staring death in the face or at the very least carted off to a German prisoner of war camp. He thought briefly about Cliff Shaw, wondered how he was bearing up in the Japanese camp on the other side of the world. The Stirling shuddered as a shell exploded only metres from them. The Germans had found their range.

'We're hit!'

It was an all too familiar cry and as always for a horrifying split second he wondered if the cry had come from his own aircraft. He recognised the voice; it was a good friend of his.

'Who's hit?' screamed Vanrenen into the radio.

John Holmes could barely speak, taking in the full horror on the starboard side of his own aircraft.

'Warrant Officer Prowd, Sir; that was Lofty Matthews's voice.'

'You sure, Flight Engineer?'

'I'm more than sure Skipper, take a look to starboard, fifty feet below.'

This wasn't happening, this couldn't be happening. Lofty's crew shouldn't have even been in the air, they'd been told the day before they had time off. He'd sat with Lofty yesterday evening enjoying a beer in the Sergeants' Mess as Keith approached the table and told them that something was wrong with another aircraft and the commanding officer had asked them to step in. He'd asked them… just asked them, it wasn't even an order. And of course Prowd had consulted with his crew and to a man they'd agreed. It was never going to be an issue, that's the way they were.

The outer starboard engine was on fire, with smoke billowing out into the night sky. It was an easy target now and John almost willed Lofty to take the necessary action and feather the engine. It was no good; John watched in horror as the aircraft started losing altitude. It wasn't just the engine on fire, it was the entire wing, and the flames were spreading along the fuselage.

On board Keith Prowd's aircraft the army dispatchers were busy pushing the containers out of the side back door but it was clear that the fire on the starboard wing was getting worse. They had dropped to around 1,500 feet and the German air batteries had locked on the stricken Stirling as another two explosions rocked the aircraft.

Lofty Matthews called into the radio.

'We've lost two more engines, Skipper – we're going down.'

Prowd couldn't increase the power to the remaining engine for fear that more petrol would cause an explosion. He knew no one would survive an explosion at that height. He gave the only command he could.

'Bail out men, bail out.'

The fire was burning fiercely now, the whole of the starboard side ablaze. One by one the crew bailed out; George Powderhill, John Wherry, Reg Gibbs and Jim Gordon. The two air dispatchers of 63rd Airborne Division also leapt out into the unknown. Lofty Matthews was the last member of the crew apart from the pilot to bail out. There was one remaining pannier left on board and Lofty was determined that whatever it was inside there would make it down to earth to help with the war effort. He heaved at the pannier and as the law of gravity kicked in and it started to slide downwards he leapt on top of it.

Prowd's altitude needle read 750 feet and he knew he had to get out of the aircraft quickly. He was satisfied that everyone had evacuated the plane and strapped his parachute on as he rushed back to the main spar, shouting to make sure it was clear. He went back to the escape hatch up at the front of the Stirling and happened to notice the altimeter which read 550 feet. He pulled back on the control column trying to level the plane up. The ground was fast approaching. It was no good – he had to go now.

Warrant Officer Keith Prowd jumped out and uttered a string of profanities as he pulled the rip cord. Within a few seconds the Stirling crashed into the ground and erupted into a ball of flames.

'No one could have survived that,' John whispered to Reg. 'Even I'm not that optimistic.'

Reg had no words of comfort for his Flight Engineer, well aware of how much he thought of Keith Prowd and Lofty Matthews.

'Did you see any chutes Sherlock?'

'None.'

'Me neither, too much smoke.'

Prowd was one of the lucky ones; he'd landed in a pine forest with his parachute caught in a tree. After a brief struggle he managed to release himself and crashed 15 feet to the forest floor. He lay there winded but nevertheless glad to be alive and he looked to the heavens.

'What do you want me for, Father?'

He was convinced he should have been killed. It wasn't long before the Germans located him and it was hopeless to resist. The twelve German soldiers stood him up against a tree and pointed their rifles at him. Keith Prowd closed his eyes as he feared the worst. The shots never came; it was the Germans' idea of a little fun.

Every member of Prowd's crew had been picked off by German rifle fire as they floated down into enemy-held territory. It was almost like a sport to the German infantrymen as they located the huge white parachutes and homed in on the bodies dangling underneath. Reggie Gibbs was killed, as was

Lofty Matthews, his body found on top of a nearby hotel still clinging to the pannier he'd forced from the plane. He'd been shot dead on the way down. The two RASC dispatchers were also killed.

Keith was immediately whisked off to a holding area in Arnhem where he was subjected to aggressive questioning by a very big blond German. His interrogator wanted to know if there were any raids planned for the next few days. Keith remained silent and the German officer whipped him with an Italian Berretta revolver he held in his hand. Prowd was beaten senseless and stripped of his watch and signet ring that were given to him by his parents in Australia for his 21st birthday. When the German aggressor realised he wasn't going to get anywhere with the stubborn pilot he gave the order to his colleagues.

Prowd was on his way to Wiesbaden where the professional interrogators would deal with him.

It was as if John had lost his brothers. Those men had meant so much to him. He lay on his bunk as Patch sat on his chest and he did everything in his power to fight back the tears. The billet was ghostly silent. George Tickner had tried to offer a few words of reassurance, said what great men they were but still John couldn't tear his eyes from Lofty's empty bunk. He fought his demons throughout the remainder of the night and sleep wouldn't come.

They'd landed late in the afternoon and at the debriefing Wing Commander Baker had confirmed his worst fears; that it was suspected there had been no survivors.

'No chutes reported gentlemen, I'm afraid,' the Wing Commander whispered quietly. 'And no contact thus far with any chaps on the ground.'

At 10.15 John climbed from his bunk.

'C'mon lad we'd better get something to eat, your stomach will think it's throat's been cut.'

Patch wagged his tail and jumped from the bed. John wandered through to the bathroom to get washed. When he returned the little dog was lying on Lofty's bed whining gently. He'd fought the tears all night but this time his defences crumbled as he picked the dog from his friend's bed and sobbed like a child.

John tried to be rational, told himself there was a war on and casualties were to be expected, but it didn't deaden the pain and he couldn't shake the thought that the war was nearly over and why did it have to happen so near to the end of hostilities. Christmas. He kept thinking of Christmas, Christmas back home and celebrations and festivities – the best ever – and reunited families and prisoners returning from overseas. Three bloody months, Lofty, why couldn't you have hung on three bloody months?

Len Jones, George Tickner, Doug Handley and Reg Tammas sat having breakfast.

'Sherlock's taking it bad, lads,' Handley said. 'He looked like shit when I left him this morning. I swear he hasn't slept all night.'

'I don't think anyone has,' said Reg. 'Sherlock and Lofty got along just great, it's only natural he's cut up about it.'

George took a mouthful of tea, looked around at the men sitting at the table.

'It gets worse. I hear we're all up again tomorrow, same place, same time.'

'You're kidding?'

'I'm not, I've just checked the briefing board, we've another meeting in that bloody gym and that can only mean one thing. As sure as eggs are eggs we're back out to Arnhem again just as quick as you like.'

Len Jones stood up as he lifted his breakfast tray.

'I'll go and tell Sherlock the good news, see if I can rally him round a bit before the meeting.'

CHAPTER SEVENTEEN

17 Stirling aircraft of 196 Squadron flew out to Arnhem at lunchtime on 20th September. No one could have envisaged that of the aircraft that took off from RAF Keevil only one of them would return to base completely unscathed. The honour on that particular evening went to Flight Sergeant J.W. Hill and his crew.

Warrant Officer Tait and his crew were shot down and crashed, the entire crew perished. Pilot Officer JF Ellis was badly injured in the cockpit and his aircraft crash landed in enemy territory. His crew survived. Warrant Officer George Oliver's Stirling was shot down at Eindhoven, though miraculously all crew members survived. Flight Sergeant Peter Avrill's plane encountered enemy flak over the drop zone and he ordered his crew to abandon the aircraft. They all survived. Flying Officer McComie's plane came under fire and the Flight Engineer Sergeant D Clough bailed out through a gaping hole in the fuselage, convinced the plane was about to break apart.

He was shot and killed by enemy fire as he parachuted to the ground. McComie managed to bring the plane under control but crash landed soon after. He survived along with the rest of his crew.

Pilot Officer Charlie King sustained heavy flak damage over the drop zone and made a forced landing at Woodbridge. His crew survived.

Pilot Officer Walter Marshall's Stirling was shot up over the drop zone and both port engines were deemed useless. They crash landed near Brussels. Marshall and his bomb aimer were badly injured but the rest of the crew escaped with minor cuts and bruises.

It was carnage, the worst day so far for 196 Squadron, and as John sat in the mess hall he took a late breakfast and looked at the glum faces of his friends and colleagues. He wondered if Allied intelligence had perhaps underestimated the strength of the German divisions on the ground.

Vanrenen had been assigned his beloved LJ 949 aircraft again. He was all smiles as he studied the board outside and prepared to walk into the converted gym. John traced his fingers down the crews he would be flying out with later that night. His finger hovered over plane LJ 810.

'Hey Skipper, Warrant Officer Azouz has been stood down. Why's that then?'

'Yom Kippur, Flight Engineer.'

'Yom what?'

Yom Kippur, the most sacred and solemn day in the Jewish calendar, a day of atonement to ask God for forgiveness for all the bad things that's happened throughout the year. The RAF recognised it as such and allowed the Jewish boys the day off.

'I see. I didn't even know he was Jewish.'

Vanrenen nodded, opened the door and waved John Holmes through.

'Only he didn't take them up on the offer.'

'No?'

'No. Azouz and his crew are flying with us tonight. Winco said he insisted on it.'

As John walked through the door he noticed Mark on the left of the aisle, sitting with a couple of members of his crew.

It was the fifth lift to Arnhem and 196 Squadron were looking a little depleted. The room seemed almost empty. He noticed the crews of George Tickner and Chuck Hoystead as he took his seat. There were ten crews flying out to Arnhem to drop supplies.

'No Horsa Gliders today. Thank God for small mercies,' John mumbled to himself.

The exercise was doomed right from the start.

John had a gut instinct, a feeling that this wasn't going to be a good night, and before they'd even crossed the English coast Chuck Hoystead radioed in to say that his rear gunner had collapsed in the back of the plane and they were having trouble resuscitating him. The order came through to return to base, it was simply too risky to fly into enemy territory without a rear gunner.

Several miles before the drop zone the flak started. It was heavier than they had ever encountered before as aircraft LJ 949 bounced around the sky like a beach ball on a windy day. Len let out a squeal from the rear gun as a shell exploded less than twenty feet away.

'Jesus Christ that was close.'

John waited for the call he knew would come.

Sure enough within seconds LJ 843, piloted by Flight Sergeant Green, radioed in to say they'd been hit. John looked out of the starboard side of the plane to see the aircraft plummeting towards the earth as flames poured from the port side fuselage. There were no more messages from the crew of the aircraft.

Vanrenen's aircraft was eerily quiet; no one needed to say anything. And still the anti-aircraft shells continued to explode all around. Chalky's voice came through the radio.

'How long till the drop zone, Tam? We need to bloody well get out of here.'

'Less than two minutes, Chalky, let the dispatchers know, get them dropped and let's fuck off home.'

I couldn't have put it better myself, thought John.

Before they'd even made it to the drop zone they'd lost another two planes. The Stirling piloted by Flight Lieutenant CFA. Brown had returned home without making the drop. The flight engineer had described the carnage vividly as the remaining crews listened in disbelief. A paratrooper had been dropped above them and they suspected his chute had failed to deploy. The unknown unfortunate had smashed into the Stirling at over a hundred miles an hour. His broken body had ripped a ten-foot gaping hole in the fuselage above the bomb bay. The inside of the plane was awash with blood, fragments of bone and body parts. One of the army dispatchers had been injured and lay on the floor of the plane, the other too traumatised to even speak.

Azouz was next to call in; they'd been hit by light flak but were okay, he'd said. They'd carry on to the drop zone and jettison their load.

Flight Sergeant Ronnie Waltrich wasn't so lucky. His Stirling had taken two direct hits. The starboard outer engine had exploded in a ball of flames and ten feet of the port wing had been blown to pieces. It was less than a few seconds before the aircraft spiralled out of control.

'Not many of us left chaps are there?'

It was Mark announcing he'd made his drop and was returning home.

'We're right behind you Warrant Officer,' said Vanrenen. 'Dropping our panniers as we speak.'

The army dispatchers had just pushed out the last of the boxes when the three Focke-Wulf 190s roared into view, cannons blazing in an explosion of tracer fire that ripped into several of the remaining planes.

'Bandit aircraft, bandit aircraft,' went up the shout from Warrant Officer Mark Azouz.

He'd spotted two at first but to his horror another two appeared on the port side. He banked the huge Stirling to starboard in a vain attempt to evade them. Flight Sergeant Bode on the rear gun had seen them too and as they brushed past the plane he rattled off a burst of machine gun fire, catching one of them on the tail. The German pilots had noticed the steady stream of smoke coming from the port outer engine. It was like a red rag to a bull.

The remaining Stirlings had found the cover of cloud but Azouz was having difficulty climbing back up to altitude, his aircraft now functioning on only two engines.

The four Focke-Wulfs regrouped and went in for the kill as they came in from behind him. Mark heard several seconds of machine gun fire as the bullets ripped into every square foot of the plane and then the Focke-Wulfs were past him again. Smoke poured into the cockpit and as he looked to both the port and starboard wings all he could see was a wall of flames on each side. And then the plane went into a dive he couldn't control.

'Bail out men, bail out immediately – we're going down.'

Azouz battled with the controls for no more than thirty

seconds until he knew his mission was impossible. The plane was in an almost vertical dive now as Azouz ran back through to the body of the plane to make sure everyone had bailed out. He screamed above the noise, barely making himself heard. The fuselage was filled with smoke.

'Everyone out, everyone out. Anyone hear me?'

He listened for no more than a couple of seconds and screamed out again. He paused, more than happy that no one called back. His men had made it out of the stricken plane safely and would live to fight another day... everyone that is but his rear gunner, Flight Sergeant Bode, who lay dead in his seat at the back of the plane.

Azouz ran for his chute as he coughed and spluttered hardly able to see a foot in front of him. He located his chute and strapped it in place as he made his way to the escape hatch. He jumped out with only seconds to spare. Stirling LJ810 ploughed into a flooded field just outside Arnhem.

Azouz was barely fifty feet from the ground when the German infantrymen opened fire. He didn't stand a chance and was killed almost instantly.

Although six successful missions were completed that day, Vanrenen's beloved LJ 949 Stirling was the only plane totally unscathed on its return to RAF Keevil. The surviving crews were in a daze as they climbed from their respective aircraft and made the short journey across the tarmac and into the mess hall. John walked with George Tickner.

'What's gone wrong, George? They said it would be over in three or four days. I swear the Nazis are getting stronger day by day.'

George hung an arm around John's shoulder and pulled him tight into him.

'I wish I knew Sherlock, my boy, I wish I knew.'

John was exhausted but still sleep wouldn't come. It was simply a nightmare, his worst possible nightmare as his good friends were being wiped out by the day. They'd been led to believe it was all but over. As far as he was concerned it was a disaster, an unmitigated disaster.

Initially, for the first few days, it seemed the Allied operation had been successful and several bridges between Eindhoven and Nijmegen were captured. But the ground forces advance was soon halted when the German forces blew up a strategic bridge over the Wilhelmina Canal at Son. This meant the Allied troops were unable to advance and failed to secure the main bridge over the Meuse in those first few crucial days.

At Arnhem, the British 1st Airborne Division were pinned down by far greater resistance than at first had been anticipated. They managed to hold one end of the Arnhem road bridge but were relying on immediate support to bolster their numbers and this did not happen. The small force of men were overrun on 21st September.

By the end of the battle the 1st Airborne division had lost three quarters of its strength.

The thoroughly exhausted men of 196 Squadron were allowed a day off on the 22nd September. They ventured no further than the Sergeants' Mess and shared a few beers. John Holmes bid goodnight to his friends at around eleven o'clock and climbed wearily into bed. He enjoyed his first night of uninterrupted sleep for six days and slept for fourteen hours. It was George Tickner who woke him just after one the following day.

'I've had Patch out, Sherlock, and he's had his sausages and toast so don't you be worrying about him.'

Sausages and toast, that sounded good. John hadn't eaten properly in days. Suddenly he was ravenous.

Tickner spoke.

'Looks like we're up again today mate.' He looked at his watch. 'There's a briefing in just under an hour. If you're quick you've time to get a bite to eat.'

John rubbed at his eyes as they slowly became accustomed to daylight.

'Thanks mate, I will… thanks.'

Vanrenen's crew had been stood down, a rare day off for Sherlock and his crew. Vanrenen had still ordered them to the briefing.

'Just in case,' he'd said.

The rest of the squadron were flying back to Arnhem, the sixth drop. Vanrenen's Stirling had been assigned to another crew.

Vanrenen caught up with Pilot Officer Sparks outside. 'Just you make sure you look after her, Flying Officer, and bring her back in one piece, that's all I'm saying.'

John pointed to Vanrenen as he walked out of the briefing with Len Jones.

'What's all that about, Jonesy?'

Len drew on a cigarette and blew a long plume of smoke into the air. 'Oh that… it's Vanrenen, he's not too happy that Sparky has been assigned to his favourite toy.'

'What? He's taking LJ 949?'

'Yep…. Van the man's little baby.'

John Holmes let out a sigh.

'Yeah he likes that plane, no doubt about that.'

13 aircraft took off for Arnhem on 23rd September 1944. There was only one casualty… aircraft LJ 949, which crash landed at Leende, 12 km southeast of Eindhoven. The Stirling broke in two on impact with the ground. The pilot and wireless operator were slightly injured and treated in a military hospital

early that morning. Within 24 hours they were back on base at RAF Keevil.

Vanrenen caught up with Sparks at lunchtime the following day.

Pilot Officer Sparks was a little sore. He'd suffered concussion, required 22 stitches in a head wound and had a fractured wrist. He could have been forgiven for thinking Vanrenen wanted to congratulate him for his bravery, welcoming him back safe and well to RAF Keevil. Not so.

'What the fucking hell have you done with my aircraft, Sparks? I hear it's in a ditch near Eindhoven.'

'But Sir, I…'

'I warned you, Pilot Officer, take care of her I said, but oh no you had to play the hot shot pilot.'

'But Sir, I was shot at, I couldn't…'

'You flew in too close, Pilot Officer, you took her too near those bastards' guns.'

'But Sir, I was at fifteen…'

'Stop making bloody excuses, Sparks, she was the best bloody plane in the squadron and you didn't take care of her.'

John and the rest of the crew looked on in amazement as Vanrenen tore into the stunned pilot. The verbal assault lasted two or three minutes before Vanrenen looked up and realised the entire mess hall were listening in. He looked around a little sheepish then turned to Sparks.

'How's the head?'

'Err… fine, Sir.'

'And the arm?'

'Good, Sir.'

'Excellent, glad to hear it.'

Vanrenen placed a hand on the pilot officer's shoulder. He leant down and whispered in his ear.

'Just don't be going anywhere near any of my fucking planes again, is that clear?'

Pilot Officer Sparks nodded, more in amazement than by way of an apology. As Vanrenen left, John and Reg walked over and pulled up a seat. The half-eaten piece of bacon dangling from Sparks's fork hung suspended in mid-air, his mouth wide open. He placed the fork onto his plate. Suddenly his appetite had diminished.

John spoke. 'Don't let him get to you, Sir, we have to put up with him all the time.'

Reg was laughing.

'That's Vanrenen, Sir, bit of a pussycat when you get to know him.

The last Arnhem drop took place the following day. Only three aircraft were detailed to make the trip into Holland. One of the planes encountered engine trouble on the runway and failed to take off. The Stirling piloted by Flying Officer Stainer returned to base because of poor visibility at the drop zone. The aircraft piloted by Flight Sergeant Draper crashed into high ground, killing three of the crew. The injured were brought back to England in a Dakota several days later.

For 196 Squadron the ill-fated and badly planned Arnhem assault had at last come to an end. It had cost them dearly.

Incredibly the man responsible for the planning and execution of the exercise, General Montgomery, claimed it had been 90 per cent successful.

He said 'In years to come it will be a great thing for a man to be able to say: "I fought at Arnhem".'

And yet uncharacteristically he owned up to the error of his ways whilst at the same time blaming outside elements. He blamed the Americans and the Canadians and ultimately the Poles who he largely ignored.

'It was a bad mistake on my part – I underestimated the difficulties of opening up the approaches to Antwerp... I reckoned the Canadian Army could do it while we were going for the Ruhr. I was wrong. In my prejudiced view, if the operation had been properly backed from its inception, and given the aircraft, ground forces, and administrative resources necessary for the job, it would have succeeded in spite of my mistakes, or the adverse weather, or the presence of the 2nd SS Panzer Corps in the Arnhem area.'

It was an incredible statement. *Given the aircraft*, he had said. Montgomery *had* been given the aircraft... thousands of them. The RAF alone had lost over 750 pilots and air crew. It had been the biggest airborne assault in military history, a fact that was not lost on the surviving crew members of 196 Squadron based at RAF Keevil.

CHAPTER EIGHTEEN

The operations flown by 196 Squadron continued through until Christmas 1944, though not on the same scale or frequency as the assault on Arnhem. They flew a few secretive missions with the SAS, dropping the crack troops into Norway and behind enemy lines in Germany, and continued dropping supplies to the freedom fighters of Scandinavia, Belgium and France as well as supplying the Allied troops pushing the Nazis ever further backwards into Germany.

When John Holmes came into contact with the SAS men and heard about their role in operations, he realised the sheer scale of the risk they undertook on every mission. It was one thing flying a Stirling under anti-aircraft fire; quite another step up the risk ladder parachuting out of the plane in pitch blackness into terrain swarming with Nazis.

On one mission into Bergen, Norway, he sat alongside Sergeant Don Baker from the 1st Special Air Service, a quiet unassuming man who told him a little about the mission they were undertaking.

'In a nutshell, Flight Engineer, we wreak havoc down there. Intelligence on the ground tells us there are at least a dozen German destroyers based in port. Our job is simply to send them to the bottom of the sea and then make our way back home.'

The briefings continued almost daily, the RAF only too keen to keep the air crews posted as to the progress of the war. There was a cheer from the assembled men when Wing Commander Baker announced the British Home Guard had been stood down, giving an indication just how toothless the German military machine had become. As Christmas Day drew ever nearer the Wing Commander announced that the Battle of the Bulge had commenced. He said it was unlikely that 196 Squadron would be called upon to assist the Allied troops in the Ardennes Region.

John and the rest of the men had one thought in their heads and one thought only. Would they be getting some Christmas leave? It had seemed like months since John had returned home to Lancaster and if 196 Squadron weren't needed for this latest offensive then surely they would be given a little time off.

He could almost see his mother's Christmas dinner, the goose and the smell of the fat and roast potatoes. Then he remembered he was married.

Wing Commander Baker's voice droned on but the words were lost on him as he tried to solve the riddle of where to spend Christmas Day. Surely Dorothy would understand; after all she was home all year round. No, that was final, he'd put his foot down if necessary. What could be better, his Mum, Dad, wife and son all at home together under one roof?

Then Wing Commander Baker dropped the bombshell.

'I'm afraid there'll be no Christmas leave, chaps.'

'What?' John sat up in shock, surely he'd got it wrong.

'Group Command instructions, I'm afraid. Apparently the chaps want you boys on standby.'

Half a dozen men raised their hands for permission to speak. Wing Commander Baker was expecting the reaction. He pointed to George.

'Yes, Tickner.'

'Sir,' he looked around his friends and colleagues nervously hopeful of a little support. 'That doesn't make sense, we can still be on standby back home and most of us can be back down here in a few hours, a day at the most.'

Len Jones spoke up. 'That's right, Sir, we Canadians and the Yanks and Aussies don't expect to be allowed home for Christmas but surely the home based boys can get a few days away? We can keep things ticking over here.'

More hands started to rise, more murmurs of discontent.

Wing Commander Baker held up his hands, he'd prepared for the moment, written down the words earlier in the day and memorised them well.

'Gentlemen, our job is not to question. I understand and sympathise with you but we are in this together and we are sacrificing just one Christmas Day so that we can be free for the rest of our days. I promise you this will be our last festive season fighting the Hun. We have him on the hook but he mustn't wriggle off and sneak under a rock to fight another day. We are talking a matter of weeks, a few months at the most and victory will be assured.'

Wing Commander Baker spoke with passion, he spoke with sincerity. Wing Commander Baker was a respected member of the team, a great pilot and his men warmed to the delivery of his speech. He spoke for no more than three minutes as the tears welled up in his eyes. He spoke of pride and of sacrifice and of absent friends and he spoke about the best bloody squadron in the Royal Air Force. When he finished there were no further questions.

Christmas dinner was held in the Officers' Mess, a three-course meal with as much beer as the squadron could drink. John couldn't quite understand the logic. They were supposed to be on standby and yet there was no way they could have taken an aircraft up at the end of the afternoon. John walked off his lunch wandering around the airfield with Patch and returned to the billet and composed a Christmas Day letter to Dorothy. He hoped that she'd had a nice time and remembered Wing Commander Baker's words as he promised he'd be home next Christmas to spend the day with her and John William.

They didn't fly on Boxing Day, or the day after. A lot of the men were angry and claimed they could have been home after all.

It was 28th December before they flew again and as they taxied along the runway Len Jones quipped that he could have quite comfortably been to Canada and back for Christmas. To rub salt in the wounds it wasn't a sortie to anywhere of any significance, just a simple cross country air test the RAF had insisted upon.

Sherlock's crew towed a Horsa Glider on another training exercise four days later. Vanrenen was livid as he fumed from the cockpit.

'Fucking training exercises, don't they know how many times we've flown in these bloody things? We don't need any bloody training or any bloody practise – I could fly one of these things with my bloody eyes shut.'

Reg Tammas turned to John. 'I don't often agree with the moaning bugger, Sherlock, but he has got a point.'

John agreed, Doug and Chalky agreed, as did Len and the

rest of the entire crew. They hadn't been given a single days leave over Christmas and the New Year and yet hadn't flown a single mission. Feelings were running high. If the war was nearing an end then why couldn't they help finish it? They had the planes, the men and the equipment surely they could help in some way.

On January 17th they were granted leave. Twenty days. It was no use crying over spilt milk. John would put the disappointment of Christmas behind him and do something really special. Why not have a Christmas Day in January, January 25th, only a month late? Why not indeed?

The manager of the Greaves Hotel thought the request a little unusual but nevertheless was happy to comply with John's wishes. Christmas dinner for 20 on January 25th. The Shaw family and the Holmes family, Len Jones, a few selected friends and Patch. John was in his element as he settled the bill at the bar and looked on at the slightly inebriated throng of people. They were all there, the people he loved and of course his son who he held on his hip as he handed the manager a five shilling tip.

'It was fantastic Walter, absolutely beautiful, couldn't have been any better. Get the girls a drink out of that.'

Walter Higgins, the manager of the Greaves Hotel basked in the approval.

'You've really pushed the boat out today young John, done your family proud.'

John stood with Jack Shaw, Dorothy's brother. John hadn't had a lot to do with Jack in the past and could only ever recall meeting him once before but the longer they stood together the longer he took to him. Coincidently Jack was on leave too and enjoying the Christmas festivities courtesy of his brother in law.

Jack placed a small tin on the bar top and opened it. To John's amazement he placed a smattering of the black powder on the back of his hand, brought it carefully up to his nose and sniffed hard.

His eyes glazed over and his skin seemed to redden.

'Lovely stuff,' he said as he looked back at John.

'What is it Jack?'

'Snuff. Do you want to try a bit?'

John shook his head.

'No thanks pal.' He raised his pint glass. 'I've everything I need right here in this glass.'

John took a mouthful of beer as his father walked over to join him.

'It's my Christmas Day, Walter, and I wanted to spend it with my family and friends. This was the only place big enough to sit everyone.'

'Quite,' said Walter as he turned and walked through to the kitchen.

William Holmes spoke. 'John, here son, let me split that bill with you – it must have cost you an arm and a leg.'

John wrapped his hand around his father's wallet and forced it back into his pocket.

'Put it away Dad, I really want to do this, I really do… it's my treat.'

William's eyes were welling up as he reached and stroked his hand.

'You're a good lad John, a good lad. Did I ever tell you how proud I am of you?'

John grinned. 'Yes, Dad, every time I'm home on leave.'

William was a little taken aback but smiled as he realised his son was probably telling the truth. He was immensely proud of him, and he told him every day right up until his leave was over.

The letter arrived the day before his leave was due to expire. It advised him to report to RAF Shepherds Grove.

196 Squadron had been relocated.

'Shepherds Grove,' he mumbled to himself. 'Where the hell is Shepherds Grove?'

Shepherds Grove was in Suffolk. The old familiar faces were there when he arrived. The two Georges, Humphreys and Tickner, Vanrenen, his crew, and even Wing Commander Baker. They re-commenced training the following day.

It was a familiar voice and a familiar cry reverberating around the aircraft radio. Vanrenen was cursing and swearing about how they could never win the war if all they ever did was bloody train. But train they did for the rest of the month and for the first ten days in February.

At the briefing room on the 12th of February Wing Commander Baker stood alongside a map of Germany with a large red circle drawn round the town of Isselberg. He was grinning like a Cheshire cat as he waited for the men to take their seats.

Reg spoke. 'What's making you so happy, Wing Commander, is the war over?'

Wing Commander Baker acknowledged the navigator and spoke. He delivered a line that stunned the whole room.

'Not quite, Sergeant… we're going bombing.'

The ground crew prepared the Stirlings the following day, refitting and fine-tuning the fuselage and the bomb bay doors. They packed each Stirling with eighteen 500lb bombs and the Squadron of Stirlings flew out for the five hour round trips. They were to drop the bombs from 7,000 feet, there would be no anti-aircraft guns and the Messerschmitts of the Luftwaffe had been all but wiped out.

Vanrenen commented on the sheer weight in the Stirling as he pulled it off the runway, informing Doug Handley that at last he'd be doing the job he was trained for. Isselberg was in Northern Germany just a few miles east of the Dutch border.

Three German Panzer divisions had dug in and were pinning the Allies back. The instructions were simple, the Allies had retreated a few miles back and four Squadrons of Allied aircraft would drop a huge tonnage of bombs inflicting as many casualties as possible and taking out as much military hardware as they possibly could. It was the easiest mission Vanrenen's crew had ever flown.

Doug dropped the bombs at the required height and the crew watched the ground until they exploded below. Isselberg seemed to erupt into a volcano of flames as the bombs from the other crews also hit home.

'Mission accomplished, Skip,' Handley called out from the front bomb aimer turret. 'Target located and hit.'

A few minutes later he appeared grinning.

'Fucking hell, lads, we drew the short straws when they converted our Stirlings, didn't we? That was the easiest run yet.'

Vanrenen radioed the other Stirlings in the formation and they turned for home. The rest of the planes called in; no casualties, no direct hits, all bombs offloaded. A 100 per cent success story.

John took an early breakfast with George Tickner and George Humphreys. Eventually it was Tickner who breathed the words everyone was thinking.

'I wonder how many lads would still be here if we'd just bombed from the outset.'

John recalled Vanrenen's words all those months ago.

Oh we'll be in the thick of the action, don't you worry about that.

196 Squadron had drawn the short straw, there was no doubt about it.

They set out on a bombing raid from Shepherds Grove on 21st February 1945. Six aircraft were flying in formation at around 8,000 feet, the group led by Wing Commander Baker. It was a pleasant evening as they crossed the channel and headed for the French coast but thirty miles over France they ran into thick cloud. It lasted for nearly thirty miles and Wing Commander Baker gave the other pilots instructions to spread their formation out. When they eventually broke through the cumulus Wing Commander Baker's plane was missing. Chuck took over as Squadron leader and one by one the other aircraft found each other. Despite constant efforts to call in Wing Commander Baker's Stirling, he could not be located. The rest of the squadron completed a successful operation. Wing Commander Baker's aircraft did not return home.

John bumped into George on 25th February as he walked Patch across the airfield just before breakfast.

'Okay Sir, what are you up to?'

George walked with his hands in his pockets as if he didn't have a care in the world.

'Back out to Norway, Sherlock, a little later on today. Are you chaps up tonight?'

John shook his head.

'No Sir, night off tonight, I think I'll wander into Trowbridge with some of the boys.'

The two men walked for some time. It was a cold, crisp morning with a hard covering of ground frost and the two men blew into their hands as their breath filled the air around them like fine smoke. They talked about home and how the end of the war was in sight. George said he looked forward to getting back home to Australia, John said there couldn't be many missions left.

'We're bombing Berlin on a regular basis now,' said George. 'Started on Dresden a few days ago I'm told, and Belgium is completely clear of the Nazis thank God.'

'They're on the run, Sir, no doubt about it.'

'Keep this to yourself Sherlock, but 9,000 planes are on their way to Germany tonight, I've a good friend up on a base in Hertfordshire who told me a couple of days ago. Says he's never seen so many bombers in one place.'

John Holmes whistled. 'My God, 9,000 you say?'

George nodded. 'And we're heading in the opposite bloody direction.'

Tickner turned to face John and shrugged his shoulders.

'Still… they know best I suppose, we're dropping a section of SAS lads just south of Stavanger. They're meeting up with the Norwegian resistance. Should be an easy enough mission and with a little bit of luck I can get back home to some bloody decent weather.'

Pilot Officer Russell George Tickner took off from RAF Shepherds Grove just after midnight on 25th February 1945. They flew northwards skirting the English coast past Newcastle upon Tyne and up towards Edinburgh. George Humphrey pinpointed RAF Lossiemouth on the flight charts right on the north coast of Scotland and wondered if they couldn't have sent a plane from a base much closer. Lossiemouth was almost on the same latitude as Stavanger. He looked at his watch. They'd been flying for an hour and forty minutes. They turned east as they approached Aberdeen and headed out into the unforgiving environment of the North Sea. The navigator called out the instructions to Tickner as he studied the coordinates on his map.

As the Stirling approached Stavanger the SAS section prepared the parachutes and checked the panniers and boxes that they would be taking with them. George Tickner looked out of the port side of the aircraft.

'Big lake down there, navigator – is that the one we are looking for?'

'Yes sir, that's it. Holen Lake, the Norwegian chaps are waiting on the south bank.'

Tickner reduced the altitude of the plane as he banked round.

'SAS boys ready?'

Thirty seconds later the panniers and boxes and six bodies of the section of the 1st Battalion SAS dropped out into the freezing cold Norwegian night air. The Germans were waiting. A small craft in the North Sea, five miles from Stavanger had reported seeing the plane approaching German occupied land. The section of German artillery concentrated on the easy target, a low flying RAF Stirling bomber. Tickner's aircraft took a direct hit in the mid-section of the fuselage. Almost immediately the aircraft was out of control and a fire broke out on board. As George battled with the controls in vain he gave the orders for the crew to bail out. Tickner fought as the Stirling went into a dive.

'Get out now,' he screamed into the radio as he realised there was no hope.

Everything happened so quickly, there was no time to locate his chute let alone strap it on and escape. His only thought was the survival of his crew as he continued to bellow into the radio.

'Going down, mayday, get out, get out.'

Three men managed to escape from the aircraft before it plunged into the frozen lake. The ice was over a foot thick and it ripped the Stirling and the men inside apart.

George Tickner, George Humphrey and John Stevenson were killed instantly. Flight Sergeant Mann and Flying Officer Caldwell made it safely to the ground and were captured by the Germans. Flight Sergeant Quirk, although badly injured was rescued by the Norwegian resistance and hidden in a house in the nearby village of Arendal.

The notice was posted at lunchtime outside the Officers Mess at Shepherds Grove. John stood with Reg. The wording was brief and to the point 'LJ925 Target Stirrup. Pilot RG Tickner 5954N O757E – Aircraft and crew missing.' John looked at his watch.

'Should have been back before six this morning, Reg.'

Reg, for once, was lost for words as he turned and walked away.

Vanrenen and his crew continued to train throughout the month of March 1945. The news in the briefings was good; all good and 196 Squadron had been warned they were to prepare for the 'final push'.

Germany was under attack from all sides, Wing Commander Turner had told them, and US and British forces had crossed the Rhine at Oppenheim. More divisions led by Montgomery had crossed the river at Wessel.

Wing Commander Turner read out the list of thirty Stirlings who would fly into Wessel to drop troops and supplies.

'Forget Arnhem,' he said. 'This is the big one, this exercise will be bigger and better than anything you have ever flown before.'

'Chaps.' He looked slowly around the room as he positioned himself on the desk. 'The Red Army is closing in on Berlin from the east and there's hardly a single plane of the Luftwaffe left in the sky. We've bombed the hell out of Wessel for the last two nights and we are ready to crush them. If we take Wessel, Dortmund and Dusseldorf will be next.'

Wing Commander Turner paused and spoke to his captive audience.

'Gentlemen… your work is nearly done. Before you know it you will be back home with your families.'

John spoke to Vanrenen as they strolled across the grass towards LJ 979.

'Do you think he's right, Skipper, do you think we're nearing the end?'

'Best not think too much about that, Flight Engineer. Just get on with the job in hand and keep your concentration. Remember, an animal is at its most dangerous when he's wounded and cornered. That's where the Bosch are at the moment… in a corner. I suspect they still have a bite or two left in them.'

They flew at first light on 24th March. As the planes flew towards the English Channel John looked out of the window. It was an incredible sight watching the hundreds of Stirlings towing fully laden Horsa Gliders. Reg stood alongside him.

'Haven't flown in daylight for a long time Sherlock, have we? You forget how gorgeous this bird looks in the sky.'

It was true. John Holmes felt the same way. There was something elegant about the Stirling aircraft especially today on such a beautiful morning against the backdrop of a glistening North Sea. On the shore he could just about make out the white waves breaking as they caressed the sand below.

In less than an hour they'd reached the Dutch coast just south of Rotterdam. It all looked calm and quiet and perhaps the Wing Commander had been right because not one Luftwaffe aircraft had been seen during the entire flight.

Tammas was studying the map and kept standing up taking a look at the terrain below.

John spoke.

'Must be an easy one today Tam, flying in broad daylight?'

The navigator nodded. 'Piece of cake today mate, I'm enjoying myself to be honest, I've never been so relaxed in my life.' He stood and pointed out of the front window. 'That's Wessel over there in the distance, we're about fifteen minutes away I think.'

The area was surrounded in what looked like a thick fog. As they got nearer John realised what it was. A shiver ran the length of his spine. It wasn't fog, it was smoke, and he could just about make out the flames from the dozens of buildings that were on fire.

Reg was clarifying the drop instructions with the commander of the paratroopers. They'd get them as near to Wessel as possible, about five miles over the Rhine. The Allied troops would amass during the day and attack the city at night fall. The flames were clearly visible now as Vanrenen brought the aircraft down to less than 2,000 feet.

'Less than a minute, chaps,' he said, 'best of luck.'

The Stirling surged forward as the tow ropes released and Vanrenen immediately increased the height of the aircraft on full throttle. The Stirling climbed slowly towards cloud level and then the anti-aircraft fire started. Small fluffy white clouds burst all around them and after each little puff of smoke a deafening explosion. The aircraft shuddered and shook; the Germans had found their range almost instantly.

'Holy shit,' said Tammas, 'I thought the city was quiet, where did these bastards come from?'

A shell exploded no more than twenty feet from the starboard wing and a horrible grinding and clunking noise reverberated through the plane as a huge piece of shrapnel flew into the outer engine.

The Germans had locked on to Stirling LJ 979, largely ignoring the others who by now were above the clouds and out of sight. The Stirling almost groaned as Vanrenen asked for more power. John watched the needle on the altimeter as it slowly dropped and still the shells exploded ever louder. John Chalk stood up and walked over to stand just behind the two pilots seats where he had a bird's eye view of everything happening down below.

John Holmes feathered the engine on the starboard side just as the flames started behind the engine housing. The plane shook again. A squeal rang through the aircraft. They'd taken a direct hit.

'Who is it? 'screamed Vanrenen. 'Who's hit?'

John looked around in horror as John Chalk lay on the floor of the aircraft in a pool of blood. He leapt through to the front of the plane.

'Chalky, Chalky speak to me!'

Chalky was conscious, cursing the Nazi bastards. It was a good sign, thought John.

'It's Chalky, Sir,' he called out to Vanrenen, 'there's a hole in the bottom of the fuselage a yard wide.'

John Chalk grimaced.

'Aye Sherlock, and a right bloody hole in my arse as well. Get something to pack it will you?'

John turned the wireless operator over and reached for the first aid box. John Chalk did indeed have a hole in his backside the size of a tennis ball. A piece of shell had ripped through the bottom of the aircraft directly behind the pilot's seat and embedded itself in his flesh. He'd picked the worst spot in the plane. The metal casing was still in there smouldering red hot, and the stinking smell of burning flesh and blood filled John's nostrils.

'You've a hole in your arse alright Chalky, two if memory serves me right, but there's a bit of a German shell in there too and I'll need to get it out.'

John Chalk nodded.

'I thought I felt something Sherlock, get it out, there's a good fella, but be gentle will you.'

Another explosion rocked the plane.

John Holmes had already taken a hold of the jagged piece of metal as he felt it beginning to burn into his hand. He gripped it harder than he would have wanted and pulled.

John Chalk screamed as the pain registered.

'You fucking Northern bastard…' He breathed hard and broke out into a sweat. 'That wasn't very gentle.'

'Better out than in you big, soft southerner, now lie back and think of England while I patch you up.'

Reg crawled over and knelt down beside them.

'You'd better get back to your seat mate, I don't know what's going on with the needles on your control panel but they don't look very clever to me. They're spinning around like buggery.'

John didn't need to check the needles on the instrument panel. The sound of the Stirling was enough. The Queen of the Skies was in distress and crying out for mercy.

Vanrenen shouted from the front of the plane.

'Diagnosis, Flight Engineer, can I keep her in the air or not?'

John took a few seconds to assess the damage.

'In one word Skipper, I'm pretty sure that our beloved lady is fucked.'

Vanrenen made the decision in less than a second. Not that he would ever tell him but his flight engineer's judgement was flawless… gospel.

'Bail out then, bail out men, I can't keep her up much longer.'

Smoke now poured through the fuselage as the plane lost even more height.

'Come on men, bail out, didn't you hear me?'

The Stirling was almost gliding, the power from three engines snuffed out and the fourth engine spluttering, a clear indication that the fuel pipe was damaged in some way. Len Jones had made his way from the rear gun and held John Chalk's head.

'We can't bail out, Sherlock. We can't leave Chalky.'

John grinned. 'My sentiments exactly, mate. I'm going to see Vanrenen.'

John jumped into the seat next to Vanrenen.

'What the hell are you doing here, Flight Engineer? I told you to bail out.'

John shook his head.

'We're going nowhere Skipper, we have two injured crewmen that won't make it and we're going nowhere without them. You'd better get this little lady on the ground and hope it's the Dutch side of the border we land on.'

'Two injured, Flight Engineer, who else is hurt?

John looked at the pool of blood on Vanrenen's seat.

'You are, sir.'

Vanrenen nodded slowly. 'You noticed.'

'I couldn't miss it Skip, it looks like you're sitting in a bowl of tomato soup.'

Vanrenen pointed to a gaping hole in the floor just below him.

'They're getting quite accurate, the bloody Huns. A bit of shrapnel I suspect.'

'Skipper, can you get her down in one piece?'

Vanrenen was already scouring the terrain as he battled with the controls.

'I don't know Sherlock, I don't know. Two pieces perhaps, maybe three.'

He looked at John Holmes and grinned.

'One piece? Highly unlikely, Sherlock, highly unlikely.'

Vanrenen had taken John by surprise. He'd never used that name before. It was always Flight Engineer or Sergeant, never John and certainly never ever the nickname that his crew used on a regular basis.

The Stirling was vibrating now and Vanrenen's white-knuckled hands were a blur on the wheel. The whole aircraft shook and John expected it to break apart at any minute. The ground was getting closer but miraculously Vanrenen was managing to keep the aircraft level.

'Fucking hell,' Vanrenen cried out, 'stay with me darling, stay with me, don't give up now.'

The nose of the aircraft dipped slightly, Vanrenen cursed and swore.

'We're not going to make it Sherlock; the bitch is fighting me every inch of the way.'

John couldn't quite describe the feeling that washed over him. They were no more than 250 feet from the ground but suddenly John knew they were going to make it. From a mild panic and a feeling of impending doom it was as if someone had flicked a switch. The ground was close now, he could see the branches of the trees, even the pine cones, the freshly ploughed fields and it was approaching a lot quicker than he wanted it to…but he knew.

'We're not going to make it, Sherlock, we're buggered.'

'Skipper.'

'Flight Engineer.'

'We are going to make it.'

Vanrenen's veins were standing out on his neck, the Stirling was almost screaming, crying out 'no more, no more'.

'What makes you so certain, Flight Engineer?'

John Holmes strapped himself into the seat and prepared for the impact.

'Because we've got the best bloody pilot on the planet flying our plane. That's why.'

Vanrenen glanced across to his right for a split second. John was calm, almost laid back. He flicked a smile.

'I certainly hope so, Sherlock… I bloody well hope so.'

They hit the ground a lot harder than John would have liked. The glass in the cockpit shattered on impact and bits of debris and soil flew into the plane, stinging and cutting into his flesh.

Vanrenen had put her down in a field of turnips and they ploughed a 200-yard road into the farmer's field before coming to a stop. The aircraft was full of smoke and it was difficult to see.

'Out, out, out. She's going to blow.'

The smell of aircraft fuel was almost overpowering as John helped Vanrenen from his seat. There was no need to locate an escape hatch. There were at least a dozen holes in the plane big enough for a man to crawl through.

'Over there Skip, get behind that wall.' John pointed across the field through a gap in the plane. 'I'll get Chalky and check on the others.'

Reg and Len had John Chalk draped across their shoulders and Doug followed behind.

'Bloody hell, we've made it, Sherlock,' Handley called out as the familiar shape of their Flight Engineer appeared like a ghostly apparition through the smoke filled plane.

'Let's just get out of here before we start jumping to

conclusions,' John said. 'I think the old girl is going to go up any minute.'

They were battered and bruised, John Chalk and Vanrenen more so than the others, but they had indeed made it and they cowered behind the dry stone wall waiting for the Stirling to explode.

'It's not going to explode,' Vanrenen announced. 'I switched everything off as we hit the ground, there's no electrics, no sparks to kick things off.'

'Well I'll be buggered,' John whispered to himself.

The crew of LJ 979 took stock of the predicament they were in.

'Where are we, navigator?' Vanrenen asked as he looked at Reg.

'In a field, Sir, a fucking muddy one at that.'

'That's not what I asked Tammas, I mean *where are we*? Are we in Germany or Holland? It could make quite a difference to our survival prospects. Are we on the German side of the Rhine or the Dutch?'

Reg Tammas hadn't even thought about where it was they'd crash landed. He remembered being a mile or two from Wessel as the aircraft was hit but was down in the hold of the plane attending to John Chalk soon after. He didn't answer. Reg just shrugged his shoulders.

Vanrenen drew his service revolver.

'Okay men, we have to assume we're on the enemy side of the fence. Let's get ready, we're going to fight these bastards to the last man.'

John looked at Len and then to Reg. Even John Chalk, who was on the verge of unconsciousness, almost telepathically gave his support to John as did Doug. John gauged their reaction and spoke. He spoke on behalf of the entire crew.

'Look Henry... man to man so to speak. We like you, we've

always liked you, even though we've neglected to tell you from time to time. In fact I'll go one step further and tell you that we love you and wouldn't swap you for all the gold reserves in the world. We consider ourselves the luckiest bastards in the RAF to have a fellow like you to fly us around and look after us.' He looked at the rest of the crew who nodded their approval.

'You're the best Henry... the best, you really are. No doubt about it.'

Vanrenen looked over the top of the wall and then back to his crew.

'But if you think we're all going to die in a shoot-out with the Bosch in the last couple of weeks of the war then you've got another thing coming.'

'Well said, Sherlock,' said Reg.

Vanrenen looked around at his crew. The best bloody crew he'd ever flown with. Sherlock was right. They had to trust what military intelligence was telling them; the war was drawing to a close.

'We're going to surrender, Henry. If the Germans come running across that field in ten minutes we're going to put our hands up and say you might have won this little scrap but you haven't won the war and if necessary we're going to sit out the rest of this insanity for a couple of months.'

John Chalk could barely keep his eyes open but he was nodding. Reg and Handley and Jones were nodding too. Even Vanrenen was nodding as he slipped his service revolver into his pocket and placed his hand on John Holmes's shoulder. Vanrenen wanted to tell him he was right, wanted to tell him what a first class Flight Engineer he was... the best. He wanted to say what a leader of men he was and even though he was still the baby of the squadron he commanded a presence and respect among his crew like no other member of the team. My

God, Vanrenen thought, even that stupid dog looks up at John Holmes as if he were the most important person in the world. He wanted to tell him all of this and more… he wanted to say the same to every member of his team. And yet something stopped him.

They'd sneaked up on the crew of Stirling LJ 979. No more than ten of them but as Vanrenen and his men listened to the reasoning of John 'Sherlock' Holmes they crept up, rifles in hand towards the wall one kilometre outside the village of Overloon just inside the Dutch border.

They were exhausted, wounded and in no mood to fight. Vanrenen and his crew heard the click of the rifles as the weapons were cocked and pointed over the wall at them. They raised their hands in surrender, resigned to their fate.

The Dutchman spotted the insignia of the RAF and broke out into a broad smile.

'My friends,' he repeated in broken English again and again. 'My dear brothers, our heroes… our saviour, we saw you come down, we are here to rescue you.'

The rest of the ramshackle band of farmers, shop keepers and builders embraced the crew of LJ 979. Soon after a truck full of British troops pulled up with two doctors on board and they treated the wounds of Vanrenen and John Chalk on the spot. They said the rest of the crew would be driven the short distance to Overloon but Vanrenen and Chalk were off to a field hospital on stretchers.

John helped two medics with Vanrenen's stretcher as they lifted it onto the truck. John jumped up and cleared a space so that the medics could position the stretcher. As they eased Vanrenen into the spot John walked to the back of the truck, preparing to jump down.

Vanrenen caught his sleeve as he passed. John stopped and

looked back at his pilot. He was pale and dirty his face encrusted with Dutch soil and his eyes welled up with tears as he spoke quietly.

'Sherlock.'

'Skipper.'

He gripped John's arm through his sleeve.

'… I… just wanted to say…'

'Sir.'

'When we get back, Sherlock…'

'Yes, Sir?'

'Would you…would you do me the honour of sharing a pint with me one evening in one of those little rancid English public houses?'

John smiled. 'I will, Skip, I will.'

Vanrenen lay his head on the pillow and sighed. He closed his eyes.

'I'd like that Sherlock… I'd like it a lot.'

John and the rest of the crew were taken to the town of Overloon where they were treated like the heroes and liberators that they were.

Despite the rations and food shortages the villagers had endured over the years they laid on a feast like nothing Sherlock and his boys had ever seen before. They plied every crew member with copious amounts of strong Dutch beer.

Towards the end of the evening the villagers introduced a dozen young Dutch girls no more than eighteen years old.

'They are here to dance with you and to make you merry,' the Dutchman announced with a wicked smile. 'They are very appreciative of everything the British have done for us.'

John Holmes explained that he had everything he needed back home and declined to get involved.

'I'll stick to the beer, Arnold,' he told his host.

Within a week the crew were heading back to England. They were driven to Brussels by car and put on planes back home. They sat in the back of a Dakota.

'Wonder how Van and Chalky are doing?' Len Jones lit up a cigarette and blew the smoke up into the air.

Doug Handley sat alongside him.

'It's kind of weird not being with them in a plane, don't tell them but I kind of miss them, especially Van the Man.'

John sat opposite twiddling his thumbs with no real purpose.

'He's the greatest, Vanrenen, isn't he? That plane was absolutely buggered, they didn't prepare you at training school for situations like that.'

Len Jones raised an eyebrow. 'They didn't?'

'It was buggered, Jonesy, I'm telling you. Every dial on that panel was at zero… nothing was functioning… nothing at all. The fuel pumps were out, the hydraulics were buggered and there wasn't a flap on the whole of the damn plane that was working. I'm not kidding Jonesy, I don't know how he brought it down, I really don't. Stirlings aren't meant to act like Horsa Gliders but that's how he flew it, like a bloody Horsa.'

'We should tell him.'

John recalled his conversation with Vanrenen in the cockpit as the plane dropped to earth. 'I already have Jonesy, don't you worry about that.'

Vanrenen and Jack Chalk spent the rest of the month in the military field hospital and were then flown back to England. They did not meet up with the rest of the crew. In fact, Sherlock's crew never got together again.

John sat on his bed and gazed around the empty room. There were too many empty beds, too many missing friends. He recalled their smiling faces, every one of them, and his thoughts drifted back to the nights they'd enjoyed in Trowbridge, in the mess halls and even just impromptu wanders around the airfield.

John was one of the lucky ones; he was going back home to his family. Tickner, Humphries, Azouz, Baker, Gribble to name a few, were not. And then there was Lofty Matthews.

John gazed over at his empty bed. The tears welled up in his eyes as he pulled the drawstring on his kit bag and he walked towards the door.

Patch cocked his head as his ears pricked up. The dog waited for a signal… a command… anything.

'Come on Patch, it's time to go… you didn't think I'd leave you here alone did you? '

The dog leapt from the bed and ran around in circles at the feet of his master, his tail wagging furiously.

John opened the door and looked out into the night sky. The sun was setting over the countryside; a crimson sheen enveloped the landscape. He picked the dog up and cradled him in his arms. John pointed up to the sky.

'Take one last look, little mate. Sherlock's going to make you a promise.'

The dog's ear pricked up again.

'It's over mate, you'll never have to look up there again, wondering and waiting if I'm coming back. We're going home Patch, just me and you. Now let's get going or we'll miss that last train to Lancaster.'

As they walked away the unmistakeable drone of a lone Stirling could be heard in the distance.

In April 1945 Buchenwald and Bergen-Belsen concentration camps were liberated by the British Army. The Soviets advanced towards the city of Berlin and reached the suburbs. The writing was on the wall for Hitler and his compatriots.

On April 20th, Hitler celebrated his 56th birthday holed up in his bunker in Berlin. Intelligence reports notified him the Russians were advancing ever closer and he knew they would want their revenge for the atrocities his troops had carried out on the eastern front. He was in an unhealthy state. Nervous and depressed.

Hermann Goering was very aware of Hitler's state of mind and was more than a little concerned about his ability to carry out his leadership duties. In the interest of the nation he sent a radiogram to the bunker asking to be declared Hitler's successor. He proclaimed that if he did not receive a response by 10pm, he would assume Hitler was incapacitated and would take over leadership of the Reich.

Hitler was furious.

He stripped Goering of his rank and his offices of power and expelled him from the Nazi Party. At the same time, Himmler, ignoring the orders of Hitler had made a secret surrender offer to the Allies. He had written in one proviso: that the Red Army was not involved.

The offer was rejected.

When Hitler heard of Himmler's betrayal, he ordered him to be shot.

On 29th April, Hitler married his companion Eva Braun. A day later they were dead. They had committed suicide.

Goebbels and his wife killed their six children and then took poison in the same bunker.

In Holland, Germany officially surrendered. Prince Bernhard of the Netherlands accepted the surrender and Denmark was liberated by the Allied troops. Formal negotiations for Germany's surrender started at Rheims in France. Soon after

Germany surrendered unconditionally to the Allies at the Western Allied Headquarters at 2:41 a.m. The ceasefire took effect at one minute past midnight on the 8th May. It was known as VE Day.

POSTSCRIPT

Christmas 1945 was just like old times. John sat with his father and Dot's father in the Greaves Hotel enjoying a pre-Christmas dinner pint. John's brothers Ernie and James, Dot's brothers Norman, Jack & Cliff were there too.

It was a miracle that the two families' sons had made it through the most destructive and devastating war in history.

Cliff had fared the worst, a shadow of his former self. He'd returned less than a month ago weighing just six stone. He was still pale and gaunt… a walking, talking skeleton and even now he just about had the strength to lift up his pint pot. He refused to discuss any details of his long incarceration. But he'd made it… he'd survived.

John stood up.

'I'd like to propose a toast, gentlemen.'

Ernie and James nodded and rose slowly from the table. Norman and John Shaw each took one of Cliff's arms and lifted him slowly to his feet. William Holmes stood too and raised his glass as he looked on proudly at his three sons.

'To the luckiest two families in Lancaster.'

'Cheers.'

'Bravo.'

'Well said, young John.'

He took a long drink of beer and placed his glass on the table.

'And of course… not forgetting absent friends.'

'Absent friends,' the men announced in unison.

BIBLIOGRAPHIES

John Holmes was born in Lancaster, England in 1923. He was the youngest of five children. He left school at 15 and trained as a fitter in a local factory.

John remained in the RAF for a further 18 months after the war, working as a trainer for future crew and finally as a drill instructor. He returned to Civvy Street and back to the same factory job he had had before the war. He continued his passion for swimming by again playing water polo for Lancaster for many years. John and Dorothy continued to live in Belle Vue Terrace with John William, and later Sandra and Stephen until the late 1950s when they bought a greengrocer's and off licence which they ran until the late seventies. John also worked as a milkman. John and Dorothy had two further children in the early 1960s, named Amanda and Mark. Later John became a taxi proprietor until his premature death in 1985 due to a brain tumour at the age of 62. John left behind his wife Dorothy, and their children John William, Sandra, Stephen, Amanda and Mark.

Dorothy Holmes passed away in 1997 followed by Sandra in 2002 and John William in 2010. John William still lived in the property that had been his parents' greengrocers when he died. Stephen now lives on the Costa Blanca in Spain while Amanda and Mark continue to live in the UK.

Henry Poleman Vanrenen was born in Melbourne, Australia, in 1912. After leaving school he returned to Avoca Forest Merino stud to assist his father.

He was awarded the DFC (Distinguished Flying Cross) in 1945. After the war he returned to Avoca Forest, then in 1948, acquired a property in Glenthompson which he called 'Wiltshire' after the county in England where he had flown operations from during the war. On the property he ran Merino sheep and Poll Hereford cattle for 40 years. He was captain of Glenthompson Fire Brigade for 16 years and treasurer of the Glenthompson branch of the Liberal Party for 11 years. Henry had three daughters, Judith, Sandra and Cynthia. Henry passed away in 1988 at the age of 76.

Reginald B. Tammas was born in Norfolk in 1920, the second of four children. His mother died when he was only 14 years old. After the war Reg became a teacher. He and his wife Jean eventually had four daughters, and over the years the family lived in many different places in England, Northern Ireland and South Australia. They lived in Australia for four years but returned to Britain when Jean's father became terminally ill. Back in England, Reg started teaching in schools with children with special needs. After he retired, he and Jean continued to move about, living in Kent, Essex and Northampton, finally settling down in Worcestershire near to where they first met. Jean passed away in 2003, just a few weeks before their 60th wedding anniversary. Reg died suddenly of heart disease in 2006 at the age of 85.

Douglas Handley was born in Wombwell, Barnsley, Yorkshire in 1922. Doug married Maggie, who he met when serving in the war. After the war, Doug and Maggie moved in with her parents in Leicester and started to think about what career he would pursue now he had left the RAF. Although teaching was his first option, he took the advice of Maggie's uncle to sit the Civil Service exam. He passed with flying colours and started his career with the Civil Service in Nottingham. After six years of married life they had two daughters, Stephanie and Lindsey Jane. With each promotion, Doug was relocated. His first move was to Exmouth in Devon where he joined the Ministry of Agriculture, Fisheries and Food. Five years on and Doug was promoted again and moved to Cambridge. After another eight years, promotion came again and he moved to Folkestone. The family moved into a beautiful house on the cliffs overlooking the sea and Doug was once again happy in a coastal environment. During this time Doug purchased an apartment in Calpe, in southern Spain, where the family enjoyed many holidays.

At the age of 62 Doug retired and moved to Spain. Unfortunately in this time Doug suffered two heart attacks but, like the fighter he was, he recovered well.

Doug and Maggie decided to head back to the UK and settled in a big house in Derby. Doug enjoyed walking his two new dogs in the beautiful Derbyshire countryside. Doug enjoyed good health for many years but shocked the family when he died peacefully in his sleep on 3rd September 1999. He had spent the day in his garden, in the sunshine wearing shorts with no sign of ill health and an almost permanent smile etched on his face.

John Leonard Jones was born in Toronto, Ontario, Canada in 1919. Len was the youngest of four children whose parents had moved to Canada in search of a better life. From a young age Len was no stranger to hard work and he always held some sort of job to help with the family expenses. After all, it was the Great Depression.

After the war Len returned to Civvy Street, and his old job awaited him. Although life appeared to be as he left it, much had changed back home. Eventually, he married his wife Margaret Dunn a few years later and following that had two daughters. He enjoyed family life outside of Toronto, namely Scarborough. Post-war, Len joined the Masonic Lodge, eventually attaining the high position of District Deputy Grand Master. He retired from his job of many years in 1984 and spent the next six years travelling with Margaret and enjoying life until, in 1990, he lost his wife and partner of 42 years. Len remained active and enjoying life for the most part until July 2008 when he passed away peacefully in his sleep at the age of 89.

John (Jack) Edward Chalk (Chalky) was born in West Ham, London in 1916. His father, also called John, came from London and his mother, Florence S Le Heup originated from France. None of the surviving family members have ever been traced.

Russell George Tickner was born in Golburn, New South Wales, Australia on 28th July 1920. He was a good sportsman, excelling in cricket and tennis and grew up playing sport in the area of Orange. He enlisted in the RAAF in Sydney on 11 October 1941. He dropped his first name and was always known as George throughout the war years. His younger brother Colin also joined the RAAF but served in Australia during the latter half of the war and for many years after that until his retirement in 1975. It is believed that he was also a member of the air crew, a navigator.

George Tickner married Phyllis Fry in London in 1944. His wife, a corporal in the WRAF, met George at one of the airfields she was stationed at near High Wycombe in Buckinghamshire. George Tickner was shot down and died in Southern Norway on 25th February 1945 in his beloved Stirling Bomber. He had been dropping supplies to the Norwegian resistance fighters in the Arendal area of the country.

George Tickner went down with his plane into Holen Lake in Norway and his remains are still in the bomber wreckage. The site is recognised as an official war graves site and demarcated by buoys. His name is on the Runnymede Memorial, Panel 283.

It is believed an RAF underwater team sent divers down to the bottom of the lake during the late 1980s. They laid a wreath in memory of George Tickner and his crew.

His son, also called Russell was born on 8th July 1945; unfortunately he never knew his father.

Phyllis Tickner died in 2002 in East London, South Africa. She never talked too much about her late husband George, it was too much of a painful memory.

Dennis Alec 'Lofty' Matthews was born in Canada in 1921. He was a member of Warrant Officer Keith Prowd's crew. On 19th September 1944 on a resupply drop to Arnhem, their aircraft EF248 'V Victory' was hit by flak at about 1500 feet, which set the outer starboard engine on fire. Due to more heavy Flak they lost another two engines. Prowd immediately ordered the crew to bail out. Lofty bailed out on one off the panniers and was killed on the way down.

Lofty Matthews is buried in the Arnhem Oosterbeek War Cemetery, Netherlands.

Keith Prowd was taken prisoner by the Germans after his aircraft crash landed. After a severe interrogation he was then sent to a POW camp. It is believed it was Stalag Luft VII at Kreitsberg near Bankau. These are his words.

'Then on 20th January 1945 we were assembled, packed up and sent on what has been declared the "German Death March", ahead of the Russian advance. We marched day and night for a couple of days with many dying from the severe cold as the temperature plunged to -20°C and more. A lot has been written about this March. For this purpose, sufficient to say that what food we received, we stole, we ate snow and any grass we saw, we stole potatoes, dehydrated silver beet and anything else we could find. At one stage I had severe bronchitis which Dr Morrison diagnosed as double bronchial pneumonia and had it not been for two friends, Frank Tait and George Pringle (both Queenslanders) I would not have survived. We were paraded at night and were forced to walk through a very, very severe blizzard which was very scary. Quite a few were lost in that blizzard, they simply fell on the spot and froze to death. We lost a ridiculous amount of weight.

'In what is now described as a "friendly fire" incident we were strafed by a USA Thunderbolt aircraft. 66 of our boys were killed.

'After about six to eight weeks of snow walking, we were entrained to Luckenwalde about 50 kilometres from Potsdam. I would like to mention with great respect and homage Captain Collins, who was a Church Of England Minister of Religion who would walk up and down the column (which at the beginning was about 1,500 POWs) saying "only a few more kilometres, fellows, keep your pecker up" or words to that effect. He did that at least twice a day. One does not have to be a genius to understand how the fellow POWs felt about him, and how many kilometres more he walked than the rest of us. Not only that, but he would always find a box to set up an altar and have a service. He was a big man, an Oxford Blue, and had two of the biggest feet I have ever seen.

'At Luckenwalde there were more than 30,000 POWs, mostly Russians, Americans, and British, some Poles and Italians. There were some scenes about obtaining wood for the fire illicitly obtained by dismantling an unoccupied building. A visit by the Red Cross inspected us, made some recommendations but none were carried out. The food was brought to us in copper clothes washers. It was foul but it was better than nothing.

'We paid 1,500 cigarettes for the purchase of a Lancaster Bomber's radio from one of the guards and were able to follow the advancement of the Allies and Russians. The Allies stopped at the River Elbe, which was only 50 kilometres away, but the Russians came our way and eventually liberated us.

'The Russian commander demanded at a meeting of all Pilots that we had to go and fly their planes which we refused to do. As a result of our refusal he closed down the camp, and reduced our food supplies.

'We then received a visit from an American reporter who hadn't been advised of our liberation, so he organised a truck to pick us up and take us to the crossing on the River Elbe; days went by and it never arrived. We decided to take matters into our own hands and went to a corner of the fence where we'd previously cut a gap. We drew lots to go out. As the last man made it through the gap he was spotted by the Russians and shot at. He was wounded and fell but the rest of us got away. A few kilometres down the road we stopped an American truck and told him of the trouble and he hid us under the seats and filled the truck with others who had decided to leave. After 36 hours and much procrastination by the Russians we managed to cross the Bailey Bridge at Magdeburgh where we were treated royally by the Americans. We were sent back to the UK via Brussels where we attended the 21 Club and had a sit down meal. It was then back to my beloved Edna and we married on 6th June 1946 one year after D Day. What a lot happened in that year.'

It is believed that Keith Prowd is still alive at the time of going to press and living in Australia.

Mark Azouz DFC was born in 1922 in Chiswick, London, to his parents Ralph and Esta. Before the war he was a law student and a talented pianist. He joined the RAF Volunteer Reserve (RAFVR) and qualified as a pilot. After flying many sorties, Azouz took his Stirling up on 21st September 1944 on a resupply drop to Arnhem, which on that day was the start of the Jewish Yom Kippur. Being Jewish himself he was allowed to stand down but he refused and after completing his mission was attacked by enemy aircraft and shot down. He fought with the plane until the rest of the crew bailed out, knowing the aircraft was going down. He himself bailed out only to be killed while floating to earth in his harness.

Mark Azouz is buried in Nijmegan Jonkerbos Cemetery, Holland.

George Alfred Humphrey was born in 1907 in High Wycombe, Buckinghamshire, to his parents Alfred and Elsie. He was married to Doris Julia prior to war breaking out. He also joined the RAF Volunteer Reserve (RAFVR).

He was a member of George Tickner's crew who perished when shot down in Norway. George is buried in Arendal Hogedal Cemetery Norway. The following words are written by his daughter Jacqueline Mary (Nee Humphrey) Hunt. She was born on June 9th, 1945, four months after George Humphrey's death.

'At 38, my father was the oldest member of the Stirling crew. He had worked in the furniture industry for many years as most young men did in High Wycombe, Buckinghamshire. He saw the opportunity to serve his country and volunteered for service in the RAF. He had a fascination for aircraft. I have letters he wrote to my mother in 1944–45 that bear this out! The crew members of the Stirling were all Australian. My dad was English, born and bred.

'Dad was the father of three daughters when he died, with me on the way. In 1997, I managed to contact two of the crew in Australia, Jack Caldwell and Eric Quirk. I received letters back from both of them. Jack Caldwell described my father as follows:

"We came by George in our crew when we went to Stradishall to convert from Wellingtons to Stirlings. In the Wellington we had a crew of five: Russell at the wheel, Rolf at his charts, me with my maps and target maps, Joe with his radio, and Eric with his rear gun turret. For the Stirling we needed two more; an upper gunner and an engineer. George had a sense of humour. Many other Englishmen may have, but, if so, most of them do a remarkably good job of hiding it. George flaunted it. I cannot remember that he ever took any situation seriously. He fitted in well. It's hard to understand how a mature man, a triple (going on for quadruple) father like George came to get mixed up with a bunch of Colonial children playing soldiers."

'Jack also explained in his letter that it was the eve of his 21st birthday when they took off that night. His mother had sent a birthday cake all the way from Australia and they took it with them to eat on the return journey. It went down with the plane. Jack explains: "It was most unsporting of the Hun to shoot us down on that particular night. The next day was my 21st birthday, and during the previous year preparations had been in progress. For months in Australia my mother and family hoarded dried fruit, flour and sugar and concocted a really impressive cake. In spite of U-boats, raiders, buzz bombs and the British postal service, I received it at the start of February and we put it away for celebration on the big day.

"'We took it with us on that trip to Norway, but were not allowed to cut it. It was overcooked in what was left of our poor little aeroplane, which had 1,500 gallons of petrol well and truly on fire when I left – without any regrets or hesitation I can recall.'"

Taffy Stimson came out of the RAF soon after the war. He joined the police force where a policeman's lot suited him down to the ground, so much so that he never pursued any other career.

196 Squadron was never far away from his thoughts and he kept in touch with his old pilot Chuck Hoystead. He was instrumental as part of the organisation to reunite some of the old comrades during the reunions that took place during the 80s and 90s.

He enjoyed a long and happy retirement though it is not known whether he is still alive.

Clive Westoby passed his Civil Service exams after the war and worked for the government in the Lincoln area until his retirement. He married his long-term girlfriend Barbara and had a son Neil and a daughter Kate. Not one to talk about the war he did however occasionally mention his role at Arnhem to his two children and always mentioned his best friend Ronald Waltrich who was killed in the campaign.

He died peacefully in his sleep aged 74.

Wing Commander Baker. Full name; Maurice William L'Isle La Vallet Baker

Died 21/02/1945, aged 33.

Mentioned in Despatches, son of Maurice Edward Thomas Baker and Esther Baker; husband of Lucienne Jacqueline Baker of Heliopolis, Cairo, Egypt. Buried in the Commonwealth War Cemetery at Mierlo in southern Holland in the province of North Brabant.

Fred Gribble was born in Long Beach, California, USA to parents Fred and Emily in 1912. After his initial training he became a member of the RAF Volunteer Reserve (RAFVR).

He then married his wife Eleanor Mohn Gribble. On 6th June 1944, The D-Day invasions, Fred's aircraft was hit on the first sortie over Normandy. The aircraft was so badly hit it plunged to earth killing Fred and all the crew.

Fred Gribble and his crew are the only Commonwealth Personnel buried in the Cagny Communial Cemetary, 9 kilometres south east of Caen.

Henry 'Chuck' Hoystead was born in Mentone, Victoria, the son of Frederick William and Ellen Francis Veronica Hoystead, his father being a famous jockey and race horse trainer.

He was educated at the Wangaratta High School. Before his enlistment to the RAAF in 1940 he was an employee of the Shell Company of Australia. He gained his wings in 1942 and was sent to England. He was awarded the DFC in 1945.

After the war Chuck returned to Melbourne where he met up with Vanrenen at the RAF reunions that they attended on a regular basis. Chuck was instrumental and took an active part in the organisation. He and others that were seconded to the RAF were part of the ODD BODS Association which was formed from those RAF members that returned to Australia. They would all march together under the ODD BODS Banner in Melbourne in the ANZAC Day Parade down St. Kilda Road to the Shrine of Remembrance. This parade is still held to remember those who fell in WW1, WWII and the Vietnam War. Chuck died in 2002.

Bill Short. At the time of writing Bill Short is alive and kicking living in Workington, Cumbria in England. He stayed with The RAF for 18 months before returning to Berwick upon Tweed and taking up his old job as a bus driver. In his mid-forties Bill bought a newsagent shop in Workington and a few years later a card shop named after his daughter Heather. Bill was a talented artist and musician and retired at 65 to pursue his other passion, fishing. Although in good health physically, macular degeneration has attacked his vision in recent years and Bill is registered blind.

Patch returned to Lancaster where he walked many miles with Sherlock along the banks of the Lune. He enjoyed a long and peaceful retirement and died peacefully in his sleep at the grand old age of 14. He is buried in the garden of 1 Belle Vue Terrace, Lancaster.

ROLL OF HONOUR

ROYAL AIR FORCE

38 GROUP

For the men who gave their lives while serving in 196 Squadron 1942–1945

THEIR NAMES LIVETH FOR EVERMORE

Donaldson James 22 Warrant Officer 4th Feb 1944

Dowzer Robert 21 Sergeant 4th Feb 1944

Glen Kenneth Albert 20 Sergeant 4th Feb 1944

Spray Alfred 20 Sergeant 4th Feb 1944

Staple Kenneth Thomas 20 Sergeant 4th Feb 1944

Vince Dennis Tunnard 23 Sergeant 4th Feb 1944

Pryke Henry Ivan 21 Pilot Officer 4th Feb 1944

SHERLOCK'S SQUADRON

Lindley John Rothwell 32 Flying Officer 5th Feb 1944

Moore Thomas 22 Flying Officer 5th Feb 1944

Woodruff Lionel Howard 21 Warrant Officer 5th Feb 1944

Simpson Charles Arthur 23 Warrant Officer 20th Feb 1944

Sawford John Edward 20 Sergeant 20th Feb 1944

Sullivan Patrick William 24 Flight Sergeant 20th Feb 1944

Lysons Ronald Cecil 23 Flight Sergeant 20th Feb 1944

McCannell Duncan Malcolm 24 Sergeant 21st Feb 1944

Claypole Sidney 23 Sergeant 4th Apr 1944

Lees John Hugh 28 Warrant Officer 4th Apr1944

Meera Shayrene 19 Sergeant 4th Apr 1944

Payne Kenrick 21 Flight Sergeant 4th Apr 1944

Teece John Robert 32 Flying Officer 4th Apr 1944

Wilkinson John Thomas 29 Flight Sergeant 4th Apr 1944

Rodrigues Alfred 24 Leading Aircraftsman 9th Apr 1944

Anderson James Kennedy 24 Flying Officer 6th Jun 1944

Bothwell Alexander Edward 27 Flying Officer 6th Jun 1944

Goddard Phillip Charles 21 Flight Sergeant 6th Jun 1944

Gribble Fred 32 Flight Lieutenant 6th Jun 1944

Luff (DFM) Richard Norman Purnell 31 Flight Lieutenant
6th Jun 1944

Whitehead Edward 21 Sergeant 6th Jun 1944

Wooton Harry Edgar 21 Flight Sergeant 6th Jun 1944

Smith Dick 33 Flying Officer 30th Jun 1944

Chalkley Frank Douglas 23 Flying Officer 19th Sep 1944

Matthews Dennis Alec 23 Sergeant 19th Sep 1944

Powderhill George Henry 33 Flying Officer 19th Sep 1944

Bancroft Earnest Walter 24 Warrant Officer 20th Sep 1944

Benning Donovan Geoffrey 22 Flight Sergeant 20th Sep 1944

Clough David Nicholson 22 Sergeant 20th Sep 1944

Cragg Trevor Bowers 21 Flight Sergeant 20th Sep 1944

Mabbot Cyril 22 Flight Sergeant 20th Sep 1944

Murphy Andrew Joseph 29 Flight Sergeant 20th Sep 1944

Tait William Robert 23 Warrant Officer 20th Sep 1944

Allaway David John 20 Flight Sergeant 21st Sep 1944

Azouz Mark 22 Warrant Officer 21st Sep 1944

Bode Peter Harold 21 Flight Sergeant 21st Sep 1944

Cowan Robert 21 Flight Sergeant 21st Sep 1944

Forrest Robert Walter 23 Flight Sergeant 21st Sep 1944

Gibbs Reginald Cuthbert 32 Flying Officer 21st Sep 1944

Grant Donald Hay 24 Flight Sergeant 21st Sep 1944

Green Charles Richard John 23 Flight Sergeant 21st Sep 1944

Marsh Leonard 20 Flight Sergeant 21st Sep 1944

Ormson Francis 21 Flight Sergeant 21st Sep 1944

Phillips Richard Glyn 26 Flight Sergeant 21st Sep 1944

Poole Sidney John 24 Flight Sergeant 21st Sep 1944

Ratcliffe Leslie Victor 28 Sergeant 21st Sep 1944

Townsend Stanley Arthur Leonard 23 Flight Sergeant
  21st Sep 1944

Waltrich Ronald Eric George 23 Flight Sergeant 21st Sep 1944

Kerton Gerald Desmond Patrick 23 Sergeant 24th Sep 1944

Turreff James Campbell 31 Sergeant 24th Sep 1944

Williamson Cedric Alfred 22 Sergeant 24th Sep 1944

Leonard James 24 Sergeant 4th Nov 1944

Moore John Charles 28 Sergeant 4th Nov 1944

Newberry Harry George 21 Flight Sergeant 4th Nov 1944

Orford John 19 Sergeant 4th Nov 1944

Raymen Frederick George 28 Sergeant 4th Nov 1944

Tolliday George William 24 Sergeant 4th Nov 1944

Webster Nelson Donald 21 Sergeant 4th Nov 1944

Eves Derek William 21 Flying Officer 9th Nov 1944

Goult Maurice Arthur 19 Sergeant 9th Nov 1944

Myers Charles Alfred 34 Flight Sergeant 9th Nov 1944

Norton John Anthony 22 Flying Officer 9th Nov 1944

Ruston Harry 27 Flight Sergeant 9th Nov 1944

Thompson John Vaas 21 Sergeant 9th Nov 1944

Baker (MID) Maurice William L'Isle La Valett Wing
  Commander 21st Feb 1945

Gordon John Robert 21 Flight Sergeant 21st Feb 1945

Hunter Calvert Hamilton 31 Warrant Officer 21st Feb 1945

McGovern John Bruce 22 Warrant Officer 21st Feb 1945

Tickner Russell George 24 Flying Officer 25th Feb 1945

Humphrey George Alfred 38 Flight Sergeant 26th Feb 1945

Stevenson Joseph Daglish 25 Warrant Officer 26th Feb 1945

Allman George Gregory 22 Warrant Officer 31st Mar 1945

Brenner Fredrick Charles 31 Flight Sergeant 31st Mar 1945

Brunton Thomas Louttit 22 Flight Sergeant 31st Mar 1945

Campbell Clarence 25 Pilot Officer 31st Mar 1945

Catterall Derek Vivian 21 Flight Sergeant 31st Mar 1945

Cross John Richard 20 Flight Sergeant 31st Mar 1945

Harding-Klimanek Paul Reginald Sergius 21 Flight Sergeant
   31st Mar 1945

Linney Kenneth William 22 Flight Sergeant 31st Mar 1945

Lloyd Edward Sidney 20 Flight Sergeant 31st Mar 1945

Matthews Francis William 31 Flight Sergeant 31st Mar 1945

Myers Paul Montefiore 20 Sergeant 31st Mar 1945

Reed George Sidney 30 Flight Sergeant 31st Mar 1945

Carroll Neville 23 Flying Officer 3rd Apr 1945

Grain Jack 24 Warrant Officer 3rd Apr 1945

Marshall Reginald Earnest 39 Flight Sergeant 3rd Apr 1945

Hughes Gilbert 33 Warrant Officer 3rd Apr 1945

Philo Stanley James Verse 22 Warrant Officer 3rd Apr 1945

Atkinson Kenneth 23 Warrant Officer 11th Apr 1945

Barnes Robert 23 Sergeant 11th Apr 1945

Jones Trevor Robert 19 Sergeant 11th Apr 1945

Tomlinson Phillip Roy 22 Sergeant 11th Apr 1945

Vernon Frederick 26 Flight Sergeant 11th Apr 1945

Whitehead James William 22 Flying Officer 11th Apr 1945

Bell Harold Alfred 32 Flight Sergeant 10th May 1945

Breed John Leonard 24 Flying Officer 10th May 1945

Gilyead Lionel James Douglas 21 Flight Sergeant 10th May 1945

Impett Raymond Charles 32 Warrant Officer 10th May 1945

Kilday Hugh Joseph 31 Warrant Officer 10th May 1945

Welch David 34 Flight Sergeant 10th May 1945's S

Bennet Arthur 20 Flight Sergeant 2nd Jun 1945